Theoretical Arch

Theoretical Archaeology

K.R. Dark

Duckworth

This impression 2002
First published in 1995 by
Gerald Duckworth & Co. Ltd.
61 Frith Street, London W1D 3JL
Tel: 020 7434 4242
Fax: 020 7434 4420
inquiries@duckworth-publishers.co.uk
www.ducknet.co.uk

A catalogue record for this book is available
from the British Library

ISBN 0 7156 2670 1

Printed in Great Britain by
Antony Rowe Ltd, Eastbourne

Contents

This book is dedicated to my family

Preface

My aim in this book is to introduce archaeological theory to undergraduate students, non-specialists, amateur archaeologists, and all those who employ archaeological work in the course of other studies and professions, such as historians, anthropologists, planners, geographers, and social and political scientists.

Although this book discusses archaeological theory as a sub-discipline, theory cannot – as a rule – be separated from other aspects of archaeology. Theory must be seen alongside and permeating practice, while practice reflects on theory. By writing an introduction to theory I no more claim that theory can be seen as standing alone than, for example, the authors of fieldwork manuals assert that their approaches can be isolated from the rest of archaeology. I have endeavoured to include in this book aspects of the conceptual basis of field methods and of post-excavation analysis, even though these might not generally be expected to appear in a work on archaeological theory.

My aim throughout has been to encourage interest in the subject and to provide a basis for further reading. When citing references, I have tended to give the article or book that first introduced a concept into archaeology, although I have not stuck to this as a hard and fast rule when another publication more easily clarifies a theoretical point. In emphasising the date when a theory was first introduced into archaeology I have frequently cited the first edition of a work that has since been revised; the reader is advised to consult the most recent edition if the current theoretical stance of that author is sought.

*

My thanks go to all those who have helped in the production of this book and given me the opportunity to learn about archaeological theory, especially my parents and my wife, who have read the text and provided continuing encouragement. Any shortcomings or omissions must, of course, be attributed to me.

March 1995   K.R.D.

Illustrations

Introduction

It would be easy to imagine that archaeological theory is daunting, or irrelevant, or both. Theorists often use jargon-laden sentences, quote obscure works, discuss periods and areas distant from those of one's own interest, and are keen to promote their own views. This hardly makes for easy reading or a balanced introduction. I aim to show the relevance of theory to all those involved or interested in archaeology, and to make accessible the major trends in modern theoretical archaeology. First, however, it is worth clarifying what I mean by archaeological theory.

I define archaeology as the study of the past using material evidence, although one might equally well apply archaeological approaches to the present. Because as soon as an event has occurred it constitutes 'the past', the scope of archaeology encompasses all but the (fleeting) present: by the time you read this book, it will be archaeological evidence that I wrote it. A modern home, workplace, college room or discotheque is as much a potential source of archaeological study as a palaeolithic cave-shelter or a Roman villa. The source materials used in archaeology are material data (of whatever date) that in some way relate to humans: *material culture*.

Archaeological theory may be defined in many ways: here I mean the conceptual basis of studying the past using material data. Theory may also be taken to include the study of archaeological methods (*methodology*), and the theory of conserving material remains and their presentation. These aspects, along with the methods and interpretations produced by archaeologists, are excluded from this book, although they are certainly founded on theory which will be discussed here. The division between theory, method, practice and presentation used here has been adopted merely for convenience (for a general introduction to the relationship between them see Renfrew and Bahn 1991).

I shall use the term 'theoretical archaeology' to refer to the study of archaeological theory. Although clumsy, 'theoretical archaeology' has become the usual term for the study of the conceptual basis of 'material culture studies' which concentrate on the past. Perhaps 'theoretical archaeology' is a regrettable term, as it gives the impression that the study itself is imagination: 'theoretical' in the negative sense. But archaeologists frequently describe the study of the archaeology of the last few hundred years as 'post-medieval archaeology', that of the middle ages

1

as 'medieval archaeology', that of the Roman period as 'Roman archaeology', and that of prehistory as 'prehistoric archaeology', so there is no reason why the study of archaeological theory should not be called 'theoretical archaeology'.

This book is also limited insofar as it is an introduction to some major themes in archaeological theory, rather than a corpus of theory or an attempt at a total overview of all theoretical archaeology. I have concentrated on introducing concepts and explaining their basis, rather than giving exhaustive accounts which reflect the full complexity of the arguments employed by proponents of each theoretical stance. I have thus left out some themes (such as theories of demography, sampling and 'style') which others might have included, and which certainly form part of theoretical archaeology. This book concentrates on those topics which, in my opinion, form the core of archaeological theory, rather than those which are aspects of method, or relevant only to specific situations.

There are two exceptions to this rule. Because works on archaeological theory are usually written by, and for, British or American prehistorians, I have attempted to redress the balance by including theory written by historical archaeologists (as well as prehistorians), and so this work contains some theory specific to historical situations, such as the Roman world or medieval Europe. I have also endeavoured to include work by scholars outside Britain and America.

In contrast to the authors of many works on theory, I have attempted to eliminate jargon from the explanations given here and to define all relevant technical terms. Around 400 terms and concepts will be explained, enabling the reader to attend a theoretical archaeology conference, understand specialist articles or books on theory, and discuss theory with professional archaeologists even if they had no knowledge of archaeological theory before reading this book. I have also given a selective glossary of technical terms (italicised in the text on their first occurrence) at the end of the book.

I aim here to represent the theoretical views of others, rather than my own, but this does not mean that I consider all of the views discussed to be of equal merit. While it is probably folly to claim to be unbiased, I have attempted to eliminate bias from the text and treat all viewpoints discussed in a fair and balanced way, whether I agree with them or not. It may be that my choice of subjects, and the subjects which I have excluded, reflect my own interests, reading, background and experience, but I have endeavoured to give a balanced representation of theoretical writings on each of the topics considered. So that my views are clear, however, I have included references to my own work where appropriate.

The remainder of this Introduction contains a brief account of the development of archaeological theory before the 1960s, tracing themes which help place into context the main chapters of this book. Finally, the major theoretical 'schools' (by which I mean informal 'groupings' of scholars rather than implying connection with an institution, or a fixed membership) will be introduced.

The emergence of a theoretical framework: developments before 1850

In order to suppose that material culture can be evidence for the past, one must have a concept that information about the past can be derived from material data. This has been realised for a surprisingly long time. (The following account is based mainly on Daniel 1975 and Malina and Vasicek 1990; I have referenced additional material.)

The earliest record of the use of material remains as evidence for investigating the distant past comes from the sixth century BC, when a Babylonian king dug among the ruins of official buildings for this purpose. In Classical Greece, the historian Thucydides argued that burials found on the island of Delos provided evidence that they were once occupied by the Carians, and so belonged to them. In the Roman period, antiquities were conserved, displayed, and visited as monuments of the past. During the fourth century AD, St Helena dug at the site of the Crucifixion looking for its material traces, and throughout the early Christian and Byzantine world much interest was shown in material evidence of both the Christian and the Roman past. Even in the late Byzantine period, law permitted the removal of buildings blocking the sight of a historical monument, such as a statue, if it could be shown that one was aware of its historical significance (Mango 1986).

Theory on this level merely represented the awareness that material remains could inform us about the past. After the Renaissance, the development of antiquarianism (scholarly speculation about the interpretation of material remains) did little to develop theory about the relationship between material culture and its interpretation. Antiquarian societies began to be founded in Italy as early as the fifteenth century, and in north-western Europe during the sixteenth and seventeenth centuries. This interest in the study of the past coincided with the exploration and colonisation by Europeans of areas outside Europe, and this contributed a new perspective, as comparison was made between the tribal peoples of, for example, America and prehistoric or early historic Europeans (see Orme 1981).

Further developments took place in the eighteenth century, such as the recognition by Rhode (in 1719) that archaeology could be a reliable source for prehistory and the classification of prehistory, by de Montfaucon (in 1734) into stone-, bronze- and iron-using periods. In the eighteenth century, too, Jefferson and Rhode recognised the chronological significance of the formation of consecutive layers of soil and archaeological features such as graves. Despite the lead given by these scholars, or the even earlier application of stratigraphy by Rudbeck in the

seventeenth century, stratigraphy was not widely employed as an archaeological concept until the later nineteenth century; much stratigraphical
information was dug away unrecorded in the meantime.

In the early nineteenth century the conceptual development of archaeology began to gather pace. In the early part of the century Thomsen built on
the earlier work of de Montfaucon by formalising the *three-age system* (the
Stone, Bronze and Iron Ages), developing this concept alongside the
division of artefacts into types (see Chapter 3). Worsaae emphasised the
significance of *assemblages*, groups of artefacts found together, rather
than isolated finds. With the concepts of prehistoric ages, assemblages and
typology, the conceptual basis of archaeology was emerging.

Archaeological concepts, 1850-1918

After the 1850s there was a rapid conceptual development in archaeology.
In 1859 Darwin demonstrated the antiquity of mankind and introduced a
concept of evolution that was rapidly applied to the cultural past. By 1865
Lubbock had divided the Stone Age into 'Old' and 'New', and in 1866
Wentropp added an intermediate 'Mesolithic' (Middle Stone Age) between
the Palaeolithic (Old Stone Age), and Neolithic (New Stone Age). While
the Mesolithic was not clearly defined until the early twentieth century,
these scholars had established the framework of prehistory. Typological
concepts became more clearly defined through the work of Hildebrand
and Montelius, writing in the 1860s and 1870s, while in 1869 de Mortillet
formulated two laws of cultural evolution: progress and analogous
development. In the 1860s Tylor introduced the concept of 'culture' into
anthropology, which was to have a major impact on twentieth-century
archaeology, and Kemble (see Latham 1856) had already recognised that
a comparison of pottery styles in adjacent areas could indicate the
migration of population groups between them. In 1869 Virchow also used
pottery to recognise population groups, to some extent pioneering the
approach developed by Childe in the next century.

Perhaps most significant for the later development of archaeological
theory, however, was the work of Pitt-Rivers and Petrie, both scholars
whose contribution to fieldwork methods is well-known to archaeologists.
Pitt-Rivers stressed the importance of stratigraphy, detailed observation,
records and publication, and integrated evolution, typology and
anthropology in his interpretation of excavated material. He saw
archaeology as a science in which the basis of interpretation must be
made known and checkable by other scholars, and an important aspect of
his conceptual framework was his emphasis on the everyday rather than
the exceptional.

The work of Petrie also integrated theory with practice. He too was a
meticulous excavator and his theoretical work concentrated on pottery
classification, laying foundations for later advances.

So, by 1900, archaeology had developed a conceptual basis which seemed to enable the scientific interpretation of material remains as sources for past culture. There were also major advances in the first two decades of the twentieth century. Chadwick (1907) used an interdisciplinary approach integrating historical and archaeological evidence to study what would today be called 'state-formation', and Haverfield, in his classic book *The Romanisation of Britain* (1912), used material sources to reconstruct society and the processes of cultural change outside an evolutionary framework.

By the middle of the second decade of the twentieth century the foundations of what would today be called 'culture-history' (which will be defined later in this book) had been laid. Archaeology had moved from speculation and collecting to the systematic description and analysis of material sources for the past. Some of the potential of those sources had already been realised, although some false leads had undoubtedly been followed.

Theory in European and American archaeology, 1918-1968

The next major advance was the development of social and economic approaches to archaeology, although, as we have seen, pioneering work on these topics had already been undertaken. This began in the 1920s with the work of Collingwood, one of the foremost archaeologists of Roman Britain, and a professor of philosophy at Oxford. Collingwood was well placed as a philosopher to develop the theoretical aspects of his work, and he later wrote an important book on the philosophy of history (Collingwood 1946), which was to prove influential in archaeology. In writing social history from material evidence, Collingwood opened up a new area of archaeological inquiry. In his book *Roman Britain* (1924), he developed this approach to archaeological evidence, but (just as importantly) in his archaeological work he formulated a method – 'the question and answer approach' – close to the deductive approach of the 'New Archaeologists' (see Chapter 2).

Collingwood's theoretical work can easily be misunderstood. If his philosophical book *The Idea of History* is misread, it is possible to suppose that he adopted an approach based on *empathy* (feeling the same way as did individuals in the past), or considered it impossible to test hypotheses. Both opinions are far from accurate when Collingwood's work is seen as a whole, and, in fact, are absent from his philosophy of history.

Kemble's lead in recognising population groups by identifying associated groups of artefacts was already being built upon by Leeds. In his book, *The Archaeology of the Anglo-Saxon Settlements* (1913), Leeds attempted to trace patterns of migration and colonisation by correlating groups of artefacts found in graves in England, and the types of burial custom employed there, with those found in northwest Europe. He interpreted these patterns in terms of both population groups and political units, anticipating Childe's famous definition of an archaeological culture in *The Danube in Prehistory* (1929) by sixteen years (see Chapter 4 and below).

The use of material evidence as a source for reconstructing past societies was a subject of interest from the 1920s onwards to several other scholars working in British archaeology, such as Hawkes, Piggott and Clark. The best-known development of this period was by the Australian archaeologist Childe, also working in Britain, who, as we have seen, introduced the concept of an archaeological culture. Childe also increasingly developed a philosophical basis for the methods which he employed, deriving this in part from his strong, and ultimately fatal, Marxist views. His approach to European prehistory, emphasising the recognition of past population groups and explaining change through migration and contact between them, came to be the dominant form of explanation in prehistoric archaeology.

The archaeological reconstruction of past economies was also being explored during this period. During the 1930s, Clark introduced the reconstruction of past economies based on material evidence alone, stressing its ecological context and the importance of understanding the environments that formed the setting of archaeological sites and finds. Although his classic book *Prehistoric Europe: The Economic Basis* was published as late as 1952, this followed two decades of work (a collection of Clark's papers on this topic is published as Clark 1989), and he went beyond this to integrate social and economic archaeology (e.g. Clark 1939; Clark and Piggott 1965) and stress the importance of a global perspective on the human past (Clark 1961).

The environmental setting of archaeological material and the role of geography and environmental factors in explaining the observed patterning in time and space had already been emphasised (most today would say over-emphasised) by Fox (1923 and 1932). Crawford (1953) identified the importance of developing a logic for the interpretation of archaeological data and sought to do this by the detailed comparison of anthropologically observed situations with archaeological material. Atkinson (1953, 1957) recognised the significance of the modification of archaeological deposits by natural processes as a potential problem in their interpretation.

Nor was the great British archaeologist, Sir Mortimer Wheeler, averse to the formulation of theory (see, especially, Wheeler 1954), although I suspect that his contribution to archaeological theory has often been overlooked. He considered that emphasis should be placed on identifying the individuals and societies responsible for producing the archaeological record, stressing the human and cognitive dimensions of archaeological evidence and the importance of incorporating these into reconstruction and explanation. Wheeler was equally keen to calibrate the archaeological record, especially in regard to historical scources, and denounced mere description in favour of interpretation and explanation.

While these archaeologists were active in Britain, a somewhat distinct and different theoretical trend was emerging in the USA. Strong (1936) and Steward (1942) suggested that archaeological data might be interpreted by comparing them with the anthropology of groups recorded in the same area (the 'direct historical approach', to which we shall return in Chapter 2). A series of scholars – Wedel, Braidwood, MacNeish and Caldwell – developed approaches stressing the importance of the natural environment in the understanding of prehistoric peoples. Other scholars, such as Kluckhohn (1940) and the social anthropologist White (1949, 1959), asserted the scientific character of archaeology and anthropology, to which archaeology was, and is, closely linked in the USA. White, and subsequently his student Meggers (1954, 1955, 1956, 1957, 1961), developed an evolutionary view of culture which placed emphasis on environmental determinism. Another aspect of explanation was discussed by Keur (1941) and Lewis and Kneberg (1941), who recognised the role of acculturation (see Chapter 7) in the way that cultures changed.

The most important American archaeologists of this period for later developments were, perhaps, Taylor and Steward. Taylor (1948) emphasised the relationship between theory and practice and adopted a 'functional' view of culture derived from anthropology. This approach (*functionalism*) was based on the premise that human cultures had a function and that institutions could usually be explained by identifying that function. While this view is no longer held by anthropologists, it was popular at the time of Taylor's book. Taylor also promoted a 'conjunctive approach', combining many different classes of evidence and examining the relationships between them, and stressed the role of speculation in considering aspects of culture unrepresented in the archaeological record. (For a recent assessment of Taylor's contribution to archaeological theory, see Deetz 1988.)

Steward (e.g. 1937, 1955) stressed the environment and cultural change. He saw archaeology as closely connected with anthropology and attempted to explain change in evolutionary terms.

It would be a mistake, however, to suppose that it was only in Britain and the USA that archaeology was developing its theoretical basis during this period. In Germany, for example, Eggers (1950, 1959) was questioning the representivity of archaeological evidence as a source for past cultures. He pointed out that material culture could be structured for religious reasons, could contain symbols and could have messages encoded within it. He emphasised that after they were deposited, archaeological data were modified by human and natural processes. Wahle (1964) was, meanwhile, stressing the importance of individuals and small groups in past societies. Nor were these scholars alone, with colleagues such as Hachmann *et al.* (1962) sharing their views.

In France, a distinct theoretical tradition was also emerging during the 1950s, and it could be argued that Gardin (1955) was the earliest scholar to call for a revolution in archaeological theory. The revolution that Gardin envisaged was, however, very different from that which occurred in Anglo-American archaeology during the 1960s; it centred on the need for more standardised, explicit and logical description of archaeological materials (for an example of a recent product of the French school, see Gallay 1986). As we shall see in Chapter 2, this has, in part, been achieved in French archaeology, where, as a consequence, a distinctive theoretical school has become established. There were also archaeologists in France developing theory to some extent parallel with that found in America during this period, such as Laplace (1957), who employed the concept of cultural evolution.

In Scandinavia, perhaps the most important theorist of this period was Malmer (e.g. Malmer 1962), who also considered explicit terminology and strict logic to be central to the development of archaeological reasoning. Malmer formulated a complete programme of archaeological procedure, from description to interpretation, based on these grounds and incorporating mathematical and statistical approaches.

These examples serve to illustrate that important developments in archaeological theory were made outside Britain and the USA during this period (for these and subsequent developments in Europe, see Hodder 1991b). Elsewhere, in years dominated by totalitarianism, the political ideologies of Nazism and Marxism controlled archaeological theory, leading to its decline as those ideologies were defeated (see Arnold 1990).

Political factors limited the involvement of Eastern European archaeologists in the 'New Archaeology' (see below) and subsequent developments until the 1980s. Marxist domination of Eastern Europe until that time meant that Marxism was used as an explanatory framework by archaeologists throughout these areas, and theoretical developments within the discipline concentrated on the scope of the subject, the definition of archaeological terms, and the description and classification of archaeological material (for reviews and examples, see Klejn 1971, 1977, 1979, 1982, 1994a and 1994b; Klejn *et al.* 1973). As these references show, this period did, however, produce a major Russian archaeological theorist, Klejn, whose work is widely read in the West, and who has offered critiques of Western archaeology since the 1960s (Klejn 1970, 1973, 1977, 1994b).

Lewis Binford, David Clarke and the 'New Archaeology' of the 1960s

1968 saw the publication of two books which may be taken to define the beginning of the modern phase of theoretical debate in archaeology, *New Perspectives in Archaeology* and *Analytical Archaeology*, in which the

American scholar Lewis R. Binford and the British scholar David L. Clarke urged a revolution in the theory of archaeology, although the importance of theoretical approaches had been developing for a decade in both Britain and America, and in fact the term 'New Archaeology' (often used for the ensuing revolution) had been coined almost at the start of this period (Caldwell 1959). Binford and Clarke had developed theory as a central concern of their research throughout the 1960s, and in Binford's case also in the 1950s (see Binford and Binford 1968; Binford 1972; Clarke 1965, 1968; Hodder *et al.* 1981). Working independently, they arrived at similar conclusions. Binford's approach was partly the outcome of his sometimes uneasy relationship with many of the leading American archaeologists of the 1950s (described in Binford 1972). In Clarke's case a key factor may be his connection with the social and economic prehistorian J.G.D. Clark, his Ph.D. supervisor at Cambridge.

Binford advocated a 'New Archaeology' consisting of a redefinition of archaeology as an anthropological science in which both the anthropological and scientific elements were accorded great importance. Binford adopted Hempel's philosophy of science, which stressed the importance of universal laws and deductive logic (see Chapter 2) as the only valid forms of inquiry and explanation. The scientific identity which Binford proposed for archaeology incorporated evolutionary explanation, ecological approaches, statistical testing, and the role of evolutionary and ecological approaches as the principal means of explaining change. Binford's anthropological identity for archaeology emphasised social and economic reconstruction, the internal differentiation of the cultures being studied, the richness of the potential evidence recoverable from material data, and the possibility of recognising cognitive aspects of culture from the archaeological record.

Binford's view was distinct from that of Clarke in many of these respects. Clarke adhered to Childe's view of the definition of an archaeological culture (see Chapter 4), and placed more importance than did Binford on geographical approaches and the role of historical evidence in understanding the archaeological record (Clarke 1968, 1972). Like Binford, Clarke put mathematical and natural scientific perspectives at the centre of his theory of archaeology. Clarke, like Binford, employed 'systems theory' (which will be explained in Chapter 7) as a means of explaining change, and stressed the role of adaptation to new circumstances as an explanation for cultural change. Clarke and Binford also agreed on the need for social and economic reconstruction, the possibility of cognitive archaeology (see Chapter 6), and the use of scientific attitudes to testing archaeological hypotheses.

The main characteristic that both scholars had in common was that they aimed at an archaeology which sought to explain change and recognise the processes by which it came about. This marked an important departure from the main traditions of both British and

American archaeology, in which description was considered more important than the explanation of change. We have already seen that there had been earlier scholars interested in these matters, but in the 1950s most archaeologists aimed at describing past cultures rather than developing theory or new explanations of cultural change.

Theoretical archaeology today

The 'New Archaeology' rapidly developed to become a major school in both Britain and America, with many other scholars contributing to its theory. There were also many critics, for example Hawkes (1968), Taylor (1969), Bayard (1969, 1978), Rouse (1970), Kushner (1970), Steiger (1971), Eggert (1976, 1978) and Trigger (1978). During the 1970s archaeologists favouring approaches derived from the 'New Archaeology' became known as 'processualists' (because of their interest in the explanation and process of change), and processual archaeology continues to be a major theoretical school today.

Processualists can be divided into those who favour forms of explanation and logic close to those of the 'New Archaeology' (*functional-processualists*) and those who consider the role of the individual, cognition, information-exchange and decision-making to be far more important than did 'New Archaeologists', reaffirm the connection between archaeology and history, and see data and theory standing in a more complex relationship (*cognitive-processualists*). Both types of processual archaeology place emphasis on the explanation and processes of change, and on testing hypotheses against data. Both consider that we are able to evaluate which interpretations of the past are likely to be correct and which are false, and both argue that, by hypothesis-testing, knowledge is accumulated and so the subject progresses (for a clear statement of this view, see Hill 1991).

At the end of the 1970s and during the 1980s, another approach, known as 'post-processualism' (or sometimes 'anti-processualism'), emerged in part due to dissatisfaction of some archaeologists with the 'New Archaeology' and its 'processual' successor. Post-processualists consider, among other things, that we are incorrect to assume that we can test archaeological hypotheses, that much more importance has to be placed upon symbolism and other cognitive factors, that the social and political context of those writing archaeology plays a major role in the interpretations they produce, and that archaeologists should strive for the production of many views of the past, rather than a single view. Post-processualists have often favoured explanations deriving from Marxism or structuralism, as we shall see in Chapter 7, and most hope to stress diversity rather than similarities between societies in the past, in contrast to the processual interest in generalities and 'laws' (e.g. Barrett 1993). This merely gives a sample of post-processual attitudes, because it is an integral part of post-processualism that there is no fixed body of theory and that the post-processual 'school' has no agreed limits (for a sample of the current diversity see MacKenzie 1994).

From the 1980s into the 1990s a debate between processual and post-processual archaeology characterised theoretical writing (e.g. Bell 1988, 1990, 1991; Preucel 1991; Embree 1992). In the early 1990s there have been indications of an emerging consensus centred on the approach referred to by Renfrew as 'cognitive-processual', although not all those concerned would call themselves 'cognitive-processualists'. While these controversies have raged, there continue to be archaeologists who adhere to the descriptive view of archaeology which preceded the 'New Archaeology' (the *culture-historical* approach), and Marxists who stand aside from both theoretical schools. Both of these groups have, themselves, very strong theoretical frameworks which, although seldom acknowledged in 'culture-history', consitute the foundation for their approaches.

This brief summary, while incomplete, should give an impression of the diversity of theoretical views to be found in modern archaeology, and of the extent to which our interpretation of the past rests upon theoretical foundations. In the chapters that follow I have tried to include theory from processual, post-processual, culture-historical and Marxist archaeo-logy. Theory from outside all these major schools, and even (where it seems especially important for understanding archaeological theory) from outside archaeology, has also been incorporated.

CHAPTER 1

The Identity and Purpose of Archaeology

There are many ways of interpreting the identity and purpose of archaeology. The way we conduct archaeological work is so closely related to our perceptions of these questions that we cannot fail to recognise their pervasive and central character (on this question, see Yoffee and Sherratt 1993). Take, for example, Renfrew (1979a), who adopts a mathematical approach and a strongly scientific identity for archaeology. Binford (1962), on the other hand, employs anthropology as a means of interpreting the material record, and sees the identity of archaeology as being with anthropology. Butzer (1982) examines sites in their environment and considers archaeology to be 'human ecology'. Wilson (1976), who sees archaeology as an 'art', uses art-historical approaches. Different scholars can approach the same subject from different perspectives, generated by their view of the character of archaeology.

This chapter attempts to outline the debate about the nature of archaeology as a subject, by considering its relationship to anthropology, history, literature, geography and ecology, and then examines the question of whether archaeology is an art or a science. This leads into a discussion of the image which others have of archaeology, and of archaeologists' own views of themselves. These, as we shall see, are not without theoretical importance, nor are they topics neglected in archaeologists' own writings.

In the last part of this chapter the second question in the title will be discussed: what is the purpose of archaeology? There are as many differences of opinion about this among archaeologists as there are about how archaeology should be defined. Take the views of, for example, Shanks and Tilley (1987a and b), who see archaeology as having a political programmme, in contrast to those of Binford (1989) who sees archaeology as an investigative natural science. It is clear that views of the identity of archaeology closely relate to the purpose of archaeology, in such a way that opinions on one reflect upon the other (a *reflexive* relationship), so that the reasons why archaeology is undertaken cannot be considered without discussing the ways in which archaeologists have sought to define it, and *vice versa*. First, however, we must consider the definition of archaeology itself. Obviously, the simplest way to define archaeology is by saying that it is a unique subject, so that, as Clarke (1968, 11) wrote, 'archaeology is archaeology'.

1. **Does archaeological practice define archaeology?** Or is it the study of material culture? In any case, excavation, like analysis, is based on theoretical concepts. (Photo: K.R. Dark)

Archaeology as archaeology

The definition of archaeology as a unique discipline is most strongly associated with the work of David L. Clarke (esp. 1968; for replies to Clarke's views, see Hawkes 1968, Hawkes 1973, and Steiger 1971). While Clarke was the first to use this definition, it is still current today (for recent uses see Wiseman 1980; Hodder 1986). Clarke saw archaeology as a separate and distinct field, not an aspect of another 'larger' or 'more established' subject, such as history or anthropology. This definition was, however, already implied in the work of such scholars as Sir Mortimer Wheeler, who stressed the distinctive character of archaeology and its independent contribution to knowledge (Wheeler 1954).

Recently, this definition has been favoured by Hodder (e.g. 1986, 1987a), especially when arguing for a *contextual* approach to archaeology, as will be discussed later in Chapter 2. It is relevant here to note that this contextual method operates by argument from one archaeological source to another, so that the reasoning employed is entirely within archaeology. This approach is distinct from that of culture-historians, and is, perhaps, unsurprising in one of Clarke's own students and an editor of a volume of studies in Clarke's honour (Hodder, Isaac and Hammond 1981).

This way of defining archaeology places emphasis on its unique characteristics within academic endeavour. It is often, however, difficult to find approaches exclusive to archaeology other than its source materials and field methods (and even these are not always completely distinct from other disciplines). It is, therefore, unsurprising that the majority of scholars have sought a definition of the subject based on its linkage with other fields (Rahtz 1985, 4 and 6). Archaeology is a very recent academic subject compared to history or philosophy, and by connecting it to these it might be supposed that it could gain academic respectability. Alternatively, there are those who would say that it is only when archaeology stands alone and separate from these subjects that academic respectability is achieved. Others again may consider academic respectability to be irrelevant.

This is not the whole story, because the overlap which has developed between archaeology and, for example, history or biology, is very large. It may well be, however, or at least have been, a factor in the search for an archaeological disciplinary identity.

In the 1960s many other 'New Archaeologists' considered that they had discovered the identity of archaeology. Archaeology, they said, was anthropology, and this is the next view that we must consider.

2. **The living past?** An Aboriginal Australian hunter-gatherer group. Some archaeologists have seen contemporary peoples as preserving pre-modern ways of life. (Photo: Royal Anthropological Institute)

Archaeology as anthropology

For many archaeologists, the association of archaeology and anthropology dates from the 1960s, when Binford (1962) wrote a classic paper connecting the two subjects. As he said, 'archaeology is the past tense of anthropology'. This viewpoint was developed by many 'New Archaeologists' in the 1960s and early 1970s, such as the contributors to Binford's volume *New Perspectives in Archaeology* (Binford and Binford 1968, Longacre 1970, Plogg 1974 and Thomas 1974), yet in origin the definition of archaeology as anthropology can be traced to the nineteenth century, as we saw in the Introduction (e.g. Pitt-Rivers 1887-98, 1906). Among culture-historians before the 1960s, this viewpoint was directly stated by Crawford (1953).

Such a definition is, therefore, long established, and has been emphasised, especially in the United States, by the combination of archaeology and anthropology in degree courses. Even in Britain, where archaeology does not in general have strong links with anthropology (though see Orme 1981 and Hodder 1982a, 1982b, and 1982c), it may be no coincidence that the 'New Archaeology' with its anthropological aspirations, as defined by Binford, developed at Cambridge, where scholars such as Clarke (who, as we have seen, defined archaeology as a distinct subject) had laid a basis, and where archaeology and anthropology were, and are, taught together (for examples of the resulting work see Clarke 1972).

The association of archaeology and anthropology has lead to some interesting 're-namings' of archaeology, such as 'palaeo-anthropology', and was connected with the most anti-historical tendencies of the 'New Archaeology' in the work of scholars such as Spaulding (1968). Some 'New Archaeologists', and even American scholars opposed to the 'New Archaeology', went so far as to take the anthropological present as a living version of the human past: 'living prehistory'. This approach lies behind Gould's classic *Living Archaeology* (1980), which is an anthropological study of the !Kung bushmen. Hodder's post-processual classic *The Present Past* (1982c), is, as its title implies, underpinned by similar concepts of the relationship between the past and present. So the definition of 'archaeology as anthropology' is not exclusive to the 'New Archaeology', and is found in culture-historical, processual and post-processual writings.

Today, the belief that archaeology is the past tense of anthropology still finds both supporters and critics (for instance, see van Dommelen 1992), but few consider that studies of the modern material culture of non-Western people (frequently called *ethno-archaeology* if it is geared to the understanding of past material culture in these or other areas) are 'living prehistory'. Structuralism, which has played an important role in forming post-processual theory (Hodder 1982b), is itself an anthropological theory of the character of the human mind (Gellner 1982), and may be taken to illustrate the constant flow of anthropological concepts into archaeology from its association with anthropology and adoption of its methods.

The fact that anthropological definitions of archaeology passed from culture-history through the 'New Archaeology' and into contemporary approaches to archaeology may reveal a continuity in archaeological self-definition. It also shows that anthropological archaeology today, despite the processualist journal of the same name, has equally strong associations with post-processual archaeology. Processualists adopting this approach have, however, developed the anthropological concepts which they derive from their self-definition in different ways from those of post-processual or culture-historical archaeologists. Notable among contemporary processual approaches is the development of *middle-range theory* in the 1980s and 1990s, especially by archaeologists with anthropological definitions of their subject, but this is a point to which we shall return in Chapter 2.

Few culture-historical archaeologists now take as strong an interest in anthropology as did their predecessors in the 1950s, and I doubt if many would follow Crawford's definition of archaeology as anthropology. Nor do all processualists consider anthropology as identical to archaeology. The anthropological definition of archaeology was, as we have seen in the previous section, not even held by both of the founders of the 'New Archaeology', so, again, this need not surprise us.

It is notable, however, that one commonly held view – that to define archaeology as anthropology is a 'New Archaeological' viewpoint – is mistaken. The anthropological definition of archaeology has its origins long before the 'New Archaeology' of the 1960s.

Archaeology as geography

An alternative to defining archaeology as anthropology has been to define it as geography (e.g. Hyenstrand 1982). This has seldom been as straightforwardly stated as have anthropological definitions, but it has been current from at least the time of Fox's geographical approach (Fox 1923). According to this viewpoint, archaeology is not the past tense of anthropology but of geography – or at least it provides a 'time-depth' in which to place geographical data about the modern world. As historical geography is a well-developed field, the inclusion of archaeology in geographical studies and the development of a geographical identity for archaeology is unsurprising, though it has never been as widespread as other definitions. Its strongest proponents today are Wenke (*Patterns in Prehistory*, 1985) and Wagstaff (*Landscape and Culture*, 1987).

It is hardly surprising that geographical definitions have been employed in archaeology, when archaeologists manipulate so many of their data by means of distribution maps and by relating them to topographical and geomorphological features, but there has never been a large body of opinion pushing archaeology entirely into a geographical mould. Archaeology has come to share frameworks of explanation with geography, such as 'world-systems theory', and both have drawn from Braudel's historical approaches to long-term change, but this has not been formalised into a movement to re-define archaeology as such (for descriptions of both approaches see Chapters 5 and 7). The archaeological study of regions is another closely related area of mutual concern in which geographical and archaeological studies have been so closely identified as sometimes to lose their distinctive characters.

Geographical definitions of archaeology have been held, usually by implication, by culture-historical, processual and post-processual archaeologists. Thus the view of archaeology as 'the past tense of geography', just as its definition as 'the past tense of anthropology', is not exclusive to any one of the major theoretical schools.

Archaeology as ecology

In his important book *Archaeology as Human Ecology*, Butzer (1982) has put forward a different definition of our subject (see also his earlier book, Butzer 1971). Ecology is not, as a scientific subject, concerned with conservation or protecting the environment – although these may be results of it – but is the study of the relationship between humans, animals, plants and their environment. So Butzer sees archaeology as the study of the past relationship between humans and the animal, plant and physical worlds, in the same way that we would study the relationship between, for example, a lion and its natural setting.

Butzer is by no means the first to have held this opinion, nor is he the first to have considered archaeology as part of ecology. Culture-historians in the nineteenth century often aimed to integrate archaeology into the biological sciences, especially with regard to evolution (Daniel 1975, 57-151). More recently, Higgs (1975 and 1978) took this approach to archaeology. It has not, however, been favoured by most post-processual archaeologists, who would rather stress the specifics of human identity than the relationship between humans and other animals. Closely related to the identification of archaeology as ecology has been the separate and distinct field of sociobiology, in which all human action is supposed to be accounted for by biological factors. As we shall see when discussing sociobiology at greater length in Chapter 7, this approach has not been held in high regard by most archaeologists – apart from objecting to its logic, many scholars have seen it as politically abhorrent or immoral. This aspect aside, archaeologists with sociobiological tendencies would probably define archaeology as part of biology.

Although ecological definitions of archaeology persist today, they have certainly lost popularity among processual and culture-historical archaeologists. For instance, cognitive-processualists would not see archaeology as an aspect of biology, nor set their explanations entirely within ecological terms, as we shall see in Chapter 7. Ecological definitions are maintained most strongly in processual studies of early prehistory, where ecological methods are widely employed (e.g. by Boyle 1990), and the close relationship of humans and their environment has to be constantly acknowledged. It is unsurprising that ecological definitions of archaeology have also found favour among environmental archaeo-logists, many of whom were trained as biologists, and where, again, ecological theory is closely related to the conduct of their discipline.

It should not be supposed, however, that an ecological identity for archaeology is held only by prehistorians. Rahtz (1988), a leading historical archaeologist, set out a similar position in his discussion of the role of decision-making in past societies.

The biological definition of archaeology might be claimed to be in decline, but it is still widespread. It is closely related to perceptions of the distinctive character of humans, and the relationship between humanity and the natural world. This is also true of the next definition we shall consider, in which the opposing view – that humanity is differentiated by distinctive characteristics from all other animals – is taken in an extreme form, to underlie the basis of a contrasting definition of archaeology.

Archaeology as literature

Post-processual scholars have sometimes gone so far as to regard archaeology as literature (e.g. Clifford and Marcus 1986). They see an archaeological report or paper as a text, as much a product of its own time and of the character of its writer as a work of fiction such as a novel. Moreover, as the hypotheses contained within it are, in the opinion of most such archaeologists, untestable, they have the same value as literary products. They may contribute to understanding the nature of current existence, or reinterpret and characterise the current social order, but they are not 'true' in the sense that a chemist would argue that a chemical reaction is true (Shanks and Tilley 1987a, 1987b). They reflect an opinion, not facts, and so are no more true than a book like *Oliver Twist*. This book, containing interpreted observations on the surrounding world seen from the viewpoint of, and through the preconceptions of the author, is, according to this school, as much an account of reality as an archaeological report on the excavation of a Victorian workhouse. Even the practice of archaeology can itself be reduced to 'theatre' (Tilley 1989).

Scholars who hold such a definition of archaeology are very rare, but these views have been suggested by post-processualists, such as Shanks and Tilley, and are, perhaps, more widespread among younger scholars holding post-processualist theoretical opinions than might at first be supposed (e.g. Bapty and Yates 1991; Baker and Thomas 1990). This perspective is closely related to the drive to reinstate emotion and emotive responses to a central role in archaeology (Shanks 1991). Scholars adopting this position may see the ability to 'feel' for past peoples, or react emotionally to archaeological evidence, as far more central to archaeology, than do other archaeologists. They evaluate academic work by attributing to it political strengths and weaknesses, such an approach being closely linked to both Marxist analyses and Hodder's definition of 'material culture as text' (Hodder 1986, 1988, 1989).

Although Hodder (1987a, 1987b, 1990, 1991a, 1992) does not take up such an extreme stance as the exponents of this school, considering as he does that the validation of hypotheses is possible, he has constantly stressed that in his opinion material culture is a *meaningfully constructed text*. In other words, material remains are ordered according to a logic held by past peoples. Hodder (1992) has stressed the importance of using literary theory, while reintroducing emotion (on which see West 1991) and the individual into the writing of archaeology. Hodder's work is, therefore, very closely related to this definition of archaeology, although he does not hold it himself.

Recently such approaches have passed, in a diluted form, to a new generation of post-processual scholars, such as Tarlow (1994). They hope to bring literary theory to bear on archaeological remains without adopting a relativist outlook or treating archaeology as literature.

The point – that if archaeological texts are literature they are not

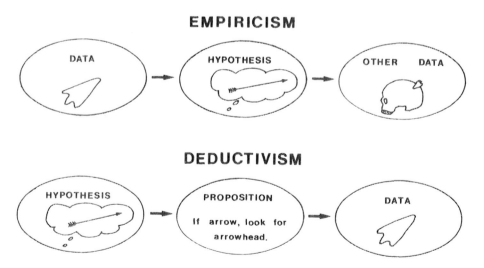

3. Empiricism and deductivism. Two approaches to archaeological reasoning.

susceptible to 'correct' or 'incorrect' interpretations – continues to play a role in the development of post-processual theory. Interestingly, a recent development of this school has been the presentation of archaeological interpretations and opinions in novel – some might say eccentric – ways, such as plays, poems and fictionalised accounts (e.g. Carman and Meredith 1992).

There is no doubt that a coherent re-definition of archaeology as literature can be formulated. This would, of course, place archaeology even more firmly in the 'arts' than would a definition of it as part of history. This seems an appropriate springboard into the muddy waters of the next question: whether archaeology, however we define it, is an art or a science.

Is archaeology a science or an art?

The early 'New Archaeologists' of the 1960s and early 1970s were certain that archaeology was a science (e.g. Binford 1968, 1972; Watson, Le Blanc and Redman 1971; Flannery 1973). They adopted a definition of science associated with the philosopher Hempel (1942, 1966: for the use of Hempel's views, Renfrew 1982, 10; Goode 1977). Hempel characterised science as based on the formulation of general laws resulting from the testing of hypotheses against evidence: the *deductive-nomological approach* (sometimes called the *hypothetico-deductive* or *H-D* approach). These general laws formed the explanation of every case to which they applied. The analogy is often made between such hypothetical laws and the theory of gravity: all cases of gravity operate as expected according to the general law of gravity, not according to the specific circumstances of each case.

The belief that hypotheses can be tested by reference to material evidence in such a way as to show that they are, without doubt, true, is known as *positivism*. Positivism characterised new archaeological thought in the 1960s and 1970s (e.g. Schiffer 1976) and could take extreme forms. Many 'New Archaeologists' felt that positivistic laws, as well as proven hypotheses, would be easily formulated, but, as we shall see in Chapter 2, that was not to be the case (for early sceptics, see Johansen 1969; Flannery 1976).

Nevertheless, in the 1960s and 1970s the definition of archaeology as a science, even a 'hard' science such as physics, found itself in bitter conflict with the overall definition preferred by culture-historians: that archaeology was an 'art' or 'humanity'. Culture-historians seldom believed in universal laws of explanation, nor in tests that moved from hypothesis to evidence (the *deductive* approach). Instead, they favoured explanation of every case individually with reference to its specifics, and used an approach moving from the data, via 'common sense', to their interpretations: an *empirical* approach. The contrast between these viewpoints was aggravated by the adoption by 'New Archaeologists' of much of the jargon and many of the methods (such as the use of computerised statistical analysis) of the natural sciences (e.g. Clarke 1968, 1972). Such a way of conducting archaeology, combined with the strident claims of the 'New Archaeology', widened and emphasised the gap between what 'New Archaeologists' considered they were doing and the standpoint of culture-historians. This led to some spectacular conflicts and virulent debates. For example, one might read the series of articles in the archaeological journal *Antiquity* during the 1960s and early 1970s, notably Hawkes's (1968) 'The proper study of mankind' and Clarke's (1973) 'Archaeology: the loss of innocence'.

The differing definitions of archaeology in the 1960s were, therefore, part of the process leading to the polarisation of archaeology into two camps, and the extreme mutual hostility that existed between them. It was not simply that 'New Archaeologists' *did* archaeology in a different way from culture-historians, but that they believed that they were doing a different type of subject.

This was in part due to the changing education of, and techniques available to, archaeologists in the 1950s and 1960s. The rise and prestige of archaeological science in the 1950s, exemplified by radiocarbon-dating, and the more scientific education of scholars active in the 1960s and 1970s, meant that the background and context of the 'New Archaeologists' contrasted with the more 'artistic' education of most culture-historians. For example, contrast Jacquetta Hawkes – a writer of fiction as much as an archaeologist – with Colin Renfrew – who has a degree in natural sciences.

This conflict of identities in archaeology persisted through the 1960s and 1970s to be further complicated by the emergence of post-processualism in the late 1970s and 1980s (Hodder 1982b, 1982c, 1982d, 1986; Shanks and Tilley 1987a and 1987b). Post-processualists characteristically rejected a scientific definition of archaeology, but they did not adopt the same view as culture-historians (e.g. Edmonds 1990; Edmonds and Thomas 1990; Baker and Thomas 1990). Instead, post-processualists usually saw archaeology as a social science (Rowlands 1982), not a natural science, although some certainly saw it as an art (Shanks 1991; Hodder 1986).

Post-processualists rejected positivism and its opposite *empiricism* (e.g. Wylie 1982). Empiricism is when we argue, as did culture-historians, from the observed data to the building of hypotheses, rather than from the hypotheses to testing against the data. Post-processualists, instead, emphasised the personal, or *subjective*, element in interpretation, and as we shall see in Chapter 2 the school is characterised by the supposition that no hypothesis can be tested. They rejected Hempel's view of what constituted science and argued instead for *pluralism*. A *pluralistic* approach sees many or all hypotheses as of equal, or potentially equal, weight (e.g. Hodder 1986; Deetz 1983). The material 'text' must be left 'open' to many 'readings' and interpretations. In their view, there is no need to arrive at a conclusion as none is possible; a post-processualist work, or museum display, might lead the reader through a discussion, culminating with the question: 'What do you think?'

As post-processualists pointed out, however, there are several alternative ways of defining science. We shall discuss Popper's views in Chapter 2, but here it is important to stress that post-processualists tended to prefer Kuhn's view (Kuhn 1962). Kuhn saw science as comprising not laws or securely tested hypotheses, but shifting over-views (*paradigms*) dependent upon their social and historical context. What constituted science at any one period was an outcome of historical circumstances, and shifts between paradigms were sudden replacements ('revolutions'), rather than gradual developments.

This alternative view underpinned post-processualist thought. It led to the rejection of Hempel's concepts of testing and universal explanation and an emphasis on the historical context in which hypotheses were proposed. Post-processualists thus defined archaeology in general terms not as a way of obtaining truth about the past, but in order to generate potentially 'useful' interpretations for understanding it (e.g. Shanks and Tilley 1987a, 1987b).

Other post-processualist views of archaeology carry with them definitions of archaeology as an art or science, and it is a characteristic of this school that it sees archaeology always in artistic (e.g. Shanks 1991) or social-science terms (e.g. Deetz 1983; Rowlands 1982). Conversely, processualists always see archaeology in scientific terms, whether as a 'natural science', a 'social science' (Rowlands 1982), or, as Bintliff (1991) has recently suggested, a 'human science' (see also Barich 1977-1982). But this debate cannot simply be described in terms of 'processualists against the rest'. Pre-processual archaeologists, such as Pitt-Rivers, also considered archaeology to be a science, and some culture-historical definitions of the identity of archaeology share as much common ground with processualist definitions as other culture-historians share with post-processualists. One could find many points of comparison between contemporary or cognitive-processualism and Wheeler's approach, and between Pitt-Rivers' approach and some functional-processualists.

Definitions of archaeology can, therefore, be set within a broader definition of whether the subject is an art or science, and what type of art or science it is. Very few scholars have attempted to make a fully integrated definition linking in detail the identity of archaeology and its relationship to other disciplines, apart from such obviously theoretical writers as Binford, Clarke and Hodder. An extreme example of the relationship of archaeology to other subjects has been put forward for debate by Rahtz (1985, 4 and 6), who sees archaeology as central to all other scholarly concerns, or at least capable of assuming such an identity;

however, this is not a view shared, at least in print, by most other archaeological theorists.

There are, therefore, conflicting definitions of the identity and disciplinary connections of archaeology, and doubtless very many more could be adduced: it has even been suggested that archaeology is not an academic subject at all, but a sport. Without indulging in terms such as 'a historical science' or 'a scientific art', it is hard to find a term reconciling these alternative views (Deetz 1983). Even if such a term were adopted, strong supporters of specific identities for archaeology would doubtless object. As mentioned above, Bintliff has recently suggested that the increasingly-used term 'human science' might be used for archaeology. This would relate archaeology to many of the disciplines discussed above, but not to all. Consequently, many archaeologists may not want to cultivate an identity as 'human scientists'. There may, of course, be non-archaeologists who doubt both the 'humanity' and the scientific character of our subject! This conveniently brings us on to the next section.

The image of archaeology

By the 'image of archaeology' I mean both how others see archaeologists and how archaeologists see themselves – considerations which are bound to have an effect on how we define our subject.   To the writer of fiction, whether novels or film scripts, an archaeologist can be anything from a crusty old professor with a white beard to an Indiana Jones. Fictional archaeologists are often seen as bumbling, boring, or simply wrong. They are also predominantly male, which is hardly an accurate depiction of the field.

Nevertheless, the predominant public image of archaeology is one of glamour, excitement and adventure. Archaeologists are seen as breaking away from a normal humdrum existence and *discovering* things. They usually do so, in the public imagination, by excavating such visually impressive monuments as Greek temples and Roman villas in idyllic or exotic settings.

As most archaeologists are well aware, most archaeology is not conducted under these circumstances. To many involved in 'rescue' archaeology, or in the more bureaucratic aspects of the subject, archaeology certainly seems a long way from this glamorous public image. Despite this reality, many non-archaeologists still link archaeo-logy with travel, exploration, pyramids and golden treasures. I know of few archaeologists who would not agree that mention of their profession often provokes such remarks as 'How glamorous', or 'I'd like to have done that'. Personally, I have heard remarkable numbers of people assert that they remember wanting to be archaeologists at the age of nine or so!

This public perception impinges on archaeology less strongly than archaeologists' own perception of their subject. The public image of archaeology, perhaps, reveals a lack of information and clarity about the subject, but the way archaeologists think about their subject may directly affect the way in which they go about it. It is hard to believe that an identification of the archaeologist with the people in the past whom he or she intends to study does not affect the way in which that archaeologist approaches the subject. For example, Scott (1990) has noted that the identification of Victorian archaeologists with the land-owning classes, and their identification of their own social system with that of the Roman period, led to the adoption of specific perspectives on the interpretation of Roman villas.

This is merely one example of the close relationship that exists between an identification with past peoples and the motivation and interpretations of archaeologists. This relationship does not exist only on the level of banal generalities such as that a scholar 'had an enquiring mind' and so was interested in prehistory, but in the detailed attractions of specific periods in the human past for particular individuals. We can use this both to evaluate the work of other scholars and as a form of self-criticism to improve the quality of our own work. Personally, I do not rule out the possibility that my interest in state-collapse and in the decline of empires derives from a childhood in 1960s London, when I lived through the collapse of much of the British Empire. The reader may well be able to recall other examples relating not only to current social, economic or political circumstances, but to the archaeologist's own upbringing, childhood or world view. Ashbee (1986) has noted that such self-critical approaches have long been found in archaeology. He quotes the following example given by Sir Osbert Lancaster (1947) in his book *Classical Landscape with Figures*: ' ... in-so-far as I employ the comparative method, my criteria, political, architectural and scenic, remain firmly Anglo-Saxon, and the standards of judgment are always those of an Anglican graduate of Oxford with a taste for architecture, turned cartoonist, approaching middle-age and living in Kensington' (Ashbee 1986, 215).

It is necessary, of course, to employ such approaches with much care. The character and attitudes of past scholars cannot simply be the subject of generalisation – 'all Victorians were class-conscious' – no matter how well-founded these generalisations may seem. Nor should we project our own preconceptions about the opinions or background of others onto present or past scholars.

Another way of using archaeologists' self-perceptions to understand the character of archaeology is more closely related to the question of how we define the subject, and consists of finding out what archaeologists consider their subject to be similar to. Such 'metaphors for archaeology' include seeing archaeologists as detectives (e.g. Adams 1983), actors, musicians, or sports-people (e.g. Carver 1988), adventurers (e.g. Hawkes

1982), political activists (e.g. Shanks and Tilley 1987a and b), fine artists such as painters or poets (Shanks 1991), and even soldiers (Carver 1988). Some of these are clearly closely related to more formal definitions of archaeology – the archaeologists who think the subject is a type of literature, for example, may consider themselves to be 'like novelists'.

To take two formalised examples, we may begin with Adams (1991), who has written of archaeology in terms of the work of fictional and real detectives; this may help us to understand why he and his colleagues were among the first archaeologists in Britain to relate archaeology to forensic science (see Boddington, Garland and Janaway 1987). This development produced important archaeological results (as had earlier work in America: Maples 1982; Stoutamie *et al.* 1983), and has contributed to police-work (what has been called *applied archaeology*).

Especially relevant is the recent evocative description of archaeologists excavating, written by Carver (1988, 11), the Director of the Sutton Hoo excavation and interestingly, in the context of this description, an ex-soldier. It contains many current self-images of archaeology:

> As we round the corner en route to our tryst, the clink of trowel and rustle of brush on the earth and stones are like the sounds of an orchestra tuning up; the shout of the chap taking levels is like the shout of the stage manager in the wings, and the members of the little company with whom we will perform the ritual are as sharply contrasted, in the crisp morning air as a group of travelling actors, or a football team, or the platoon of ill-assorted mercenaries which is shortly to throw itself on hill 779, and survive.

It might be claimed that self-definitions, often made in the introductions to academic works, in humour, or in popular writing, tell us more about what archaeologists really think they are doing than do formal expressions of theory about the nature and purpose of archaeology. Archaeologists who consider themselves 'like detectives' are liable to operate differently from archaeologists who consider themselves 'artists' (e.g. Barker 1977, who is himself an accomplished painter). Little information is available about this aspect of archaeology and no coherent study has been made of it. It does, however, seem that the perception of their subject by archaeologists, outside formalised theoretical debate and public images, should be taken into account in any consideration of the identity and purpose of archaeology.

Having discussed some definitions of archaeology, we may now turn to some of the reasons why archaeologists consider the subject to be worthwhile.

Why do we do archaeology?

Archaeologists have been very straightforward in expressing opinions about the purpose of their subject (e.g. Dark 1985; Bintliff 1988;

Gathercole and Lowenthal 1989; Layton 1989a). As we saw when defining post-processualism in the Introduction, the purpose of archaeology can be very strongly linked to the theoretical school to which the archaeologist belongs. It is probably true that reasons for doing archaeology condition the definitions of archaeology that are given, and the definitions condition the reasons. Clearly there are many reasons why one might want to study past material culture. These include the belief that knowledge is itself always valuable, the search for evidence to support religious, political, or other (e.g. aesthetic) ideas, the search for 'origins', or for entertainment alone (Rahtz 1985). One might wish to study material culture to emphasise differences or similarities between the past and the present, or to recognise the distinctive identity of humanity. As we shall see below, some have wished to study it to emphasise similarities or differences between nations. Archaeologists might be seeking to advance history, art-history, classics, geography, biology, or some other academic subject. Alternatively, archaeology might be undertaken simply from curiosity about what material things were like in the past, or about elements of the landscape or environment.

Archaeology has certainly been undertaken in the past for political or personal gain, e.g. as a career strategy. We have seen that personal identification with a specific period or group in the past might encourage one to undertake archaeology, or the subject could be done as a form of 'escape' from the present. Conversely, some might study archaeology to bring themselves 'down to earth'. Anyone dissecting a medieval sewage pit with a trowel would agree that the experience might well have this effect. Alternatively, archaeology might be a way of seeking one's personal 'roots', or, less dramatically, it might be studied at university, or entered into as a hobby, because the subject is of interest to one's relatives or friends, or in order to meet new people. These non-academic reasons must be considered if we are to understand why people spend their leisure time working at archaeology, and why highly-qualified graduates often undertake very poorly-paid insecure work.

This brief discussion should leave no doubt about the wide range of different reasons that cause people to consider the subject worthwhile and to become archaeologists. Archaeology is certainly attractive to an extremely wide cross-section of personalities and backgrounds. In the remainder of this chapter I shall look at some specific academic and political reasons for the study of archaeology.

Marxism

Some of the most unambiguous statements of the purpose of archaeology have come from Marxists such as Gathercole, Shanks and Tilley (Gathercole 1984; Tilley 1989; Shanks and Tilley 1987a and b).

Archaeology has long contained scholars motivated by the political ideology of Marxism, such as Childe (e.g. 1979).

In accordance with the overall perspective provided by their Marxist views, such scholars consider that all archaeology is a political activity (e.g. Trigger 1984b). The aims of Marxism in political terms are furthered, according to these scholars, by the subject, which after all is often described as 'historical materialism'. It is hardly surprising that such a subject plays a role in the theory of the study of the past through its material remains.

Although Childe strongly supported Stalinist Russia, modern Marxist archaeologists do not all conform to a single Marxist ideology. Some have 'classical Marxist' views, such as Roskams, and others, such as Gathercole, more broadly interpret a Marxist approach. A key difference between these two very broad groups within Marxist archaeology is over the question of ideology (see Spriggs 1984; McGuire 1992) – not Marxist ideology today, but the role of ideology in past societies. To a classical Marxist, past ideology is no more than a reflection of its economic basis (for a sceptical review see Gathercole 1984). Non-classical Marxists, as we may group them very broadly here, mostly see ideology as not simply a reflection of economic relations, but as playing a crucial role in pre-capitalist, e.g. prehistoric, societies (see Friedman 1974). We shall return to these divisions among Marxists in Chapter 7.

This broad division leads to a different concept of the purpose of archaeology among classical and non-classical Marxists. To a classical Marxist the role of archaeology is to support and expand upon Marx's writings, and on Marxist 'classics' such as those produced by Engels and Lenin. For such a scholar archaeology can add data unknown in the nineteenth and early twentieth centuries, and incorporate new geographical areas and timespans into Marx's framework (Saunders forthcoming). It can also examine in more detail the workings of the relationships already explained, according to these scholars, by Marx (Saunders forthcoming).

The alternative Marxist view is to suppose that Marx's work itself needs revision or can be added to by later studies. Such scholars might introduce concepts derived from Marxist scholars such as Foucault and Althusser (e.g. Shanks and Tilley 1987a), whose work will be mentioned again in a later chapter. The purpose of their archaeology is consequently very different from that of classical Marxists. Marxism itself provides them with a motivation and many analytical concepts, but unlike classical Marxists, for them archaeology has the potential to reflect back upon their fundamental political views. If this still seems extremely biased, it must be noted that such scholars argue that all views of the past are unavoidably biased (Shanks and Tilley 1987a and b), and usually that they are products of specific historical circumstances themselves (Saitta 1983, 1991).

However, by no means all politically motivated archaeologists are Marxists (e.g. Gero 1985; Andah 1983; Ford 1973; Renfrew and Bahn 1991; Bintliff 1988), and some archaeologists with strong political views seek to prevent them from influencing their archaeological interpretations (see Boado and Damm 1988). One might well find archaeologists whose purpose in studying the past is to support conservative points of view, or to discern the true political development of their own (or another) country (e.g. Andah 1983). Especially notable among politically motivated archaeologists are feminist scholars.

Feminism

The 1980s and 1990s have seen the growth of a large feminist movement within archaeology (e.g. Schmitz and Steffgen 1989; Ehrenberg 1989; Gero and Conkey 1990; Walde and Willows 1991). This has explicit political aims: the redefinition of the role of women in the past and present and the redefinition of the attitudes to women in the study of the past and in the conduct of archaeological research.

The viewpoints and aims of feminist writers have varied greatly in archaeology (e.g. Gero 1985; Gero and Conkey 1990; Walde and Willows 1991; Engelstead 1991; Gilchrist 1991; Wylie 1992). Some have sought to demonstrate the past domination, or universal oppression, of women by men. Others have had a less extreme aim – to bring women more into the centre stage of reconstructions of the past, and to expunge negative attitudes to women from both the interpretations of archaeologists and the profession of archaeology itself.

Leading figures among the feminist movement in archaeology have come from both processual and post-processual schools, although not from culture-history. Post-processualism has been strongly associated with feminism through the work of scholars such as Moore (1982, 1986, 1988) and Braithwaite (1982). Feminist approaches have mostly been adopted by archaeologists working in Britain, the United States, and other English-speaking countries, with leading figures including Ehrenburg (e.g. 1989), Hastorf (e.g. 1990), Wylie (e.g. 1990), Gero and Conkey (e.g. 1990) setting the agenda. But not all feminist archaeologists are from English-speaking countries: the school is strongly represented, for example, in Scandinavia and among Scandinavian scholars working elsewhere, such as Sorensen (1988) and Dommasnes (1992). Rather than discuss examples of feminist archaeology in this section, I have integrated them wherever appropriate in the thematic chapters on reconstructing society, economy, etc., and I would stress that political feminism is to some extent separate from 'gender studies', which will be discussed in Chapter 4.

4. The political role of the past. Welsh participants asserting a shared identity with their Breton hosts at a 'Celtic' festival in Brittany in 1983. The link being celebrated is that of the fifth- and sixth-century AD migrations from Western Britain to Brittany. (Photo: K.R. Dark)

Other political motivations

One area where archaeology has played an especially interesting role in politics, and where political motivations have underlain much archaeological research, has been in the post-colonial archaeological study of developing countries by their own archaeologists (see Miller 1980; Gathercole and Lowenthal 1989; Stone and Mackenzie 1989; Layton 1989). Archaeology can play a significant role in the formation of contemporary identity and in the symbolism of new states. Most striking is the use of Zimbabwe, an archaeological monument, as a symbol of a post-colonial state (Garlake 1973; Segobye *et al.* 1990). Political impetus of this kind has often derived from the need to consolidate national unity and strengthen feelings of group solidarity, for example in Israel (Shay 1989). It has been considered useful to seek a shared, and preferably glorious, past. John Muke, a Papuan archaeologist, has pointed out to me (personal communication 1986) a fine example of this from Papua New

Guinea, where scholars have attempted to show that in the prehistoric past, diverse peoples, now speaking hundreds of distinct languages, shared a similar material culture, and so, perhaps, were less markedly differentiated. It has also been considered valuable to show that in the distant prehistoric past the peoples of Papua New Guinea were technologically advanced compared to their contemporaries elsewhere. By seeking a common heritage in this way it has been hoped to increase both the unity and self-confidence of this new nation.

Without a doubt, the discovery of a rich archaeological past can play a role in formulating modern national identity. It can also be a valuable boost to tourism. Alternatively, indigenous peoples may be strongly opposed to interference with archaeological sites which they consider to be their own exclusive heritage (Miller 1980). (For the role of archaeology in the developing world, see Layton 1989a; Stone and Mackenzie 1989.)

5. Racism and progress. Although this Roman centurion, buried at Colchester (Essex), was Italian, Roman law made no racial distinctions between citizens: what does this tell us about questions of racism or of 'progress'? (Photo: K.R. Dark)

Anti-racist motives

Another motivation for studying the past, not wholly unrelated to the previous one, is to combat racism (e.g. Trigger 1980). Scholars have attempted to use archaeology to show that all humanity derived from the same palaeolithic origins, or to show that non-Europeans were capable of great cultural and technological achievements before the colonial period. This is, in part, the significance of Zimbabwe (Garlake 1973): the site of the deserted city was so magnificent that some pre-modern scholars could not believe that it was built by Africans alone. Archaeology has shown that this assumption is ungrounded and that the site was built by local people, unaided by Europeans. Although it is difficult to assess from published comments whether there are archaeologists wholly motivated by the aim of countering racism, it is certainly a factor in contemporary archaeology.

The construction of a global or European identity

Some archaeologists have viewed the subject as capable of providing a greater sense of global community, or of European unity. Archaeology certainly has the potential to demonstrate linkages between areas, and their inter-relationships in the past, and so might be seen as able to recognise periods in the past in which Europe was more united than at present. Such views have, however, recently been the subject of some scepticism from scholars with their own political motivation, the emphasis of regionalism.

The diversity of human experience

One reason for undertaking archaeology, which post-processual theorists have supported, is to demonstrate the diversity of human experience. By seeking multiple pasts and openness to different interpretations, they have hoped to challenge the 'taken-for-granted' assumptions, or as they sometimes call them, the 'givens', of contemporary society. They have sought to show that in the past there were many other ways of 'being human'. This has sometimes been combined with *critical theory* (see Chapter 7) which seeks to undermine the way in which scholarly endeavour (in this case archaeology) supports the status quo in the modern world.

6. Does progress exist? Underfloor heating system (hypocaust) in the Roman villa at Fishbourne (Sussex). 500 years later, the technology was lost in Britain. Does this show that there is no 'law of progress'? (Photo: S.P. Dark)

The demonstration of progress

An important motivation, particularly in the early twentieth century and before, was the ability of archaeology to show the progress of culture and technology from the earliest times to the present. This will be discussed at greater length later in this book, but here it may be noted that there are many problems with the concept of progress itself. It is probably a less notable motivation for the study of archaeology today than it was, for example, in the 1930s.

The futility of war, or of political domination

Another reason that some scholars have studied archaeology has been, at least in part, to show that military victories, or political domination, are irrelevant when seen in the broader context of long-term cultural change. Such scholars have hoped to emphasise that weapons or fortifications proved ineffectual or irrelevant, and have hoped to show that political independence re-emerges even from the harshest domination. Their aim has been to promote peace, and it was from this viewpoint that, in the early 1980s, an 'Archaeologists for Peace' movement emerged in Britain, although this did not prove an enduring group. Although this has an

obvious appeal, I can think of no archaeologist who has stated in print
that this was his or her sole motivation for taking up the subject.

Conservation

There are now several theorists who have set out a case for a 'green'
archaeology, in which the study of the effects of humanity's
inter-relationship with the environment over the long timespans capable
of being studied by archaeology helps to inform current debate about
environmental conservation (e.g. Greeves 1989; Pryor 1990; Macinnes
and Wickham-Jones 1992). Bell (Boardman and Bell 1992) has recently
suggested that archaeology might provide evidence for the evaluation of
coastal change, and related projects have begun at, for example, Romney
Marsh in England. Bell has also played a leading role in attempts to use
archaeological evidence in studies of geomorphological landscape change
(Boardman and Bell 1992). Archaeologists are also involved in current
studies of long-term 'desertification': environmental change leading
to the transformation of areas into deserts (personal communication,
J. McGlade 1991).

A long-term perspective on the present
and a guide to the future

The view that the study of the past may help inform us about the future
has a very long history in scholarship. Processual archaeologists, whether
arguing from the point of view of universal laws concerning how cultures
change, or from broad generalisations, have often considered it possible
that archaeology may help us to understand how our own societies are
changing, and to learn something of the way they may change in the
future (see Dark 1985; Renfrew and Bahn 1991). An excellent example of
this approach is Tainter's (1988) fascinating study of the collapse of
complex societies (see also Yoffee and Cowgill 1988). Having formulated a
general explanation on the basis of archaeological evidence from ancient
Mesoamerica, the Roman world, and other past states, Tainter attempts
to relate this explanation to our own state societies. Others have
attempted to identify long-term cycles of change and regularities in the
processes underlying political and social transformation, extending from
the archaeological past into the present, and potentially into the future
(for a review of such attempts in archaeology and other disciplines, see
Dark forthcoming). The assumption behind this approach is that if such
cycles can be verified on the grounds of data about the past, and if no
reason can be shown to discount their operation in the present and
immediate future, we can use them to argue about possible future
developments in our own societies.

The use of archaeology in this way is not restricted to processualist scholars. Culture-historical scholars have taken the view that societies universally grow more complex, or progress. This is a well established avenue of research, and certainly forms at least part of the motivation for many archaeologists, including me (see Dark 1985). It is closely related to similar developments in ecological modelling, mathematics, history and political theory.

Conclusion

It is by no means clear that a widely held definition of archaeology, or statement of its purpose, can be set forward in detail today. It would certainly be difficult to find a unifying motivation for archaeologists, other than, perhaps, the impulse to discover more about the past. Archaeologists, whether intellectually or emotionally, define themselves, and are seen by others, according to a wide range of formal connections and informal images.

All archaeologists, professional or amateur, must therefore consider where they stand on each of these issues. These are not insignificant matters; how we do archaeology is a product of how we define archaeology, and why we do archaeology is encompassed within both of these aspects. Even if one said only, 'I am an archaeologist because I enjoy digging up things', this would simply be another theoretical position.

CHAPTER 2

The Framework of Archaeological Reasoning

Data and evidence

Archaeologists recover many *data* each year. Every artefact, structure, or bone, can be seen as a piece of data (correctly a *datum*), which might yield archaeological information.

But data only constitute information about their own existence; they are not in themselves archaeological evidence. They become evidence only when they are employed within a framework of interpretation. A pot does not tell us that it is (for example) Roman, or what it was used for. We derive this information from analysing that pot within a framework of concepts, from which we establish ways of reasoning about it and techniques for examining it. The results of archaeological analysis are not, however, 'facts' in the same sense that material data are 'facts', except to the positivist (who believes that it is possible to prove interpretations). They are interpretations derived from, or in some way related to, data.

Many archaeologists fail to make these simple but crucial distinctions. Thus, 'corn-drying kilns' become as much facts as their constituent bricks, or 'social organisation' as much a fact as a layer of clay. Even the most ardent positivist scholar does not dispute the crucial distinction between data and evidence, and yet this is seldom recognised, at least explicitly. For example, in early Anglo-Saxon cemetery archaeology there are plenty of data, but it is by no means clear that there is plentiful *evidence* until the logical frameworks have been set out which enable the interpretation of that data.

The distinction between data and evidence is not a trivial point, for it deeply affects our attitudes to the archaeological record, and to the importance of *middle-range theory*.

Epistemology and middle-range theory

Epistemology is the study of how we know what we know. It is the most philosophical branch of theoretical archaeology, and could be construed as both the most important and the most complex theoretical subject (for

36

a sample of relevant approaches, see Binford and Binford 1968; Salmon 1982; Binford 1982, 1983a, 1989; Watson 1984; Hodder 1986, 1992; Kelly and Hanen 1988; Gibbon 1989; Embree 1992 and its bibliography on this theme, 319-26). It might initially appear that the answer to the questions how we can test hypotheses concerning the past, or whether we can at all, are either obvious or so vastly complex as to be insoluble. The problem posed by epistemology is, however, a simple one. Epistemology can be reduced to the questions of whether we think that we can prove or disprove things, and whether we think that we can evaluate the likelihood of their being true or not.

One way of looking at this question has already been mentioned: positivism. The positivist believes that it is possible to test hypotheses and show them to be true or false. Testing in this way usually involves comparing the hypothesis to new data other than that which was used to generate it. The subsequent test is often mathematical – for instance statistical – and if it shows a fit between the hypothesis and the new data, the hypothesis is said to be true.

Positivism in archaeology is mainly associated with the 'New Archaeology', but there are still positivist archaeologists working in processualist and culture-historical archaeology, although many process-ualists and most post-processual archaeologists have taken a negative view of positivism (e.g. Renfrew and Bahn 1991, 432). To give an example of how these differing attitudes work in practice: many of those who have worked on an excavation will know the experience of finding the remains of a stone-built wall running across the excavated area, and of a new area being dug 'expecting' to find more of it. If the remains of a similar wall is found, then the hypothesis that the wall ran across the new area is said to be true. This may seem self-evident, but it is a positivist view of testing.

Another viewpoint is *probabilistic* evaluation. If we do not accept that proof is possible we might favour a probabilistic view of testing. This is often associated with a *refutationist* epistemology, based on the work of Popper and championed in archaeology by Renfrew and Bell (Popper 1985; Renfrew 1982; Bell 1981, 1982). The refutationist holds that we cannot show what is 'true', only what is 'false'. If a hypothesis is tested and found not to be refuted by further evidence, it is considered *corroborated*. That is, while it is not proved to be true, the more tests it passes, the more confidence we can place in it. So the wall running across the site in our example is not certainly proved to exist in the new area, but it is far more likely that it does. If, on the other hand, more remains had *not* been found, it would have been shown that the wall did not exist in that area, which a refutationist would be happy to accept. Archaeologists who have been involved in the re-interpretation of old excavations may well find this an attractive view, in contrast to what might otherwise be seen as 'commonsense'.

Finally, there is testing by *concordance*. Concordance is the fit observed between the hypothesis and some, or all, of the other information available. Some would take this to include other hypotheses as well as other 'facts'. This approach is based on how the hypothesis 'fits in' with other information. Concordance testing is often implicitly used by archaeologists, for example, when we say that it is most likely that the grand building in the centre of a Roman town was a forum (market square), because it fits in with the other things we know about that town and other similar towns. More explicitly, concordance testing (its supporters often prefer to call it *validation*) lies at the basis of the *contextual* theory of hypothesis evaluation proposed by Hodder (1987a, 1992; see also Barrett 1987).

Contextual archaeology

Hodder's (1987a, 1992) contextual archaeology is the use of the relationship of each element of material culture to each other element to elucidate its interpretation. That is, if we wish to understand a type of artefact we must see it in the context of the site where it is found, the other artefacts, and seemingly unrelated aspects of material culture such as burial customs or agricultural residues.

Hodder has suggested that this gives a post-processual logic for

7. How can we tell? Is this reconstruction at West Stow (Suffolk) a true picture of early Anglo-Saxon life? Or is it a form of historical fiction? (Photo: S.P. Dark)

archaeological interpretation, which supersedes both relativism and processualist views of middle-range theory. Yet others have found this argument 'circular', as each part of the material record depends for its interpretation on other parts of that record, themselves interpreted by reference to it. So, pot A is understood in relation to its point of recovery (site B), but site B is understood in relation to pot A. The debate is currently unresolved, but post-processualists have tended to adopt other forms of argument.

Political and moral validation

Post-processual archaeologists have suggested that another possibility is to evaluate hypotheses with reference to political or moral value in the present. In this view, a Marxist archaeologist might, for example, believe only those hypotheses which would further the cause of Marxism. Barrett has suggested, in as yet unpublished work, that moral universals might serve to validate archaeological hypotheses. This view stands somewhere between those who favour some form of testing (or validation), and post-processualists adopting a relativist viewpoint.

Relativism and objectivity

All these options suppose that we can evaluate hypotheses. Those who do not believe in testing are called *relativists*. Relativism is based on complex philosophical arguments, but is centred around the concept that all knowledge is entirely *subjective* (for an important critique, see Bell 1988) since all information is processed by the perception and preconceptions of the observer (see Leone 1986). This contrasts with the view that there can be *objective* knowledge consisting of what is true under any circumstances. Clearly, positivists consider that objective knowledge can be obtained relatively simply through testing hypotheses, and in probablistic evaluation both objective and subjective knowledge are believed to exist, the link between them ultimately depending upon a threshold beyond which the observer believes something is true or not. A relativist, however, says that we cannot even know that we exist, let alone that the wall running across our site does.

In relativist archaeology we have to decide between hypotheses on personal grounds: whether we like an interpretation or find it useful, not whether it is true or not. The relativist does not believe in truth, only in perception.

Truth is something strongly associated with testing, and the 'truth' produced by positivistic testing and, say, concordance testing, may be taken to mean different things. So, when one prehistorian says, 'In the Neolithic this settlement was used by farmers', it may not mean the same in epistemological terms as when another makes the same remark (e.g. Barrett 1990).

Few archaeologists have openly declared themselves as adopting a relativist approach, although a volume of such studies has been published (Baker and Thomas 1990). This approach has, however, been employed in recent work by post-processualist scholars, and it forms the principal post-processualist alternative to contextual and *structuralist* theories of truth (Wylie 1982; Hodder 1992). Structuralists consider that perception does recover patterning from the real world but that that patterning has been filtered through the conceptual structures of the mind, and so reflects those structures as much as what is perceived (e.g. Gellner 1982; Small 1987).

There are, therefore, many different ways of approaching the validation of hypotheses, and the logic employed to form them is central to archaeological thought. All archaeologists, other than a few post-processual scholars favouring relativist perspectives, consider that archaeological interpretations have to be based on some form of logical argument. Post-processualists may consider, however, that what we would recognise as logic is a product of our own time and place, so that it, too, is a result of our cultural setting. This can lead to the view that there is no logic which may be applied to any time or place, or to the material remains of past societies. Consequently, some post-processualists would reject logic as a basis for archaeological reasoning, and favour, for example, emotion. This is not, however, usually considered a credible view by archaeologists, and it would be fair to say that archaeological arguments are generally based on logical reasoning.

Logic linking material data and interpretation is called (especially by processualists), middle-range theory (e.g. Binford 1982, 1983a; Raab and Goodyear 1984). As soon as we look at a site and claim, 'That's a wall', or 'That's a post-hole', we are making use of such logic – in processualist terms we are using middle-range theory. This is a convenient term and will be used here.

It is impossible for archaeologists, whatever their theoretical stance (even if the stance is to be 'uninterested in theory'), to operate without such linking logic, unless they are relativists who reject logic as a basis for reasoning. So, generally, archaeologists would recognise that archaeology necessarily has to take place 'within' middle-range logic, as much as it necessarily takes place 'within' a theory of truth.

To the relativist the question of logic is, of course, irrelevant and misleading, because no such logic can exist. To the culture-historian that logic is usually claimed to be 'commonsense'. In archaeology, common sense is supposed to be what the material data 'obviously' mean to the interpreter. That is, the culture-historian may claim that there is no such thing as non-intuitive meaning to be derived from material culture, and that the meaning of material remains can be discovered from their careful consideration within a logical framework, which might equally be applied to modern objects or structures. This view assumes that we can intrinsically 'read' material data, or, to put it another way, that their meaning is self-evident. 'Self-evidence' is, in fact, central to much culture-historical reasoning. It claims that material culture 'speaks for itself', and can be read by any logical and critical observer. Such views are sometimes combined with a critical method based on the analysis of the logic of archaeological inferences, but often also by criticism based on (so-called) *ad hominem* assessments: X is a skilled archaeologist, therefore what X says is more likely to be true than what Y (who lacks such skill) says. Such critiques are often grounded as much in assessments of the 'perceptiveness' and intelligence of the analyst – sometimes, even, in how well-known the analyst is to the archaeologist assessing the work – as on the methods employed. This contrasts with the processualist view which emphasises the methods and structures of interpretation rather than the archaeologist who is using them, and especially the ability of the hypothesis proposed to withstand further testing.

Processualists have made middle-range theory a central concern in the 1980s and 1990s, and have based this upon the study both of how archaeological materials are formed, and of how they are *modified* after their formation (*formation processes*): what have been called *depositional* and *post-depositional* factors. Depositional factors may include natural processes (or *N-transforms*) such as erosion (depositing a soil layer), or human processes (*C-transforms*) such as the dumping of refuse (for examples, see Schiffer 1976, 1987; Moore and Keen 1983; Sommer 1990). Post-depositional factors (also described in terms of C- and N-transforms) include the organic decay of buried wood, and human factors such as the deliberate robbing of graves. Such factors structure the archaeological record. Data are never exactly the same as represented in the archaeological record as they were before entering that record: for example, a broken sherd of medieval pottery is not the same as that pot when it was in use. The archaeological data, therefore, can be taken to represent the past but do not present us with that past in a unmodified state. Even in a shipwreck, what we recover as the archaeological record of the ship is not the same as the ship as it existed in the past. Nor is the archaeological record itself static; it is constantly being modified, and usually this involves the loss of information (e.g. Bonnischen 1989; Adams 1991). If a Bronze-Age barrow is left unexcavated for a century, the continuing processes of root and animal action, and the chemical and hydrological modification of the deposits comprising it, will result in the modification of the archaeological data. Seldom does this involve the addition of information, so a basic tenet of depositional and post-depositional theory must be that the potential information contained in the archaeological record is always decreasing (Adams 1991).

To give another example of how rapidly and extensively the archaeological record is modified: even if, in a medieval siege, an attacker was killed in action and instantly buried by the collapse of rubble, the manner in which the corpse fell and the modification of the body by natural processes constitute depositional and post-depositional modifications to the record. Processes resulting from the collapse of rubble onto the body may further modify its position and preservation. Even before post-depositional processes resulting from centuries of burial, which might, for example, dissolve the bones of the skeleton in an acidic soil, the warrior killed in action might be represented in the archaeological record as a partly disarticulated skeleton, with a few corroded iron artefacts found beneath the rubble surrounding it. Most archaeological deposits are not formed so dramatically, but nor do they have the same opportunity for preservation as discrete representations of human history.

An alternative is the post-processualist stance that material remains are not passively formed and modified by natural and human processes, but 'meaningfully constituted' into 'text'. That is, people structure their material world, and natural processes do not entirely remove this structuring. This 'text' is perceived as having both a 'passive' and an 'active' role even when it has become part of the archaeological record: it can both be acted upon and 'act' within culture. The resulting interpretations – for example, that pots were manipulating their owners – have been among the most widely criticised post-processualist views and also among the most widely employed. Some post-processualists have agreed with processualists that natural processes can be reconstructed, and that their role in structuring the material record can be discerned (e.g. Hodder 1992). Others have felt this too to be impossible – as it is if examined from a relativist viewpoint.

Archaeologists of all of these different opinions have agreed that anthropology, historical sources, the study of natural processes and experimental archaeology can form part of a debate about these questions, and it is to these areas of inquiry that we may now turn.

Anthropology

Archaeologists, even those who do not favour an anthropological identity for archaeology, have long recognised the middle-range value of anthropology. It might be hoped that anthropological study would elucidate the relationship between material and non-material culture, and so enable us 'to do archaeology' as perhaps shown by aspects of Bloch's studies (e.g. Bloch 1971).

Anthropology has been used in many ways by archaeologists seeking to derive middle-range theory from it (for a sample of these, see Robbins 1966; Binford and Binford 1968, 1972, 1983a; David 1971; Donan and Clewlow 1974; Yellen 1977; Sabloff 1978; Gould 1978; Kramer 1979). To some, such as Bryony Coles (Orme 1981), it provides caution against

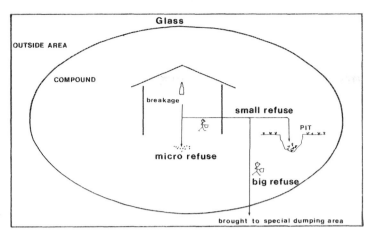

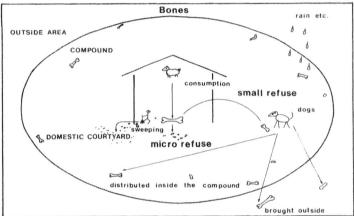

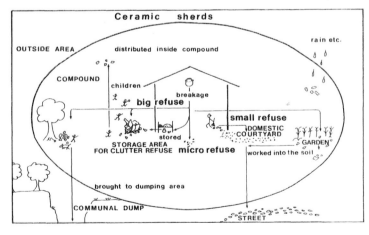

8. The theory of rubbish. Three examples of human and natural factors in the formation of archaeological deposits. (Reproduced with the kind permission of Ulrike Sommer)

over-optimistic interpretations of settlement or burial evidence and artefacts (see also Heider 1967; Ucko 1969). To others, such as Binford (e.g. 1983a) and Hodder (e.g. 1982b and c), it provides a direct source of information concerning the detailed relationship between material culture and archaeological reconstruction, although each would take a very different view of this. Yet others have seen it as an over-rated source of interpretive logic (e.g. Wobst 1978).

Some of the most interesting work has been done by American scholars, especially Binford, who coined the term 'middle-range theory' and has made this the centre of his recent research (e.g. Binford 1981, 1983a, 1989). An excellent example of the processualist view is his important study of archaeological patterning produced by people sitting around a hearth (Binford 1983a). He considers that anthropological information reveals a general, if not universal, way in which people place themselves around an open-air hearth. This can be confirmed from anthropological descriptions and even photographs, and provides an idealised picture (a *model*) of how people sit and where they throw their rubbish. This can, therefore, be tested by comparing the distribution of rubbish relative to the hearth, and the resulting patterning to the model. This model has proved to be a starting point for refinements and discussion by other scholars (e.g. contributors in Kroll and Price 1991; Stapert 1984, 1990).

Hodder (1982b and c) suggests that detailed consideration of how material culture relates to non-material culture – for example, how house plans relate to social organisation – shows such a wide range of possible relationships that no universal archaeological arguments can be employed relating archaeological remains to their interpretation. He has suggested instead that a plurality of interpretations, to be validated on assessed data, have to be formed, and that symbolism is so widely found as an important part of material culture in anthropological studies that its study must be central to archaeology (Hodder 1982b and c).

It is from anthropology that the view of material culture as text derives. That is, anthropological studies can be taken to show that material culture remains are 'meaningfully' structured by human action – even if they are latrine or rubbish deposits. By this is meant that human attitudes, whether unintentionally or deliberately, structure the material with which humans come into contact.

These two views emphasise the different ways in which, when considering anthropology in the formulation of middle-range theory, inferences have been drawn from anthropological evidence and applied to archaeological study. Many of these inferences have been contradictory and unable to be held in combination, but many can be complementary within the same theoretical overview.

A specialised field within anthropological study is the use of anthropological evidence specifically to answer archaeological questions of this type – *ethnoarchaeology* – and this has tended to be practised entirely by archaeologists (e.g. Bonnischen 1973; Donan and Clewlow 1974; Binford 1978; Gould 1978, 1980; Kramer 1979; Tooker 1982; Staski and Sutro 1991; Cameron and Tomka 1993). The rise of ethnoarchaeology since the 1970s has largely been in response to the lack of relevant information available from anthropological studies which have tended to concentrate on issues such as kinship, gender, sex, social and religious organisation, but not on the material evidence for them.

Another specialised field in this approach is the study of 'modern material culture', occasionally called 'the archaeology of us' after the well-known book of the same title (Gould and Schiffer 1981; see also Rathje 1974, 1979). Modern material culture studies have applied anthropological techniques to the solution of archaeological problems by reference to modern material remains in the 'developed' countries, although these remains are, of course, no less 'modern' than those of the contemporary Bushmen or Australian Aborigines. Miller (1984) has, for example, examined the material culture of contemporary suburbia as a source for cognitive archaeology, and there is a wealth of ethnoarchaeo-logical data deriving from the British Isles and Europe, as yet underemployed by archaeologists (e.g. Evans 1957).

Such studies, whether ethnoarchaeology or 'modern material culture', have produced a similar range of interpretations and problems to anthropological studies: the breadth of interpretations of similar material by anthropologists and by archaeologists; the range of ways in which participants in the societies studied interpret identical material culture; the issue of generalisations from specific cases and of 'universals'; and the difficulties in obtaining accurate or unbiased evidence of the interpretation of material from members of the society under study. Again, these studies have been used to formulate detailed interpretations and logic (Schiffer 1976, 1987), and as cautionary tales (Parker-Pearson 1982). They have also been interpreted as providing evidence of the symbolic character and active role of material culture (Shanks and Tilley 1987a and 1987b; Tilley 1989).

Differences in the preservation of archaeological evidence itself have also been used to evaluate how we may reconstruct the past from its material remains. There has been little explicit theoretical debate about the implications of sites with exceptional preservation when debating middle-range theory, but John and Bryony Coles have drawn attention to this important issue (e.g. see Coles 1991).

The questions raised by comparing sites of different forms of preservation are to some extent different from, but overlap with, those raised by ethnoarchaeology and modern 'material culture studies'. Central to these is the prospect of 'calibrating' the representivity of archaeological remains on sites with poor preservation by reference to those with exceptionally well-preserved material. This does not help us to construct a logical framework for deriving social or economic information

9. The problem of representivity. Of this seventeenth-century bedchamber, only accidental losses, a few metal fittings, the stone walls and, perhaps, window-glass and pieces of plaster would usually survive on a European site. The organic elements (wood, cloth, etc.) would rot away and portable objects would probably be removed when the house was deserted. (Photo: Courtesy of Sheffield City Museums)

from the archaeological record, but it does help to counteract the effects of post-depositional factors 'scrambling' the way in which archaeological material presents us with evidence of the past.

The theoretical implications of differential preservation

Archaeologists have generally been aware that they work with samples. An archaeological excavation or a survey is a sample of a site or region. These, however, represent no more than samples of already processed material evidence – the results of the post-depositional and depositional processes already mentioned. Such processes, in removing the organic element from most of our artefacts and structures, and by destroying the skeletons and the bone elements of these artefacts in acidic soils, leave us with only a partial representation of what once existed at any site; even those artefacts which are recovered may lack substantial elements. Take the example of the room, a photograph of which is reproduced here as Fig. 9. There are few elements of this well-furnished bedroom which would survive if it was found in a typical archaeological context in temperate

Europe or North America. Natural and, especially, human factors will have sorted the components of artefacts so as to render some elements of the surviving material culture more visible than others in most situations. All that may survive on a site from a room such as this may be a few metal fittings and the foundation of the walls.

The theoretical implications of this affect archaeological interpretation in two main ways. Any correlation between surviving material and non-material culture may be unreliable, as substantial elements of material culture may no longer survive, or may not be recovered by archaeologists. Moreover, we may lack the elements of artefacts which would enable us to assign functions to them, or even to categorise them. That is, a consideration of the problems of differential preservation has, even at this level, an important theoretical role. It can help us to realise the limitations of our data and caution against interpretations which do not take its partial quality into account.

In an interesting study, Vickers (1990) has drawn attention to the way in which socially important classes of artefact may be poorly represented in the archaeological record due to social factors alone. Vickers observes that high-value metal vessels existed in Classical Antiquity, but are less strongly represented in the archaeological record than lower-value decorated pottery because precious metal was liable to be melted down and re-used. This has meant that archaeologists have placed undue importance on decorated ceramics and overlooked a socially important but archaeologically (almost) invisible type of artefact. This highlights a point made independently by other scholars in the case of specific examples (e.g. Barker 1986), that material culture does not reflect the sophistication or complexity of the culture of its users: that is to say, there is no certain correlation between the two (Dark 1994a).

But we may go beyond this. The recovery of material from waterlogged or other exceptionally preserved contexts can place into clearer perspective material culture recovered from dry sites. Quite simply, it can tell us what elements of the material record we may be missing. Yet we must be constantly aware of the danger of assuming that every site is similar to its better preserved counterparts, or speculating that it is necessarily more complex than the excavated evidence would otherwise lead us to suppose. We must recall that even waterlogged deposits represent a partial and modified sample.

Most well-known examples of differential preservation depend upon natural processes of waterlogging and desiccation. The middle-range importance of studying natural processes involved in forming the archaeological record has long been realised, and is no less important today.

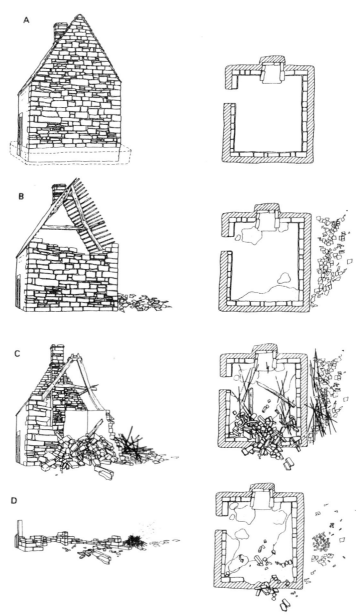

10. Natural and 'cultural' formation processes. The collapse of a small stone building. A. The structure in use (broken line shows foundation trench for walls). B. The same building abandoned: note the tiles scattered at back and floor beginning to break up. C. The same process of decay accelerates and the roof timbers fall into and around the building. D. Human factors further accelerate disintegration of the building. Most of the stone is removed for re-use elsewhere, as is some of the timber, the rest being burnt near the building. (Reproduced with the kind permission of Philip Barker)

Natural processes

Since the recognition of archaeological stratification and of the importance of its study – *stratigraphy* – in archaeological reasoning, archaeologists have employed natural processes to explain archaeological materials (for a modern account of stratigraphy, see Harris 1979). Other widely employed examples include the use of terms such as 'erosion' and 'silting' to introduce natural factors into studies of the formation of archaeological deposits.

Not only geological and geomorphological processes (e.g. Raikes 1967; Gladfelter 1977; Vita-Finzi 1978; Nash and Petraglia 1987) have been used in this way, but also biological factors. We readily talk about the decay of organic materials on 'dry' sites (so long as they are not *too* dry), and the realisation that artefacts are moved (post-depositionally) by earthworms has been part of archaeological interpretation since the 1950s (Atkinson 1957). Interestingly, the way in which the latter factor has been discussed illustrates the often half-hearted use of many such concepts – few archaeologists have been prepared to eliminate a crucial sherd of pottery as dating evidence on the grounds of possible worm-disturbance. Still fewer archaeologists are well acquainted with the literature, produced for non-archaeological purposes, on the decay rate of materials such as wood, or on the modification of these by, for example, fire (see Barker 1977, 1986; Stewart 1990).

Natural processes also underlie some of our other middle-range arguments – notably our interpretations of environmental and skeletal data (e.g. Binford 1981). They also form, as O'Conner (1991) has pointed out, some of the most widely acknowledged 'universals' used in archaeology. For instance, few (if any) scholars, whatever their theoretical views, have doubted that humanity is united by the need to eat.

Even such basic universals can, however, be used to generate a logic for interpreting material culture. For instance, light and shade and the solidity of material itself have been used to assist in archaeological interpretation. These form useful examples of how simple generalisations about the natural world can be employed.

Light and materiality

The distribution of well-lit and shaded areas in a building, room, or site, is a factor which we might use to interpret archaeological patterning. An excellent example of this is Drewett's analysis of the excavated data from Black Patch, Sussex (1982). The areas of the excavated buildings which would be shaded or well-lit were used to interpret the pattern of artefacts found. It was shown that tasks (represented by artefacts) requiring precision and, therefore, light, were situated in what might be seen as

BLACK PATCH
HUT 3

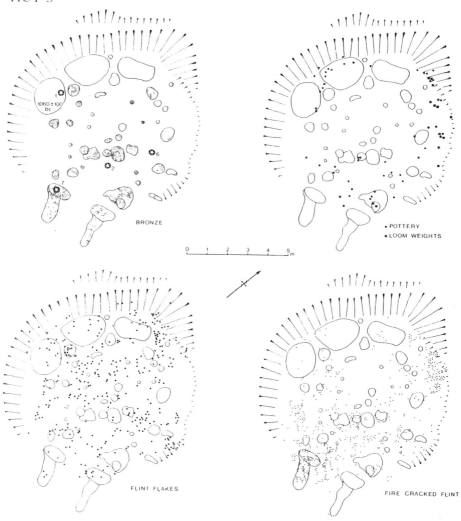

Hut 3. Artefact distributions

11. Light and materiality at Black Patch, Sussex. The distribution of finds in Hut 3 and the use of lighting to interpret them. The artefacts relating to activities needing light were found in areas which received it, while activities for which light was unimportant may have been located in darker areas. (Reproduced with the kind permission of Dr P.L. Drewett and The Institute of Archaeology, University College, London)

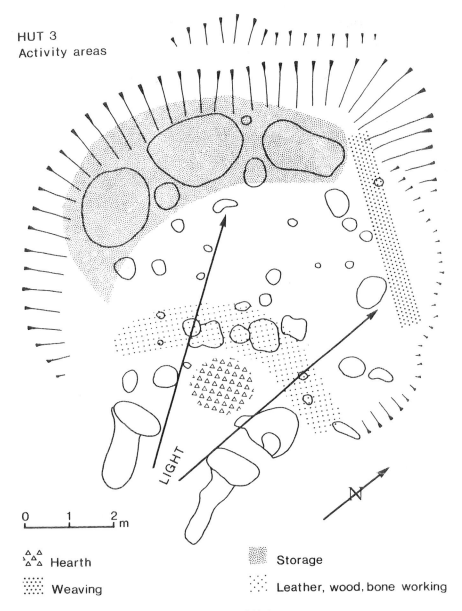

HUT 3
Activity areas

LIGHT

0   1   2 m

△△ Hearth
△△

∵ Weaving

▦ Storage

∴ Leather, wood, bone working

Activity areas within hut 3

well-lit locations (by the doorway and hearth) and others away from these areas. That is, the distribution of dark and light was employed as a basis of interpretation to analyse the archaeological artefacts.

Materiality, the state of being material, has also been used in a similar way. As a solid object (a flint, for example) cannot pass through another solid object, such as a wall made of wattle and daub (unless this has already been broken or damaged), if we find artefacts in relation to walls, or other solid barriers, we can assume that, if the artefacts were deposited after the barriers were constructed, they did not pass through these barriers to their present locations. This is obvious, but it has been usefully employed, for example, by Bradley at Belle Toute, as a method of assessing artefact-distribution and establishing the way in which artefacts were originally deposited (Bradley 1970).

Materiality and the distribution of light and shade have been used in other ways: for example, in the case of O'Kelly's well-known use of lighting in the interpretation of the megalithic structure at Newgrange, Ireland (O'Kelly 1982, 123-4; see also Patrick 1974), or Bradley's (1989) analysis of light and shade in megaliths. A related approach employs the visibility of sites, monuments, works of art or rooms as a way of analysing them. For example, we might use the ability to see one site from another (*intervisibility*) as evidence that people could have seen, or signalled to, each other (e.g. the fascinating approach of Irwin 1992, using intervisibility to understand the colonisation of Pacific islands).

When we have more information about complex natural processes this can underpin equally specific interpretations founded upon them. The recent use of forensic science in archaeology is an excellent example of how the detailed understanding of natural processes can enable the detailed interpretation of archaeological data.

Forensic science

Forensic science (loosely, the science of detection) is a well-developed field. Cooperation between archaeologists and forensic scientists has enabled archaeology to tap this theoretical and methodological knowledge, leading to a far wider awareness of the value of each field to the other (e.g. Garland *et al.* 1988).

Special attention has focussed on burial archaeology, as this is an area in which forensic science is very highly sophisticated. Experimental and observational data collated during and after the Second World War have led to an understanding of the way in which a body decays and is modified both between death and burial (*diagenesis*) and after burial. The modification of body tissue and bone occurs in predictable ways, dependent upon treatment of the body, cause of death and mode of deposition. This enables forensic pathologists to determine the circumstances of death and the time which elapsed between death and burial. Archaeologists can use this data in a similar way – there is no reason to suppose that such processes differed much in the past from today.

Forensic science is still an under-exploited area of middle-range theory. Applications stretch beyond burial data into far less obviously relevant areas. In a fascinating but still unpublished study, the late T.C.M. Brewster used forensic methods of finger-printing to establish that pottery from two nearby sites in Yorkshire was made by the same potter (see Chapter 6). The pottery was decorated by being impressed with finger marks, and these yielded sufficiently detailed characteristics of fingerprints for forensic scientists to declare that they belonged to the same individual. An archaeological conclusion thus resulted from the application of forensic science.

Perhaps the greatest value of the work so far, however, has been to urge caution on excavators as interpreters of burial evidence. The rapid modification of burials means that what is recovered by the excavator is always liable to represent a modified sample. The movement of artefacts in what are often considered to be 'sealed' contexts, such as burial pits and sarcophagi, has, for example, been demonstrated. Likewise, even such a simple observation as the regular slumping of the heads of inhumation burials to one side due to decay alone, has been useful in preventing undue importance from being placed on this in the archaeological record.

Very few archaeologists today fail to consider natural processes as evidence of depositional or post-depositional modification of the archaeological record. Another widely employed source for middle-range logic is the use of experimental archaeology.

Experimental archaeology

Experimental archaeology is the attempted reconstruction of past events under controlled circumstances (Coles 1979; Grebingen 1978; Ingersoll *et al.* 1977). Experiments have been made in manufacturing techniques and structural reconstruction, as well as in the destruction of reconstructed artefacts and structures. Take, for example, the Danish experiment which reconstructed an Iron-Age roundhouse and then burnt it down (Coles 1973): the site was subsequently excavated and the excavated remains compared with the original building. The comparison enabled the excavator to calibrate the excavated data by reference to the experimental reconstruction, resulting in a logic of interpretation which could be applied elsewhere.

Another type of experiment involves the striking of flints to reproduce ancient tools. The resulting debris is mapped and recorded in detail, so that when similar debris is found in archaeological contexts comparison can assist the interpretation of the archaeological data. One can go further and experiment in cutting different types of material with the tools produced, examining (after cutting) their traces macro- or micro-scopically for indications of characteristic patterns of damage or wear. Likewise, we can examine experimentally post-depositional modification of archaeological features, as at Overton Down (Fowler 1988/9), or of artefacts (Adkins *et al.* 1989).

To take a well-known example of this type of middle-range theory in action: John Coles (1962) reconstructed a copy of a copper-alloy Bronze-Age shield. He also made a copper-alloy copy of a Bronze-Age sword contemporary with the shield. The alloys and designs were excellent facsimiles of the Bronze-Age originals, and they were used in an experiment in which the sword was struck against the shield, as if in warfare. This showed that the copper-alloy sword sliced through the copper-alloy shield. Coles argued that copper-alloy shields of that design would not have been used functionally in warfare as protection against such swords. He went on to suggest that this may be evidence of their symbolic or ceremonial function.

Here we see middle-range theory formulated from experiment. Such experiments have even included the running of whole settlements or farming regimes, and are exemplified by British and Danish experimental farms, such as Butser and West Stow.

12. **Archaeology by experiment:** reconstructing Iron Age structures at Castell Henllys, Wales. (Photo: K.R. Dark)

Although not widely employed by post-processualists, experimental archaeology has formed a mainstay of processualist and culture-historical theories of the relationship of material culture to its interpretation. It is widely used today (in Europe especially) for this purpose.

Historical evidence

Written sources, including maps, have also been widely used in archaeology, but their middle-range relevance has generally been restricted to detailed identifications of 'specifics'. A specific site has been associated with a name or term found in texts, and that identification has then played a large part in the interpretation of the archaeological monument to which it has been applied. Conversely, scholars have sought a specific site mentioned in historical sources – one has only to consider the futile attempts in the 1970s to identify King Arthur's court and Mount Badon, the site of a pivotal battle in the war between the Dark Age Britons and Anglo-Saxon invaders (see Alcock 1971).

Maps have been used to make very precise identifications, which have even included the identification of structures visible in the archaeological record with those shown on maps of settlements as 'the house of ...'. Such identifications, for instance in colonial America or in the study of medieval European towns, have made a major contribution to archaeological interpretation (examples can be found in Deetz 1977). Pottery assemblages have, for instance, been interpreted by reference to historically known occupants of the buildings in which they were found, or with which the buildings could be associated – e.g. traders or mayors. Such interpretations clearly take only a narrow view of the middle-range potential of texts, however, and recently new perspectives in the use of historical sources for middle-range arguments have been developed. Before discussing these, it is necessary to mention some of the criticisms addressed to the types of arguments already mentioned.

These methods are open to criticism based both on their *particularism* (the emphasis placed on detail rather than on obtaining a broader picture) and on their failure to address archaeological rather than historical or topographical questions. This type of criticism has usually been associated with Reece and Rahtz, who have advocated the rejection of textual sources as aids to archaeological interpretation (Reece 1981, 1982, 1983, 1987; Rahtz 1983). Both scholars have proposed a method of archaeological research in historical periods which rejects any argument based on historical evidence being applied to archaeological data, in favour, in Rahtz's case, of their parallel study. When such parallel approaches have been followed to their conclusion, then, Rahtz suggests, the results might be compared or even combined.

Reece has adopted a more extreme view, which concentrates solely on

13. **The limits of 'commonsense' interpretation?** The 'dark earth' at Pevensey Roman fort (Sussex). Similar deposits form the final Roman (or earliest post-Roman) layer at many Late Roman sites, but their interpretation has defied 'commonsense' reasoning. (Photo: S.P. Dark)

archaeological sources. As an empiricist (see Chapter 1) he sees such sources as capable of 'speaking for themselves'. In the case of Romano-British archaeology, the subject of much of Reece's work, he says that archaeological sources tell a different story from historical sources, but are to be preferred as evidence: 'the spade never lies', as the saying goes. Many archaeologists would disagree with this viewpoint: for instance, according to processual archaeologists we need middle-range theory to 'interpret' or 'decode' the messages provided by the archaeological sources. To them, the excavated data for Roman Britain is unable to 'speak for itself', but needs to be interpreted within a logical framework linking material and non-material culture. These and other contradictory views have sparked off a long debate in historical archaeology (e.g. Deagan 1982; Reynolds 1983; Austin and Alcock 1990; Dark 1994b).

Both Reece and Rahtz favour a rejection of the historical underpinning of archaeological research, and this is a view adhered to by many 'historical' archaeologists in Britain, such as Arnold (1984, 1988) and Hills (1978). A widespread approach has been to consider that textual evidence provides information about non-material culture or aspects of past societies otherwise difficult to reconstruct, in contrast to complementary evidence about those societies afforded by archaeological interpretation (e.g. Champion 1985). On the other hand Richards (1987, 1988, 1992) and Mytum (1992) have attempted to use Rahtz's parallel method, combined in Richards's case with an interest in post-processualist symbolic analysis, and in Mytum's with a processualist viewpoint close to that of Clarke.

This is in contrast to the way in which historical sources have been used by scholars aiming to use textual, or cartographic, information for primarily archaeological purposes, in order to answer archaeological questions. Such scholars include Binford (e.g. 1982), South (1977a and b), and Hodges (1983). For example, Binford emphasised the possibility of generating middle-range theory from textual evidence. This approach has recently been developed in conjunction with structuration theory (Dark 1994b; for structuration theory see Chapter 6).

These archaeologists argue that their perspective overcomes the particularism of the historical approach outlined above, and so has superseded the criticism of Reece and Rahtz. Textual sources used in this way can generate middle-range theory on several separate bases: by direct identification of archaeological sites or artefacts, by the recognition of codes of action and systems of value (Deetz 1977; Spencer-Wood 1987; Little 1992; Beaudry 1993; Dark 1994b), by the clarification of consistent patterning associated with specific activities, and by enabling direct inter-regional comparisons (Dark 1994b).

It could be claimed that these approaches represent an archaeological use of history, rather than the earlier approach which used archaeology historically (Dark 1994b). If so, then it places texts and maps in the same role as anthropological descriptions or natural scientific laws, in their relationship to the logic of the interpretation of archaeological materials. Unlike these sources, as products of the society under study, they enable *interpretation from within* that society. That is, they may enable us to give the same interpretations to archaeological materials as people within that society would have given.

Not to be confused with the historical approach to middle-range theory is the *direct historical approach*, as it is called by American archaeologists (Wedel 1938). This uses anthropological descriptions retrospectively – an anthropologically established situation is said to have been the same as that in the past if past material culture produced by the same people in the same place leaves an identical patterning in the archaeological record.

Although now seldom employed because of the seemingly insurmountable logical problems presented by cultural change, the direct historical approach is still evidenced in contemporary archaeology although (especially in British and European archaeology) it is not widely identified as such. While strictly an anthropological mode of middle-range argument, it is included here so as to avoid confusion over truly historical approaches.

14. An artefact,
monument or text? The
Dark Age Latin inscribed
stone at St Clement,
Cornwall. (Photo: S.P.
Dark)

Recognition, ambiguity and archaeological method

Underlying all arguments about how we interpret material culture are the inter-linked aspects of recognition and ambiguity. Recognition is at the heart of all middle-range theory in that we aim to recognise both the meaning of material culture and the processes which led to its present state. We also aim to recognise the way in which our own approach – whether the area we excavate or the methods of excavation and conservation used — structures the material record available to us.

A related issue is whether material culture is open to ambiguous interpretations (interestingly approached, from different standpoints, by Leigh 1980, and Tilley 1991). This is important theoretically, because where one is faced with ambiguities in the possible interpretation of the archaeological record, ways must be found to discern which of the potentially many options to choose, or whether to reject the possibility of a single interpretation. The latter course can lead to the generation of multiple interpretations of the same material, of which a notable instance is the attempt to show multiple possible interpretations of the same structural evidence (e.g. Millett and James 1983, 245-6). Often, however, ambiguities may have existed concerning the interpretation or use of material culture in the society under study. These ambiguities may have existed in the perception of those making, using or depositing the artefacts which we examine (as argued, in the case of Anglo-Saxon brooch decoration, by Leigh 1980). Our material data may *always* have had ambiguous meanings and multiple functions. To post-processualists these ambiguities facilitate, as we have seen, a plurality of interpretations, while processualists have tended to view conflicting interpretations of the same material as *multiple-working hypotheses*: alternative 'explanations' to be tested against data.

If problems of ambiguity are incorporated into archaeological reasoning, the complexity of formulating usable middle-range theory is made more extreme. We have to provide not only a logic enabling an interpretation to be made, but one showing that this interpretation is the only possible one, or enabling us to recognise the range of possibilities. Alternatively, this question can be approached by building a probabilistic scale of interpretations: data A *could* be B, but is more likely to be C.

These two questions of recognition and of ambiguity are at the heart of archaeological interpretation and have a profound effect on how we prepare interpretations. These points, as is the case with all middle-range theory, apply equally whether we are discussing a Romano-British post-hole or the collapse of the Maya civilisation.

The nature of archaeological arguments

A different way of analysing archaeological logic is to examine the structures of archaeological argumentation, by reference either to their internal framework or to their formal logic. This has been attempted in two ways and is a main theoretical concern of French archaeology. Gardin (1980, 1987) has pioneered the simulation (by using 'artificial intelligence' computer systems) of archaeological reasoning (see also Lagrange and Bonnet 1978; Lagrange and Renaud 1984). This approach has the potential to expose logical flaws in argumentation and so to improve the logical execution of reasoning. Another closely related approach is the study of archaeological logic itself. This has also been developed by French scholars in their theory of *logicism*: the analysis of the structure of archaeological reasoning in order to evaluate the validity of the arguments proposed (for an overview of this theory, see Gallay 1989).

Another point of view is that adopted by Adams (1991). He has suggested a formal logic of archaeological analysis based on the concept of inference quotas: how much information each part of the archaeological resource will yield. Adams's approach may seem more formulaic than many archaeologists would favour, but it has the advantage of setting out, in explicit form, every step in the evaluation of the archaeological data.

The analysis of archaeological arguments is not incompatible with other forms of middle-range theory. It can, as Adams would affirm (1991), be employed alongside other studies of formation processes and archaeological interpretation. On a rather more straightforward level, there has long been pressure from processualists for the clarification of the way in which we talk about archaeology – although, conversely, culture-historians have often been sceptical of processualist jargon. Mathematical analyses can be seen as another aspect of this development of archaeological theory, since they require a prescribed and formally expounded series of steps in reasoning from the recognition of archaeological data to the explanation of cultural change.

A central element in most archaeological reasoning is the use of either analogy or correlation. These have been of special interest to archaeological theorists and the subject of much debate.

Analogy and correlation

Anthropological evidence can be used to seek direct evidence for archaeological intereperetation, or to provide correlations between non-material and material culture which do not depend upon *direct* artefact-artefact or site-site comparisons. Comparisons between specific objects, buildings, site-types or distributions, and anthropological examples use the concept of *analogy*, i.e. comparison with a similar object, building, site-type or distribution found in the anthropological record. If the archaeological and anthropological examples look the same, then they are assigned similar interpretations. That is, the archaeological materials are claimed to have the same interpretation as the anthropological examples.

Analogy as defined in archaeology has been much criticised, but it is the mainstay of much research (to give some examples: Ascher 1961; Binford 1967; Hodder 1982c; Wylie 1985, 1988; Walker 1988; Gifford-Gonzalez 1991). Analogy is one of the most widely-employed types of direct evidence for interpretation, alongside the implications of natural processes and 'laws'. Anthropological evidence is used *indirectly* in the form of generalisations which have implications that might be met by many different specific types of evidence.

An excellent example of such a generalisation is provided by Ian Hodder's early work in Kenya (Hodder 1979). Hodder showed that *social stress* (social, economic or military pressure on individuals and institutions) results in the emphasis of group-characteristics. Such stress is especially strong in isolated or peripheral communities or in isolated or peripheral individuals, so that they tend to show emphasised 'cultural' or identity-related characteristics. As these might be found only in specific aspects of material culture, this generalisation is far from a 'law', but it may be used to interpret material culture patterns showing emphasised group-characteristics, even if specific analogies with the anthropological artefacts are unable to be found. While Hodder would himself place little or no importance on this aspect of this study, it seems to me an especially clear example of the use of anthropology to produce generalisations yielding *material culture correlates* (other examples are Simek 1987; Corillo 1975; Peebles and Kus 1977).

Source-criticism

Scandinavian archaeologists in particular have developed a different way of assessing the logical basis of archaeological interpretation: *source-criticism*. This consists of two aspects: establishing which patterns in data are produced by archaeological approaches and methods, and putting earlier and contemporary interpretations into their historical and social contexts.

The first way of criticising archaeological sources has been widely used. When archaeological data are patterned because of the approaches used to recover and interpret them, rather than because of past events or processes, these approaches are said to have *structured the record*, usually resulting in the over- or under-representation of some classes of material. Examples of this sort could be found relating to almost all periods. Infamously, for example, medieval layers in historic European and Middle Eastern towns were dug away unrecorded in order to get down to Roman deposits, because scholars were not interested in these later remains.

Similarly, it has long been recognised that ease of access and choice of methods structure the archaeological record. Distribution-maps of sites or artefacts can be affected by modern patterns of discovery, such as road-building, quarrying or the difference in agricultural regimes between farms or fields.

In an interesting theoretical study, Kristiansen (1985) observed that if a majority of artefacts or sites of a specific type were discovered already, we might expect their numbers plotted against dates of discovery to form a modal curve. This enables us to recognise potentially representative data-sets from those which are potentially unrepresentative.

Even such a simple consideration as the proximity of roads, or the amount of undergrowth, can play a part in structuring patterns of recovery. Human factors can be important too: a hostile farmer can hinder discovery on his land for decades. Likewise, the academic interests of archaeologists, themselves unevenly distributed across the landscape, can structure the patterns of recovery, as can their choice of study-areas. So patterns represented by archaeological distributions always require critical assessment of this kind, whether on- or off-site.

Another form of source-criticism is the setting of patterns of archaeological discoveries in their historical and social contexts. Obviously much favoured by post-processualists, this approach is common to all theoretical schools, although some 'hard-line' functional-processualists might discount it as irrelevant. Yet it is hard to deny that trends in wider intellectual life -- evolutionary concepts, for instance -- can encourage the production of archaeological interpretations based on theory rather than the data themselves. One might say that the recent interest of some processual archaeologists in non-linear dynamics and of post-processualists in *post-modernist theory* (see Chapter 7), are examples of this, as both are broad trends in academic writing.

Another form of such criticism is to seek 'bias', whether in the form of individual or group-views, expressed in the selection of interpretations or evidence. Post-processualist scholars may claim that any interpretation is 'biased', but most processualists and culture-historians consider 'bias' a misguided basis for archaeological interpretation. Many would, however, agree with the post-processualist view that interpretation, especially, is *value-laden*, i.e. that it expresses the values of the interpreter(s). This is an extension of the view that all practice is *theory-laden*: i.e. rooted in theory.

Other examples of source-criticism can be found as they are used elsewhere in this book, but these may illustrate the utility of both such approaches. There are, of course, archaeologists who, while disagreeing with a relativist view, are doubtful as to the possibility of interpreting archaeological material at all, and their viewpoint must now be mentioned.

The minimalist or descriptivist stance

An alternative to using middle-range theory is to assert that all the archaeologist can do is to describe the data relating to past material culture. That is not necessarily to say that we cannot make what sound like interpretive comments – 'this type of pottery was a burial urn, is from Frisia, and belongs to the early to mid-fifth century' – but these are, in fact, only levels of description. In this case they describe the function, cultural affinity, and date of the material: the 'explanation', insofar as it is possible, lies in that definition (usually combined in historical archaeology with the historical facts about the period), and hence we can get 'interpretations' based wholly on such descriptions.

Closely related is the *minimalist* view. This asserts that an essentially *descriptivist* framework can be supplemented by 'commonsense' interpretations, such as 'a line of stone blocks set in mortar, forming a rectangle, may be called a building'. Such views of archaeological 'interpretation' have associated claims that they are more critical and realistic than more 'ambitious' interpretations.

Unsurprisingly, they are strongly associated with the culture-historical school and rejected by both processual and post-processual archaeologists. Moreover, they are also strongly associated with the archaeology of specific periods and places as a result of the development of modern archaeology. The archaeology of Anglo-Saxon England is, today, still dominated by such opinons, and minimalists can be found in Roman-period archaeology also.

Minimalists and descriptivists would generally reject any middle-range theory as irrelevant and over-ambitious ('optimistic' is a term often used), and would see 'commonsense' as the basis of their approach. Minimalism is no less a 'theoretical' viewpoint than that held by processualists or post-processualists. For example, their use of 'commonsense', employed as the basis for what processualists call 'middle-range theory', is universalist, or at least generalising. Probably few minimalists or descriptivists would acknowledge the theoretical character of their approach, and they have generally stood outside modern theoretical debate within the discipline.

Conclusion

There are, therefore, a very wide range of views on middle-range theory and a smaller, but no less deep-running, series of controversies about epistemology. Moreover, as we have seen, by no means all archaeologists find all, or even any, of these approaches fruitful – although few, if any, do not subscribe to one of the views outlined here.

Often, the effect of these controversies is to cause the conclusions and methods of one school to seem naïve or incorrect to another. That such debate continues in archaeology could be viewed in several ways: we might see it as a reflection of the vitality of the subject, or of the relatively recent growth of archaeology compared, for instance, to biology. Another view, would, of course, be to claim that archaeologists don't know what they are doing.

Few archaeologists, and none apart from the minimalists and descriptivists, have considered such matters irrelevant or a waste of time, even if they have questioned the very existence of a 'material record' (e.g. Patrik 1985). Indeed, the importance of middle-range theory has been stressed again and again by scholars with such different views as Binford, Hodder and Barker (Binford 1983a; Hodder 1982c, 1992; Barker 1977, 1986). It is, therefore, impossible to exclude it from any general account of archaeological theory.

CHAPTER 3

Classification and the Measurement of Time

Chronology is seldom considered a theoretical issue, but all archaeology rests upon the assumption that the past was not identical to the present. Archaeologists approach their subject with a bias towards change over time. If change is to be measured we need to be able to measure time.

Classification is also closely related to change. By putting things into groups – i.e. classifying them – we can recognise how these groups relate one to another and place this against the time-scales established by other means. Alternatively, by placing material remains into groups and establishing the relationship between groups, we may hope to establish chronological relationships. Classification, therefore, becomes an important tool for the measurement of time.

Although classification and chronology are closely related in archaeology, the uses of classification extend far beyond temporal studies. If, for instance, we want to map sites of a specific type in the landscape we must first define that type. If we want to compare societies in two different areas by reference to material evidence, we have to employ our classification of these societies or aspects of their material culture.

Chronological studies include both the concepts and the methods used to establish dating, but it is only the conceptual aspect that needs to be discussed here. Archaeologists use a number of such concepts in their work, e.g. stratigraphy, calibration and *terminus post quem* dating. Often, these are not thought of as being theoretical concepts, but they are as much theory as epistemological arguments, being based on philosophical and logical studies rather than deriving from self-evident facts about the archaeological record. I shall discuss them first, before going on to examine the theoretical aspects of archaeological classification. Finally, some general issues concerning the nature of time and the theory of progress will be considered.

Dating

First, it is worth clarifying two concepts central to all chronological studies. These are absolute and relative forms of dating.

64

Absolute and relative dates

Archaeologists often write about absolute and relative dates. *Absolute dates* are those related to calendar dates so that an archaeologically derived date of AD 100 represents a date in the year AD 100. *Relative dates* relate the date of one thing (for instance, one pot) to another. An example of a relative date is if we say 'Pot-A is earlier than pot-B' but do not assign either a date in calendar years. 'Earlier', 'later', or 'contemporary with', are relative, not absolute, chronological terms, and all discussion involving such terms employs relative dating, whether or not it also involves absolute dates.

Obviously we would ideally want always to have absolute dates in archaeology, especially in historical archaeology, when the comparison of historical and archaeological evidence is otherwise extremely difficult. We must have absolute dates if we want to compare an archaeological site dated to AD 100 with a historical event of AD 100. Because we can date both to the same year does not mean to say that they are related, of course, any more than our inability to do so shows that they are unrelated. But we cannot usually resolve the question of their relationship unless both can be placed within an absolute chronology of calendar years.

15. Relative dating: the uppermost mosaic floor must be later than that which it overlies. (Photo: S.P. Dark)

Stratigraphy

The simplest form of dating, and one which should be used on any excavation, is stratigraphy (for a recent consideration of the theory of archaeological stratigraphy, see Harris 1979 and later editions). Archaeology, as we saw in the Introduction, began to adopt a theory of stratigraphy from the eighteenth century, but did not widely employ it until the late nineteenth century. Stratigraphy came to archaeology in the nineteenth century as a 'ready-made' theory of how to date layers of soil or stone from geology, where it had been formulated by Hutton in 1785. In origin stratigraphy is not, therefore, an archaeological theory, but, like other theoretical concepts (such as 'central place theory'), was borrowed by archaeology from another subject.

By the study of natural layers in the soil – not itself evident to most archaeologists earlier than the nineteenth century – and the recognition that their relationship one to another could give a relative sequence, stratigraphy provided a simple way of assigning relative dates to excavated sites. Many archaeological dates are founded on the relative dating of stratigraphy, which is then assigned 'absolute' dates (those in calendar years) by means shortly to be discussed.

Stratigraphy itself was not immediately developed in its present form. What to scholars of the nineteenth and early twentieth centuries seemed logical stratigraphical methods are today seen as misguided. The most well known of these is *arbitrary stratigraphy*, which rests on the basis that soil forms at a constant rate and, therefore, that horizontal slices through a site afford a sequence of deposits. Wheeler (1954) conclusively demonstrated the inadequacy of this method. Later, depositional and post-depositional studies were to make us more cautious about evaluating the relationship between artefacts found in layers of soil and the layers themselves.

These examples serve to illustrate that stratigraphical theory has not been static over a century of its archaeological use. The most important developments have derived from studies of the formation and modification of archaeological deposits, such as those mentioned in Chapter 2. Darwin (1881) showed how the study of earthworms could illuminate how, and at what speed, archaeological deposits formed. Atkinson (1957) employed Darwin's work, alongside his own observations, to recognise that objects found within a layer of soil could only be considered securely stratified within it if it could be established that they had not been moved by animal action. Subsequent work by soil scientists, such as Limbrey (e.g. 1975), and excavators including Barker (e.g. 1977), shows that an appreciation of chemical and hydrological processes operating in the soil, and of the effects of root-action, can prevent us from misinterpreting buried deposits. A simple illustration is provided by the observation that rust-coloured iron-pan, forming in patches on the surface of buried deposits, results from natural processes of this kind (e.g. Keeley and MacPhail 1981). Such reddened patches found on the surface of seemingly well-stratified deposits had previously been regarded as hearths.

The 1970s saw a rapid development in stratigraphy. Hirst and Carver prompted the use of a 'neutral' language for discussing stratification in which, instead of terms like 'posthole', 'pit' and 'wall', units of stratification would be initially called by terms devoid of interpretation (Hirst 1976). Carver suggested that the term *context* might be generally employed to mean 'stratigraphical unit', and this has been adopted by most British archaeologists.

The next major development came in the late 1970s and early 1980s through the work of Harris, who produced the first formalised exposition of the theoretical basis of archaeological stratigraphy. Harris also re-emphasised the importance of surfaces of layers, and of what Hirst (1976) had called 'negative' or 'positive' features. 'Negative features', in Hirst's definition, were those cut into layers, such as pits and postholes, and 'positive features' were those built up from the surface of layers, such as walls. Harris called such surfaces *interfaces*, and so introduced a new type of stratigraphical unit into the archaeological repertoire.

These seemingly minor developments in the theory of stratigraphy are of great importance in several ways. Their significance to the practice of archaeology is obvious, but is not the main concern here. What is especially interesting is that an established theoretical 'tool' – stratigraphical dating – has been conceptually developed from the 1970s to the 1990s: that is, during a period when most archaeologists would consider it part of the conventional range of their subject. Because the relative chronology of most excavated sites depends upon stratigraphical evidence, these conceptual changes have important chronological implications and caution wariness in using stratigraphical evidence in too simplistic a way.

In order to convert relative dates based on stratigraphy into 'absolute' dates, it is necessary to employ additional evidence. This evidence is provided by our ability to date artefacts or deposits independently of their stratigraphical position. These independent dates are then used in stratigraphical arguments by means of two crucial concepts, *terminus post quem* and *terminus ante quem*.

Terminus post quem and terminus ante quem

Stratigraphy, as we have already seen, is theory. Layers of soil and rocks do not label themselves as 'earlier' or 'later', let alone 'Roman' or 'medieval' – these are interpretations which we make, and all interpretations have necessarily to be made inside a theoretical framework. In this case the framework has been 'stratigraphy'. This does

not undermine the truth of stratigraphy, nor of the relative dates it
produces, but we must be aware of their theoretical element, and that
conceptual improvements can enhance our ability to recognise and
interpret stratigraphical units and relationships.

Most stratigraphical sequences are assigned 'absolute' dates by means
of another theory, that of *terminus post quem* dating. This depends on the
discovery of a datable object or feature within the stratigraphical
sequence, such as a Roman coin in a layer of gravel. The date of the
stratigraphical unit containing this datable item, and of all subsequent
stratigraphical units in the sequence, is said to be of the same date, or
later than, that item. If there is more than one datable element, it is said
to be of the same date, or later than, the latest. This sounds simple, but as
soon as we start to examine the theoretical basis of this concept the
situation becomes far more complex.

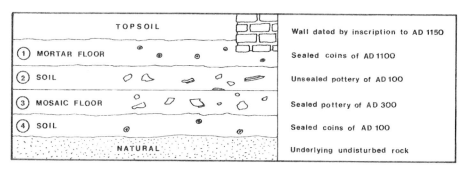

16. *Terminus post quem* and *terminus ante quem* dating. Layer 4 is given a *TPQ* of AD
100 by the coins sealed in it. It cannot be earlier than AD 100, but might be later. Layer 3 is
given a *TPQ* of AD 300 by the pottery sealed in it and therefore dates from AD 300 or later.
Layer 2 contains unsealed pottery which, because it is unsealed, does not give it a *TPQ*. As
Layer 2 overlies Layer 3 it is therefore given a *TPQ* by the pottery sealed in Layer 3, so it
dates from AD 300 or later also. Layer 1 is given a *TPQ* by the coins of AD 1100 sealed in it
but a *TAQ* by the wall cutting it. On this basis, it can be dated to no earlier than AD 1100
but no later than AD 1150.

First, there is the problem of establishing the relationship between a
datable artefact or feature and the stratigraphical units making up the
sequence. Usually *terminus post quem* dates depend upon the
stratification of artefacts in layers of soil or in the make-up of walls or
floors.

The relationship between finds and layers, or other stratigraphical
units, is, however, dependent upon the methods we use to analyse the
significance of their locations. These methods are themselves dependent
upon the concepts used to formulate them. That is, theory permeates the
way in which we understand the stratification of artefacts; our
understanding of this is highly *theory-laden*.

For example, if we find object A (say, a Samian ware bowl), in layer B (say, a layer of soil within a pit), then we frequently make the assumption (which is what it is), that object A is stratified in layer B. But consideration of post-depositional factors such as those mentioned in Chapter 2 shows that it could have derived from later layers C, or D, or earlier layer E. We cannot simply say 'Well, it might have been redeposited', or 'I can't see any roots or burrows' – such processes are among many operating on the archaeological material which we use, and are not in any case recognisable without theory enabling us to construct the methods to do so.

But suppose find A is *sealed* in layer B, that is, it is impossible for it to have derived from either earlier or later inputs. Can we use find A to provide a date for layer B? This is, again, a far from obvious conclusion – and even if it were obvious, this would not make it true. Whether we can use find A in this way depends upon the theoretical basis underlying *terminus post quem* dating.

Find A may be preserved, or re-used, and so have been deposited in a layer far later in date than the date of find A. For instance, Anglo-Saxon jewellery contains Roman coins centuries earlier in date than the artefacts in which they were re-used: this shows that such coins were available to be re-used at the time at which the brooches were made. It is possible, therefore, to find an Anglo-Saxon pit which, although filled in the sixth century, contains only Roman coins.

Any find can thus represent a possible date-range from the date of its manufacture to the present time. Quantity does not alter this quality: if we have a thousand finds of a single date – say, a thousand coins of AD 100 – they still do not date the layer in which they occur more certainly to their own date than if a single coin of AD 100 was found in it. It is possible that one might have a layer containing a thousand coins of the same date, all deriving from earlier deposits, on the same site as a layer with a single well-stratified coin of that date. It would be the layer with the single coin which was the better dated, but we would still have to recall that even a well-stratified find provides only a *terminus post quem* date.

Terminus post quem dates have, therefore, to be used very precisely and critically. Only the latest sealed find in any stratigraphical unit can assign it a *terminus post quem* date: the remainder, however numerous or well-dated, are irrelevant to its date.

A related, and even more complicated concept to apply is *terminus ante quem* dating. If a stratigraphical sequence contains a unit – such as a layer or wall – which is so well-dated that it can be assigned an 'absolute' date without reference to the stratigraphical sequence, or to *terminus post quem* dating, it can be used to recognise the date before which the stratigraphical sequence preceding it must have occurred. The layer or feature immediately preceding that providing the *terminus ante quem* date is then said to be of the same date, or earlier than it. Once again this sounds straightforward, but there are again problems: how many features can we internally date sufficently well to use in this way, even in historical archaeology?

To give an example: if we have a cathedral wall overlying an archaeological layer, such as an earlier floor, which has a building inscription dating its construction to, say, AD 1100 incorporated into it, then we must be sure that the inscription is a primary part of the wall if we are to use it to assign the underlying layer a *terminus ante quem* date. If the inscription *is* a primary part of the wall it dates that wall to AD 1100, and provides a *terminus ante quem* for the layer underneath it. If the inscription could have been incorporated in the wall at a later date, or could have derived from an earlier building, then it can be used to provide a *terminus post quem* date for the wall, but this does not enable us to employ *terminus ante quem* dating.

Terminus ante quem dating must never be allowed to rest upon assumptions or interpretations of the association between, for example, historical texts and archaeological features. This means that without epigraphic evidence or dates derived from natural science methods (see below) it is often impossible to employ *terminus ante quem* dating.

So, for instance, consider a churchyard in which a hundred tombstones dated by inscriptions to between AD 1700 and 1800, are set in the uppermost layer of soil. The earliest of these tombstones – if it can be shown that it is in its original position – gives a *terminus ante quem* for the layer of soil in which it is set. But a coin of AD 1700 in the same layer of soil gives only a *terminus post quem* date for that layer. This is because the coin could have been deposited in AD 1700 or at any later date, while we know the date at which the tombstone was set up. Only when the date of a stratigraphical unit (such as a floor or wall or, in this case, a tombstone) can be fixed with absolute certainty may it be used to provide a *terminus ante quem* date. It is important to note that *terminus post quem* dating alone cannot provide this level of certainty. Consequently, it is seldom possible to use *terminus ante quem* dating in archaeology. Such is the logic of *terminus post quem* and *terminus ante quem* dating. The need to assess the relationship between those finds and stratigraphical units which are able to be dated in 'absolute' terms and the relative dates assigned to the remainder, and to distinguish between 'sealed' and 'unsealed' finds, connects these forms of dating very closely with both stratigraphy and the matters discussed in Chapter 2.

An interesting theoretical problem is whether consistency of association increases the likelihood of a specific date. We have already seen that quantity does not affect the qualitative arguments concerning *terminus post quem* dating, and the same is, of course, true for *terminus ante quem* dating; no amount of secondary inscriptions can alter their stratigraphical and chronological significance compared to those found integral to the wall in our example.

So, if we find a certain type of structure – say, a megalithic monument –

and inside it we find pottery which is not in sealed contexts where it can date the structure by the application of *terminus post quem* dating, it is of no chronological significance whatsoever for the date of the structure itself (e.g. Rault 1992). That is, even if the same type of Neolithic pottery is found inside a thousand megalithic structures of the same type it does not show them to be Neolithic. Quantity and consistency of association do not affect *terminus post quem* and *terminus ante quem* arguments.

But does the pottery in this example afford a *terminus ante quem* date for the megaliths? The answer is again 'no', because quantity of data does not make any difference to the logical procedure involved. On the basis of this evidence alone, and even if we can rule out *residuality*, all the Neolithic pottery could have been deposited in all the megaliths at the date of its manufacture, or at any subsequent time.

Terminus post quem and *terminus ante quem* dates are unaffected by how consistently finds and stratigraphical units are associated. The quantity of material involved is also irrelevant. What is crucial is to establish the relationship between the 'absolutely' datable element – whether an artefact, or, for instance, a radiocarbon-dated deposit of charcoal – and the stratigraphical sequence, together with the strict application of the logic underlying each type of dating. This raises the question of how we arrive at 'absolute' dates for stratigraphical units and artefacts. Obviously, it is possible to answer this question in terms of method alone, but here it is the underlying conceptual basis of these methods which is of interest. There are four principal ways in which this can be attempted: through the application of natural science (e.g. in radiocarbon dating), by the use of historical evidence, by reference to intrinsically dated objects, such as coins, bearing a date in calendar years, and by fitting artefacts or structures within a system of classification.

Natural science and absolute chronology

The application of natural scientific theories to archaeological dating is well known. This is how radiocarbon dating works, but these theories are, although seemingly 'natural laws', conceptual frameworks invented by people, as much as are archaeological theories. They may be amenable to the same sorts of revision and criticism as are other scholarly theories. Consequently, it is unwise to see them as completely certain and absolute, although this does not necessarily mean that we should not base our dating systems on them, nor that they are necessarily incorrect. It is extremely important to recognise, however, that the natural sciences are also developing fields of enquiry and, while some of the assumptions underlying the archaeological use of natural scientific theory are almost certainly correct (such as many of those involved in tree-ring studies), others may be subject to change as natural scientific research progresses.

From the archaeological point of view, the principal conceptual question facing us when we use any natural scientific approach purporting to afford 'absolute' dates is whether *calibration* (the re-adjusting of dates derived from such methods to make what seem more accurate or credible determinations) renders these dates no longer 'absolute' (reviewed by Aitken 1990). An absolute date needs to be directly related to calendar dating.

It is, therefore, the conceptual problems with calibration which will be reviewed, albeit extremely briefly, here. Other aspects of natural scientific dating, such as the methods involved and their physical and biological bases, are well covered in other works and are not as closely related to questions of theory in archaeology, so they will not be outlined here.

Calibration and the illusion of absolute dating

Renfrew has pointed out that absolute dates based on natural scientific analyses rarely exist (Renfrew and Bahn 1991, 136). As soon as we recalculate dates by comparing them to other evidence, or calibrating them, we alter them from absolute dates to relative dates. This is because they are now dated by a relationship between the evidence used to produce them and the evidence used for calibration. Such dates are not necessarily incorrect, and few archaeologists would doubt the approximate validity of radiocarbon dates, for example, but they are no longer truly absolute.

As radiocarbon, archaeomagnetic, and luminescence dating all require calibration of one sort or another, they produce not absolute but relative dates. Moreover, we must recognise that most of these approaches generate date-ranges within which the (relative) date of the artefacts or stratigraphical unit which is being dated may lie. They provide only a date bracket which contains the true absolute date. The only exception, Renfrew has noted, is tree-ring dating (*dendrochronology*), which forms the absolute timescale against which radiocarbon dates have to be calibrated.

Dendrochronology has formed the mainstay of the recent development of 'high-precision dating' in archaeology. This is of major theoretical importance as it affords sufficiently accurate dates for absolute dating to specific years, even in prehistory, to be achieved.

Baillie (Baillie and Munro 1988; Baillie 1989, 1991a, 1992, 1994) has noted that such precise dates enable correlations between archaeological deposits and natural or historical events which were previously unavailable. They open up important new opportunities for archaeologists, but they also cause new problems. The implications of such accurate dating have yet to be fully worked out, but Baillie (1991b) notes the propensity for such dates to encourage archaeologists to ascribe to them other potentially simultaneous occurrences. Conversely, we can now use them to observe that radiocarbon dating leads the archaeologist to 'smear' discrete, short events into longer time spans.

High-precision dating also has important implications for historical archaeology. It has the potential to ascribe specific structures or sites to the lifetimes and therefore (potentially) the actions, of named historical individuals. Because it is based on dendrochronology, this ability extends to some forms of artefact, e.g. the covers of medieval manuscripts (Fletcher and Tapper 1984). Again, the potential of such correlations has yet to be realised, but high-precision dating may cause us to redefine aspects of the relationship between archaeology and history in theoretical as well as practical terms.

Another problem derived from calibration is the possibility that different calibrators could give different date-ranges as a result of their

17. Historical dating.
Even at Hadrian's Wall,
written and archaeologi-
cal evidence for dating are
difficult to correlate.
(Photo: S.P. Dark)

differing approaches and methods. This has recently been illustrated by scholars using Bayesian statistics in radiocarbon calibration (Buck *et al.* 1991). This, again, emphasises that calibrated dates are not truly absolute. It also shows that there is a theoretical, as well as practical, reason for always stating the type of calibration employed when using radiocarbon and other forms of natural scientific dating.

Historical dating

Another type of absolute dating is that based on historical correlations. This may be achieved by recognising a site as that mentioned in a historical text by the use of epigraphic evidence relating an archaeological monument or artefact to written evidence, or by making more generalised comparisons between the construction or disuse of a specific site and historically recorded periods of site construction and disuse.

The final method presents greater, many would say insuperable, difficulties in correlating the historical and archaeological record. Studies of deserted medieval villages have often found it difficult to correlate archaeological and historical periods of landscape change, for example, and false assumptions about the date of disuse of many ancient cities have derived from the preconception that they were abandoned following historically attested sieges.

This approach – the correlation of a historical event with archaeological evidence – is the logic underlying the ascription of specific archaeologically-identified burials to historical kings, in cases where no inscriptions have been found. It is, for example, the method that conventionally ascribes Sutton Hoo Mound 1 to King Raedwald of East Anglia (Carver 1992a).

As was mentioned in Chapter 2, there are many problems in making identifications of this sort, and aside from historical evidence related to the archaeological record by inscriptions and, perhaps, tree-ring dates, we may doubt if any approach based on the use of historical evidence to date archaeological materials can provide us with absolute dates.

Internally-dated artefacts

There are, of course, artefacts which bear calendar dates moulded on them. Coins and inscriptions are the most frequently found, unless one allows manuscripts and other documents to be included. Occasionally, however, pottery and metal artefacts, or even structures themselves, can have calendar dates shown on them. If these dates can be demonstrated by stratigraphical analysis in the case of buildings, and by critical examination of, for example, their relationship to glazes or corrosion products, to have formed a part of the original object or structure, they

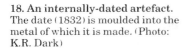

18. An internally-dated artefact.
The date (1832) is moulded into the
metal of which it is made. (Photo:
K.R. Dark)

form an important tool for the absolute dating of archaeological sources.
This, of course, assumes that the calendrical information shown can be
related to our own calendar.

Absolute chronology and artefacts

Apart from those artefacts carrying intrinsic dates, any use of artefactual
evidence for chronological purposes rests on the classification of the
artefacts themselves and their relationship to stratigraphical and other
forms of dating. Without intrinsic dates, as we shall see, artefact
classification does not permit the use of objects to assign absolute dates.
Artefactual dating is, however, an important element in relative
chronology, and relative chronologies based on artefacts can often be
'calibrated' against absolute chronologies derived from other means, as in
the association of artefacts and coins. The importance of classification
extends far beyond artefact studies, however, and even beyond

chronology, for it is one of the most fundamental tools which the archaeologist uses to order, and seek pattern within, the material remains of the past (for a recent review, see Adams and Adams 1991).

Before considering how artefacts and other archaeological evidence are classified, it is first necessary to evaluate the chronological importance of artefacts themselves, and the conceptual problems involved in dating them.

Date of manufacture and date of deposition

The first problem affecting all artefacts is the contrast between date of manufacture and date of deposition. Suppose we have a pot intrinsically datable by an inscription to AD 1750. When it is discovered, even if whole, it could have been *deposited* (lost, deliberately disposed of, or moved by natural processes) the second after it was made, or at any time subsequently. If it is found on a building site today it might, if unstratified, have been lost this morning by a collector of eighteenth-century pottery. This is obviously a somewhat implausible and extreme example, but it illustrates the general rule, clearly related to the rule of *terminus post quem*, discussed earlier.

There is also a complex relationship between the date at which an artefact is deposited, and how it is perceived by those who encounter it,

19. The problem of re-use. A Roman inscription built into a medieval wall at Lanercost Priory (Cumbria). (Photo: S.P. Dark)

whether its manufacturer(s), user(s), or depositor(s). If any of these assign to the object a quality – such as 'ugly', 'rubbish', 'precious', or 'special' – they will treat it differently from others assigning it other values (Sommer 1990).

Moreover, if the object has a potential for re-use – as a part of, or raw material for, another object – then it may be treated in this way, preserving its material but changing the form in which that material enters the archaeological record (Sommer 1990). For example, much Roman coinage probably survives only as the melted-down metal forming early medieval artefacts.

A particular type of re-use takes place if artefacts are regarded as heirlooms, or of religious significance. They may be carefully kept for far longer periods than would normally be expected. Medieval Europe contained many artefacts preserved for centuries because they were correctly, or incorrectly, considered as the remains of saints, or associated with them in some way. For instance, an excavator unaware that this was the case might not assign to the pig bones, which Chaucer depicts as false relics in his *Canterbury Tales*, the value ascribed to them by those misled into supposing them the bones of a saint. Without anthropological or historical information it might, therefore, be hard or even impossible to identify value-systems from archaeological evidence of this sort.

Coins present other problems. They may be in circulation very briefly, at least officially, be re-used as non-economic objects (given to children as toys, for example), or remain in circulation for very long periods. Studies of Roman coinage afford many fine examples of how coins are used and how they may be archaeologically studied (Casey 1986). Notably, we see that coins which 'officially' belong to a short period can remain in circulation for centuries (Reece 1984). In the early twentieth century it was still possible to encounter Roman coins in circulation in the currency of the Middle East (for examples, see Boon 1991).

The hoarding of objects does not affect these questions: coins, for example, can pass in and out of hoards for many reasons and at many periods, without economic motivation always being present. Hoarding may help us to recognise value, as hoards usually comprise artefacts someone felt worth conserving or concealing. The hoarding of non-valuable objects is, of course, another possibility, and we also have to ask, 'value to whom?'. So the implications of studying hoards are far from straightforward. Coin hoards may be compiled for purposes of storage, in order to re-use the coins as currency, or as scrap metal, or for purposes of disposal, when currency has ceased to have value, or for religious reasons. Such arguments can be applied to hoards of any material, and this subject will be further discussed in Chapter 5.

A hoard of Roman coins is not necessarily a 'Roman coin hoard', unless it can be dated to the Roman period. For example, a hoard of Roman coins might have been gathered together because they were being used in an eleventh-century children's game as counters, or because they were concealed by a coin collector to escape the notice of an angry twentieth-century spouse! In order to interpret a hoard we have to attempt to reconstruct the circumstances of its deposition – but that is a 'middle-range', not a dating, question. It shows, however, that, as with stratigraphical dating, it is important to recognise the relationship between chronology and the processes which form and modify the archaeological record.

These points touch upon only a few of the theoretical problems involved in archeological dating, but I hope they have shown that dating is a highly technical matter, and that it is closely related to other areas of theory. Classification forms another bridge between theory and dating.

Classification

When archaeologists prepare a report on excavated pottery, for example, they assign artefacts to types, and attempt to date the artefacts by dates assigned to the groups into which they have been placed. Classification is, therefore, able to be viewed as both description and interpretation (one might, of course, say that all description is interpretation or *vice versa*) and is a mainstay of archaeological chronology (for a range of discussions: Dunell 1971; Hill and Evans 1972; Klejn 1979, 1982; Whallon and Brown 1982; Adams 1988; Adams and Adams 1991).

By using the concept of types and the study of their classification (*typology*) archaeologists assert that they can recognise difference through classification (for a recent discussion see Adams and Adams 1991). In doing so, they immediately raise so many theoretical questions that it will be possible only to discuss a few of the vast range here.

First, there is the problem of recognising what it is significant to classify (see Malina and Vasicek 1990). Each artefact can present a huge range of obvious and non-obvious characteristics which one might classify (known as *attributes* or *traits*). Each of these traits may vary, and such traits (*variables*) are those most often used in classification, since most classifiers divide their material into groups. But what traits do we choose in order to classify an artefact or site? How do we measure these: for example, how do we estimate an object's 'shape' (e.g. Tyldesley, Johnson and Snape 1985)?

Take, for example, a piece of pottery: is it the dimensions (or some of them), or the fabric (for an interesting paper on this, see Monaghan 1982), which we consider worthy of classification? Do we consider the surface treatment of the inside or the outside of the pot? How much variation is 'significant' (e.g. see Impey and Pollard 1985)? Do we assign importance to the weight of the pottery sherd, where it was found, its colours, its possible function, or the way it has broken? The choice between these options is not obvious, although most classification of

20. Formal classification. It is possible to put amphorae (storage jars) such as these into groups according to their shape, but why classify them in this way? (Photo: K.R. Dark)

objects tends to be on the basis of form (*formal classification*) or function (*functional classification*). Not all of the variables used in classification are visible: some may be miscrosopic (such as mineral inclusions in the clay) and others may be physical properties (such as magnetism). These are but a few of the many possible variables upon which we might base the classification of a single artefact.

Of course, faced with a site which may contain complex structures and might change over time, or with art containing sophisticated designs, one is presented with further problems of defining exactly what one is classifying and, not least, of deciding where patterns 'end'. The question of whether we group phases or features together or classify them separately is a further problem when discussing settlement evidence.

So, even on this level, knowing *what* to classify is not easy. Knowing *why* to classify is a related, but no less complex, problem. It is necessary to consider whether we aim to recover classifications identical to those employed by the maker(s) or user(s) of artefacts or sites, which may themselves have varied (see White and Thomas 1972), or whether we seek to construct our own classifications, bearing no, or only partial, relation to these.

If we decide to develop a classification for our own purposes, we must

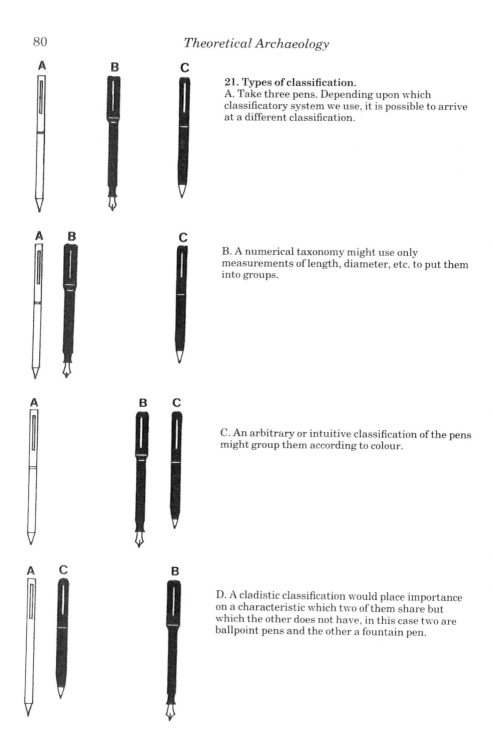

21. Types of classification.
A. Take three pens. Depending upon which classificatory system we use, it is possible to arrive at a different classification.

B. A numerical taxonomy might use only measurements of length, diameter, etc. to put them into groups.

C. An arbitrary or intuitive classification of the pens might group them according to colour.

D. A cladistic classification would place importance on a characteristic which two of them share but which the other does not have, in this case two are ballpoint pens and the other a fountain pen.

decide what questions we want it to answer, or whether we seek a universally useful classification. What we classify is a product of our reasons for classification, because it, too, must be based on a selection of a number of possible attributes which might be used in classification. Conversely, in the same way as we classify in accordance with the questions which we aim to answer, what we classify may be affected by how we go about classification.

Surprisingly, perhaps, archaeologists have developed few of their own theories about classification, rather than classifications themselves. Although post-processualist writers have attempted to suggest that 'folk classifications' (e.g. Miller 1985a) might form the basis of classification in archaeology, or that we might employ linguistic concepts of grammar (used much earlier, incidentally, in historical archaeology by culture-historians), most archaeologists fall into one of two main groups so far as classification is concerned. The first, strongly associated with culture-history, is *arbitrary* or *intuitive classification*. The second, strongly associated with the 'New Archaeology', is numerical classification -- or *numerical taxonomy*, as it is called (for overviews, see Doran and Hodson 1975; Orton 1980). Another mathematical theory of classification has also recently been introduced into archaeology, *cladistic classification*, although its introduction in the late 1980s has not yet led to a large-scale published archaeological case-study, it is however, one of the most important classificatory theories in contemporary biology.

Arbitrary, or intuitive, classification

Arbitrary classification works on the basis that one can select, by skill, or from the questions asked, the attributes required for classification. These attributes are used to define types, which are arranged into a sequence by the relationship of their groups of attributes one to another. Underlying this arrangement is usually a concept of evolution or degeneration, and it is often based on using a few dated examples to form a 'direction' in which the sequence should run.

Take the following example. Brooch A is found in a layer dated to AD 500, brooch B shares some characteristics with brooch A, and some with brooch C. Brooch C is found in a layer dated to AD 800. Therefore, it is argued, brooch B dates to between brooch A and brooch C. In other words, it dates from AD 500-800.

Closely allied to arbitrary taxonomy is the concept of *dating by association*. This method works by the association of artefacts found together in groups, or *assemblages*. If, in our example, brooch A is found with brooch B, but brooch C is found with brooch D but not with brooches A or B, it can be argued that, as we know the date of brooches A and C, we can date brooches B and D.

But if we take a further assemblage which contains a brooch of the same type as brooch D and a new type (E), we can date brooch D by reference to the assemblage containing brooches D and C, and so (it is claimed) date brooch E by reference to brooch D. This string of 'associations' forms the basis of *cross-dating*, once the mainstay of archaeological chronology.

Since the 1960s, arbitrary classification has been severely criticised, especially by those favouring numerical methods of classification. They have said that it is illogical, or based on far too ill-defined or 'unproven' concepts. In placing importance on the skill of the archaeologist to evaluate the correct attributes for classification, arbitrary classification has been criticised as unscientific, or even 'élitist'. It can be depicted in this way because the classification method is not exactly repeatable by any scholar applying set methods, and depends upon *ad hominem* judgments concerning the classifier. Such critics have pointed to the differing classifications of the same artefacts produced by contemporary archaeologists using arbitrary classification.

Another criticism has centred on the lack of precision with which the chosen attributes to be used in a classification have been published. This lack of *explicitness*, as it is called, has been countered by the adoption (by some archaeologists using arbitrary classification) of schematic methods for consistently recording artefacts, setting out in detail the attributes which have been chosen for classification. An interesting study of this type was undertaken by Avent (1975) who made use of both written and diagrammatic means of presentation to make it clear exactly what attributes were used in his classification of Anglo-Saxon brooches.

Consistent schematic recording and publication such as this ensures that it is clear what is being classified and how the attributes/traits are being selected and recorded. They also ensure consistency throughout a classification. French scholars such as Gardin (1978) have been keen to adopt a similar method proposing extensive conventions and codes for use in all archaeological classification (see Swain and Fu 1972; Breeding and Amoss 1972; Uhr 1973; Kamenetsky, Marshak and Sher 1975; Borillo 1975). These so-called *shape grammars* have also been shared by many numerical taxonomists, especially in the USA (e.g. Gero and Mazzullo 1984), where the approach has a long history in the work of Rouse and Spaulding. Similarly, other, often mathematical, systems have been proposed in an attempt to standardise classification (Cullberg 1968).

Archaeologists using arbitrary classification have usually been given to supposing that they can retrieve the 'original' or 'natural' classification of their subject (see Malina and Vasicek 1990, 168-87; Gardin 1978). More sophisticated recent classifications in this school have stressed the use of concepts such as symmetry and the problem-orientated character of classifications. These have enabled even more exactness and rigour to be applied by those using this approach.

The principal critics of arbitrary classification have been numerical taxonomists, and these were perceived to be at the forefront of studies in classification during the 1960s and 1970s. Numerical taxonomy had a great appeal to 'New Archaeologists' and is very closely associated with the 'New Archaeology' movement. It seemed to promise absolute and 'scientifically-based' means of classifying archaeological material, and so coincided with the scientific aspirations of the 'New Archaeologists'.

Numerical taxonomy

Numerical taxonomy is a vastly complex subject (the standard starting points are Sokal and Sneath 1963; Sneath and Sokal 1973), introduced into archaeology by Clarke (1965, with a major published study in 1970), in his classic study of the classification of beakers. Numerical taxonomy is based upon developments in biological classification (especially Sokal and Sneath 1963) which seemed to archaeologists in the 1970s to have swept away arbitrary classification (e.g. Doran and Hodson 1975; Orton 1980). During the 1960s biological classification switched from arbitrary to numerical methods, although, as we shall see, cladistics was introduced into biological classification during the same decade.

Numerical taxonomy is based on a simple theory, despite its huge methodological complexity. Many archaeologists have considered the complex mathematics employed in numerical taxonomy daunting, but it can be explained by reference to extremely simple concepts.

The basis of numerical taxonomy is this: if we turn attributes into numerical codes (hence, in part, the co-existence with shape grammars), we can compare artefacts as groups of numbers (*matrices*) made up of such codes. Because these are numerical groups, they can measure quantities (such as the diameter of the rim of a jar) as well as qualities (such as whether a pot is red or not). These groups can be compared with one another in statistical terms, and we can then classify them according to the number of shared attributes. This enables us to arrange them in an order in which the relationship between each group, representing a single artefact, and every other group, is capable of being expressed in statistical terms. Such relationships can be shown in family-tree-like diagrams (*dendrograms*) that express the linkages between groups. These linkages can, therefore, be taken to represent the relationships (e.g. chronological) between the artefacts.

Unlike arbitrary classification, numerical taxonomy defines each type as a group of characteristics rather than placing importance on a specially distinctive characteristic. Grouping things according to a combination of shared characteristics, some of which are found in each member of the type, is called *polythetic classification*, in contrast to importance being placed on a single 'significant' characteristic (*monothetic classification*).

This pattern of relationships is then related to dated examples of the artefacts being classified. The relationships between these otherwise datable artefacts and the pattern of groups (representing the relationships between all the artefacts) enables the overall pattern to be dated. In this way a combination of statistical methods and otherwise datable fixed points can afford both a classification and chronology for any type of artefact, or even for types of sites.

Numerical taxonomists claim that their approach is less biased, more explicit, and – unlike arbitrary taxonomy – has a firmer mathematical underpinning than arbitrary classification. This, they say, makes their theory of classification capable of producing truer and superior classifications to those of the arbitrary taxonomists.

Since the 1960s numerical taxonomy has spread to become the principal form of classification in prehistory, although historical archaeology has remained mainly the province of arbitrary taxonomy, with some notable exceptions. There has also been a tendency for culture-historians to favour arbitrary classification, and for processualists to favour numerical taxonomy, as already mentioned. So the division between these approaches has partly taken on a relationship with different types of archaeology and overall perspectives on the subject.

Critics of numerical approaches have pointed out that attribute definition and choice are still 'arbitrary', i.e. based on the observer's own decisions (Thomas 1971, 1972, 1978). Therefore, they suggest, the claim to objectivity made by numerical taxonomists is unwarranted. Moreover they point out the contrasting classifications which can be produced by applying different numerical techniques to the same data. They criticise numerical methods in similar ways to those in which numerical taxonomists criticise arbitrary classification.

These were the only two schools of archaeological classification until the 1980s, when post-processualist scholars developed grammatical approaches and methods emphasising folk-taxonomy. Unsurprisingly, in view of their overall orientation, they considered classification to be always subjective and contextual. They saw classifications as reflecting only the concerns and requirements of the observer or classifier. This is the only possible relativist position on classification, outside the denial that it is possible to classify archaeological material at all.

Another method was introduced in the late 1970s and 1980s, outside the post-processualist movement (Bellman 1979; Dark 1987). This is the theory of *cladistic classification*.

Cladistics

Cladistics is a mathematically-based system of classification derived from the work of the German biologist Willi Henig (1966). It has become the dominant theory of classification in biology, especially zoology, adopted by such august organisations as the British Museum of Natural History.

Although it is based on mathematics, one need not have any mathematical ability to employ cladistics, and in theory it is, again, simple. Its basis is to classify according to unique characteristics so that, for example, every time an artefact is found to have a unique feature it forms a new group.

In a cladistic classification we group artefacts or sites according to attributes they share together but which are not found in the wider range of artefacts or sites. Cladistics claims not total objectivity, but the systematisation of decision-making in classification. Like numerical taxonomy it has a mathematical basis: in this case, in set-theory mathematics.

In practice, the attributes considered in classifying artefacts or sites are only those occurring more than once but having a restricted distribution in a group of objects or sites. The objects or sites are then divided into groups (each defined by unique characteristics within the overall range of artefacts or sites under consideration), according to the number of shared characteristics occurring in this way. The closeness of relationship between these groups is ascertained by using the number of shared, but restricted, characteristics to form a family-tree-like diagram (a dendrogram, called in cladistics a *cladogram*).

The result is a pattern of related groups, each with a distinct mathematical identity similar to that produced by numerical taxonomy. At this point cladistic classifications can be divided into two types dependent upon the attitudes of the classifier to the meaning of this sequence. Some believe that the cladogram represents, in itself, a relative dating sequence, others (known as *pattern cladists*) hold that it simply represents a relationship between the groups identified. In archaeology, dating evidence, other than that provided by classification itself, can assist in solving this issue.

Cladistic approaches enable us to choose the variables to be classified on a systematic basis, but we still have the problem that when we define the complete group of variables and choose traits for classification, it is according to our own perceptions. So cladistics, too, can be criticised on the grounds that the classifier makes arbitrary decisions both in terms of what constitutes an attribute and in establishing the total range of attributes. It is also open to the criticism that, as it is based on non-numerical mathematics (set-theory), it is not amenable to statistical tests in the same way as is possible in numerical taxonomy, although *numerical cladistics* does represent characteristics as numbers.

Conclusion

These theories of classification represent all those in current use. Archaeologists are much divided over this issue, but it is probably fair to say that arbitrary taxonomy has been losing ground. Both cladistic and post-processual approaches are, arguably, too new to have made an impact comparable to that of arbitrary and numerical views.

An obvious question is whether there is any way of independently evaluating the effectiveness of classification: can we expect classifications to answer the questions frequently asked of them, such as date, function and affinity? Surprisingly, perhaps, as we usually think of experimental archaeology in relation to the functions of artefacts and types of production, classification has also been an area in which experimental research has been undertaken.

Experiments in classification

The best known experiment in classification was undertaken by Deetz (Deetz and Dethlefsen 1965, 1971; Dethlefsen and Deetz 1966), who examined the historical period tombstones of the USA in order to test archaeological concepts of classification. He showed that these well-dated monuments did indeed show the sort of sequence of styles which he might have expected in an archaeological classification. That is, typology could have been used to date these monuments.

Quite a different experiment was conducted by Miller (1985a). Working on locally-produced pottery in India, he noted that the classification given to the pots by their users and makers was dependent upon how they were used, not upon their form. A similar result had already been reached in Roman-period archaeology by Wheeler, who (in a famous but unpublished lecture) noted that the form of pottery was not related in an 'obvious' way to its function – although often described as 'storage jars', amphorae could be used for storage, or as coffins, or urinals, or musical instruments. The work of these two scholars produced complementary conclusions, insofar as they suggest that form alone is not a key to functional classification.

Another form of experimentation is to give the same data-set to a number of scholars to analyse using one method, or to apply a number of methods to a single data-set. Such a data-set need not exist in reality but could, for instance, be a mathematical simulation.

Experimentation of this sort has been widely seen as showing both the possibilities and the difficulties of archaeological classifications. It can also form a valuable test in assessing the relative merits of theories or specific methods of classification, as well as in evaluating the resulting classifications and the interpretations placed upon them.

In conclusion, a further problem associated with classification can be summarised. Archaeological approaches to dating using all of the above classificatory systems depend upon change taking place over time. There are instances, however, where the form of artefacts or sites does not change over time and these, of course, present a major difficulty for all attempts at chronology based upon classification.

Typological conservatism

The continued production of an artefact or site-type without change in its form is called *typological conservatism*. To take a couple of examples: in the French colonies of the Arab Near East, a distinctive type of French coin was in use in the eighteenth century (Carver 1987, 42). It became so established as the definition of coinage in itself that when the production of this form of coin ceased in the eighteenth century, its design was exactly reproduced (*fossilised*) in the local production of these colonies. Exact copies of its final form – complete with the last date of minting – continued to be produced into recent times.

A second example is afforded by stone bowls produced in Italy from the early Roman period until the middle ages (Carver 1987, 42). The forms of these did not change much over a millennium of manufacture, rendering them very difficult to date.

Both of these types of artefacts did not change in form over long periods of manufacture, yet we frequently assume that lack of typological change implies that an artefact-type is becoming obsolete or its production is losing vigour (e.g. Fulford 1979). Both illustrate the difficulty posed by typological conservatism for chronologies based on classification.

Comparison between different classes of artefact (pottery and metalwork, for example) is unlikely to help us to solve this problem. It has often been noted that little typological change occurs in wood-working tools between the fourth and eighteenth centuries even though, strictly speaking, typological conservatism was not present. The possibility of typological conservatism must therefore be evaluated before a chronology based on classification alone is used.

The problems of chronology and classification are closely related, and their theoretical study has a major contribution to make to the practice of archaeology. They serve to illustrate, once again, that even the most basic archaeological procedures involve the application of theoretical concepts.

CHAPTER 4

Social Archaeology

Social archaeology is the archaeology of society, and so encompasses a very wide range of topics (for a sample of the range, see Redman *et al.* 1978; Renfrew 1984; Renfrew and Bahn 1991, ch. 5). This chapter examines those aspects of the field which, for example, concern approaches to reconstructing social organisation, understanding the role of women and children, establishing political boundaries and centres, and identifying competition and conflict.

Social archaeology is undertaken by processualist, post-processualist and culture-historical archaeologists (e.g. Gjessing 1975; Hodder 1992; Renfrew 1984). Unsurprisingly, this field of study has been characterised by a very great variety of approaches, of which only a limited selection can be outlined here.

We may begin with a classic archaeological question: can we reconstruct social organisation from archaeological sources? Most excavators aim to make some comments concerning the social organisation of settlements and of communities represented by cemeteries; when they do so they are undertaking social archaeology.

Social organisation: ranks, roles and status

There have been so many varied studies concerning this subject that it is difficult to know where to start (for a detailed introduction to current approaches, see Renfrew and Shennan 1982; Hodder 1986, 1992; Renfrew and Bahn 1991, ch. 5). Many types of data and differing approaches have been employed to try to reconstruct social structure: burial, settlements, artefacts and human remains (e.g. Ucko 1972; Rathje 1975; Cherry 1978; Miller and Tilley 1984; McGuire and Paynter 1991; Paynter 1992; Lubar and Kingery 1993). These types of evidence each have associated theoretical problems which have been hotly discussed in archaeology since the 1960s.

On a general level, there has been debate over the philosophical and anthropological possibility of the existence of non-ranked, or non-exploitative, social structures, with some political attraction to each interpretation. The possibility of non-ranked but socially differentiated societies – divided among kin-groups, occupation, gender, or age – has been widely acknowledged, however, and such societies are referred to by the anthropological term *segmentary* when a kin-basis is adduced.

Marxist scholars have tended to adopt a more rigid view of past social structure, favouring terms such as *primitive communism* for the non-stratified societies which, they have argued, existed in early prehistory. One Marxist scholar (Tilley 1984) has tended to view all societies as based on exploitation, and others have adopted Engels' classification of social evolution into savagery, barbarism and civilisation in their analyses of prehistory, although this is now largely outmoded.

Another method has been to employ Service's order of band, tribe, chiefdom, state (Service 1971, 1975) to clarify all cultures according to their social organisation, and Service's criteria can be sought in the archaeological record. Later work, especially that undertaken by Claessen (1983; Claessen and Skalnik 1984) has been taken up by other scholars.

Others feel that societies (either past, present, or both) cannot, or should not, be classified. Yet others doubt the existence of such a thing as society at all, while the concept of *culture* remains prevalent in many archaeological studies, either explicitly or implicitly. Culture is used in two ways in archaeology. The first of these refers to the way of life or total range of institutions, customs and beliefs in a past society. The second is the equation between a group of archaeological characteristics and a 'people'. This latter usage is sometimes referred to as an 'archaeological culture'. An archaeological culture was defined by Gordon Childe as

> ... an assemblage of artefacts that recur repeatedly associated together in dwellings of the same kind and with burials by the same rite. The arbitrary peculiarities of implements, weapons, ornaments, houses, burial rites and ritual objects are assumed to be the concrete expression of common social traditions that bind together the people. And sometimes we can see the whole complex move about; that must signify a folk movement (Childe 1950, 2).

Certainly this was the dominant theoretical tool for understanding social organisation between the 1930s and the 1960s (Meindander 1981), leading to such cultural definitions as 'the Beaker folk'.

The concept of an archaeological culture was still being employed by Clarke in 1968, and in his writings perhaps reached its most formalised and intricately worked-out form. It was challenged as a concept by Renfrew (1979b) and others in the 1970s (notably Shennan 1978), and has now largely disappeared from theoretical writings (but see Shennan 1989). Nevertheless, a concept of 'culture' still persists in historical archaeology – for example, in the correlation of the Sintana de Mures/Chernyakov 'culture' with the historical Goths (Heather and

Matthews 1991) – and in later prehistory, when one may still, it seems, speak of 'Celtic' or 'Germanic' culture. Classical archaeology also persists in 'cultural labels': for instance, in discussing Mycenaean or Minoan cultures.

Recently, continuing (and as yet unpublished) work by Karen Hoilund Nielsen has produced a series of correlations between groups of artefacts and tribes in the first millennium AD, whose location at the date of the artefact-group is known from written sources. This, she suggests, enables us to link the artefact-groups with these historical tribes. Interestingly, the geographical areas in which these artefact-groups are found change over time in accordance with the way in which textual sources tell us that the tribes moved within Europe during the Migration Period.

Some attempted replacements for the term 'culture' – such as the 'Beaker package' (Shennan 1978) – have been widely adopted. But archaeologists have still aimed to establish consistent correlations in the material record in space, with the aim of discovering group-identities.

Although this gives only the briefest outline of the debates concerning 'culture' over the last thirty years, it will be clear that even at an abstract level of argument the problems of recognising social organisation have generated much controversy and many irreconcilable differences of opinion. This is expressed even more clearly when we turn to the question of social structure as evidenced by burial.

The social archaeology of burial

Perhaps the most regularly used approach to reconstructing social structure is the use of burial evidence (see Saxe 1970; Struever 1971; Brown 1971; Rahtz *et al.* 1980; Chapman *et al.* 1981; Bartel 1982; O'Shea 1984; Roberts *et. al.* 1989). Usually the method employed has been to take one or more aspects of burial customs – artefacts deposited in or near the grave, the form or scale of a tomb, or the layout or location of the cemetery – and to correlate these factors with rank or status (e.g. Brown 1981; O'Shea 1981a).

So, if the presupposition is that burial mounds are specific to a given rank and so is gold, then that rank is recognised by the burial mounds containing gold. Alternatively, if a rank is correlated with a burial location – let us say, in a prominent place – then those burials in that location are assigned the rank proposed.

A more subtle approach to recognising rank is that of symbolic analysis. The search for likely status symbols in graves might be carried out in order to enable us to identify rank or social position without the preconception that wealth correlates with rank (Pader 1982; Hodder 1982d). But the difficulty has been in recognising such status symbols in the archaeological record. One way might be to claim that some materials are intrinsically symbolic of the status of specific ranks. On the other

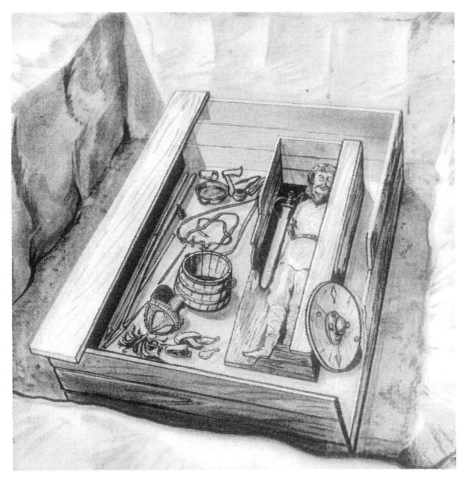

22. From material remains to past activities. A reconstruction of the burial shown in figure 23. The first step to social reconstruction is to establish the way in which the excavated evidence represents past activity: in this case, the original circumstances of burial. (Reproduced with the kind permission of Rheinisches Landesmuseum)

hand, a relativist, in particular, might assert that a specific symbol correlates with a specific rank on no other grounds than the assertion itself. This, it might be assumed, would enable us to engage in an interesting discussion about such evidence, but most archaeologists would consider this form of argument uncritical and unusable.

The principal problems with using burial evidence for studies of social structure are, however, that the representation of burial in the archaeological record may have obscured the very material affording information about social organisation (Ucko 1969). Even if social position is signalled in burial customs, it may be in an idealised form. Social ideals can, as we are aware, be very different from social reality (on the anthropology of death, see Huntingdon and Metcalf 1979).

Burial customs themselves can obscure social organisation even if it was once represented by aspects of the burials being studied. For example, exposure of the body before burial, and the deliberate or accidental mixing of bones from different bodies may present major difficulties, as does the loss of bones on the funeral pyre for cremations. These factors mean that while we can usually be assured that a skeleton articulated within an inhumation grave comprises the bones of one individual, detached mixed or cremated bones may come from several bodies. It is therefore often difficult to be sure that every case in a cemetery of what we would archaeologically recognise as an individual burial actually represents an individual in the past society under study.

Even if, as in an articulated inhumation burial, all parts of the skeleton certainly belong to a single individual, the association of that individual with the objects (if any) found in the grave is another theoretical problem. Anthropological and historical studies certainly contain references to the deposition of objects in the grave for (or in order to get to) the afterlife, or to facilitate reincarnation, but objects in the grave might also be, for instance, gifts to the dead representing debts, or burial dues, or sacrifices to a deity, or expressions of social status or economic wealth (which may not be the same thing), or representations of the role of the dead in life. They may also, of course, represent sentimental tokens associated with the individual by those taking part in the burial. These options merely touch upon a few possibilities.

So the reconstruction of social position from artefacts in the grave, or from cremations, is fraught with theoretical problems (Ucko 1969). So, too, is the use of burial customs or cemetery layout and location, because we seldom have the evidence to assign significance to the variations visible within a cemetery. Variations in burial customs, or location of graves, may represent no more than chronological patterning, change occurring over the period in which the cemetery was in use. They may represent religious differences between those buried, or between those burying them, or differences in local customs between scattered communities using the same cemetery. They could represent different population groups, some migrants into the area, others local to it. Or they might represent customs specific to groups in society defined on other grounds than social status, such as occupation, or membership of a specific clan or burial club (e.g. see O'Shea 1981a).

In short, although there is much written about burial as a source for rank, status and social role, scholars differ over almost every issue involved. There is, at present, no consensus over whether burial can, or cannot, be used as such a source, or, even if it can, over how it can be used to generate social organisation. This is not, however, to detract from the extremely interesting and sophisticated analyses of this type which have been undertaken (e.g. Shennan 1975; Peebles and Kus 1977; Tainter 1980; Gibbs 1987; Morris 1987, 1992; Cannon 1989; Hedeager 1992; Van Velzen 1992).

This discussion merely addresses a few salient points concerning the use of burial in social reconstruction. Other issues include difficulties in ranking artefacts (a problem to which we shall shortly return) and differences arising from the sampling strategy, or methods of excavation and recording, employed in the recovery of data. The most significant data for social studies might be those less often recovered: for example, evidence of occupational or hygiene-related diseases, or of levels of nutrition.

Yet another view is to claim that burial, by its ideological character, informs us only of non-social factors, and not at all about social organisation. This opinion supposes that the 'scrambling' process of burial customs renders social position not recoverable from burial data, or even not represented within it. A variant on the same critical approach is to argue that although social position might well be expressed in archaeological evidence for burial, it is impossible to recognise when this has, or has not, occurred.

A related problem is the possibility of 'invisible' funerary customs. These might take two forms: the first is when the method of deposition of the corpse renders it irrecoverable – the scattering of cremated ashes into the deep sea is an excellent example; the second is when disposal occurs in such a way as to bias the archaeological record against its recovery. Examples would be the deposition of bodies in rivers, or by sailing them off – like Hrothgar in *Beowulf* – in a burning boat. Doubtless the reader will be able to imagine many other theoretical possibilities of this type. The social organisation visible in burial may, therefore, lack the 'top' or 'bottom', or for that matter any other part (women, children, etc.) of the social scale, because some groups within the population have been 'buried' in archaeologically irrecoverable ways.

The segregation of specific classes or social groups (e.g. warriors) into separate cemeteries, or into zones of (usually partially sampled) cemeteries, also presents theoretical problems, while cremation brings difficulties of its own. How do we know that a pot used to contain cremated ashes was made for that purpose, or specially selected so as to ascribe significance to the cremation? Richards (1987) has suggested that the correlation of grave-goods and pot-shapes with the age and biological sex of ashes within is a key to recognising such relationships, but there are obvious problems with assigning significance to any one of these correlations, and the same problems that affect the social archaeology of inhumation burials still apply.

Complications arise, too, from the re-use of urns or non-funerary pottery for cremation, and from multiple cremations in a single urn. All these factors need to be taken into consideration when evaluating such evidence.

One of the principal ways in which archaeologists have tried to assign social status to burial evidence has been to examine the artefacts associated with burials. Artefacts found outside burial contexts (e.g. on domestic sites) have also been seen as a potential source of information about society. As we have seen, however, the social archaeology of artefacts is not without its own problems.

23. Assigning significance. The seventh-century Frankish 'warrior grave' at Morken, Germany. On which of the finds, if any, do we place special importance? Or is it the total assemblage which is socially significant? Alternatively, is it the manner of burial itself which tells us of social position? Even if we can decide upon answers to these questions, are we seeing an accurate picture of Frankish society or no more than an idealised representation of it? (Photo: Rheinisches Landesmuseum)

The social archaeology of artefacts

The simplest way in which artefacts are used by archaeologists to form the basis of their conclusions about social structure is by ordering them according to their value or significance as perceived by the archaeologist concerned. When such ordering is said to correlate with social status, or with the value of the artefacts concerned, it is described as *ranking*, although, confusingly, this term is also used elsewhere in social archaeology to refer to the way in which social status itself is apportioned.

Artefacts may be ranked on the grounds of their material (e.g. gold, silver, etc.) or their scarcity (e.g. the rarity of amber outside those areas in which it is naturally found), or the amount of effort required to produce them. The latter – known as *energy input* (or *energy expenditure*) *ranking* – is based on an estimation of how long it would take to produce the artefact, the value residing in the length of time that the producer(s) would have to spend away from primary food production. That is, those making the artefact were not producing the food which they ate while doing so. Alternatively, we can consider the amount of raw materials used in production (*resource expenditure*) in a similar way. These approaches can also be applied to the ranking of structures, as in the interesting experimental study by Reynolds (1982), who demonstrated the costs in time and resources involved in building a timber roundhouse.

Other methods, less widely employed, include ranking by colour, or weight, or according to the specialist skills required for manufacture. Ranking by the type or complexity of the artefacts involved is also often used. But with many of these criteria there are severe problems associated with differences in classification, and with the differing perceptions of the manufacturers, users, and modern scholars. We cannot even be sure that colour or size perceptions remained consistent through time and space, according to some anthropologists.

As indirectly mentioned in Chapter 2, middle-range problems with depositional and post-depositional differences in representation between types of, or parts of, artefacts are major problems here. The most important artefacts for use in establishing social organisation may be the least preserved or obvious. In many medieval chapels the most valued item – a relic – does not survive in the archaeological record even though it was consciously preserved and sealed into a substantial stone, wood or metal container during the use of the building.

There are, then, major problems facing the archaeologist when trying to assign value to artefacts, and the difficulties already mentioned can be multiplied many times. The most important thing about a specific type of prehistoric pottery (such as beakers) to its users in prehistory could (as with Dark-Age E-Ware or Roman amphorae) have been not the pottery vessel but the contents. To give another example, throughout medieval Europe artefacts such as swords were valued by associations ideologically

24. A reconstruction of an early Anglo-Saxon burial. The burial has to be seen in a context comprising not merely the burial itself and the contents of the grave, but activities surrounding it and its relationship to settlement evidence. (Photo: Hampshire County Museum)

constructed around them, yet these associations are not consistent with any one category of artefacts or aspect of material culture, nor with any one area. Such theoretical possibilities suggest that the information about social organisation once encoded within material culture might in these cases be irrecoverable in the archaeological record when seen in isolation.

Other problems are presented when artefacts are transferred by trade or gift-giving up or down the social scale, or from one political unit or population group to another with different customs or values. It seems that value is neither consistent from one culture to another nor through time, even though some scholars have considered that it is.

Another interesting approach has been to attempt to establish correlations between artefacts and symbolic roles, so as to assign them an association. For example, McGhee (1977) noted that ivory and sea mammal bone were used for some types of artefact, whereas antler was used for others, and by considering the functional and gender associations of these objects, he suggested that the different use of material was for symbolic rather than practical purposes. Using anthropological evidence, he suggested that women were associated with the sea and men with the land, and that a land:sea contrast existed in the perception of the users of the artefacts. By constructing a series of contrasts and associations, he attempted to assign a symbolic role to these artefacts on the basis of the material of which they were made.

Without the contextual evidence provided by anthropological or historical data relating to that specific society, however, such approaches are hindered by the difficulty in recognising symbolism and in constructing a series of associations in the past. This, however, brings us into the scope of cognitive archaeology, which will be discussed in Chapter 6.

Structures and settlement evidence form the other main source of social archaeology. Buildings have been examined in isolation, for example, in terms of their architecture or in relation to their layout in settlements (see Chapter 2; Hill 1968, 1970; Hietala 1984; Kent 1984, 1990; Samson 1990). Settlements themselves have been examined individually, or in terms of their relationships to one another and to the surrounding landscape: *settlement-patterns*.

The social archaeology of structures and settlements

It has been assumed that structures reflect social organisation in several ways (e.g. Ucko 1972; Glassie 1975; Kent 1984, 1990; Samson 1990; Parker-Pearson and Richards 1994). The architecture of buildings has been seen as representing functions related to specific social divisions, or symbolising social positions or relationships. One might, for example, see a medieval castle as reflecting the functions of the feudal aristocracy – warfare, feasting, political and resource control etc. – or as a symbol, in its height, manner of construction, or location, of the political or social role of the élite.

The analysis of the layout of buildings and activities on a site (*intra-site analysis*) has been a major subject of interest. Architecture has also been considered in relation to the way it constrains our movements within it (e.g. Reid 1989). In applying *access analysis*, Foster has aimed to show social organisation through assessing access to different areas of structures and settlements (Foster 1989). A related concept, developed earlier and separately, is Fleming's (1982) theory that social boundaries (e.g. of class) are reflected in physical boundaries (e.g. of property).

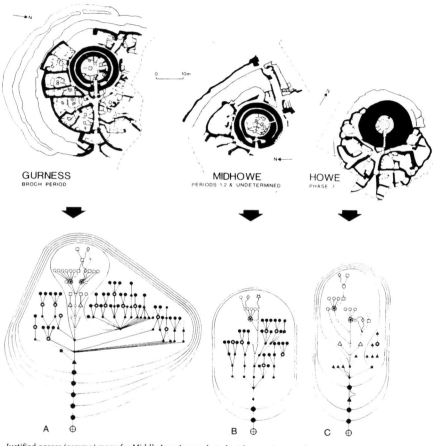

Justified access (gamma) maps for Middle Iron Age nucleated settlements (reversed/open symbols distinguish the broch from other structures).

KEY
⊕ carrier space
• transitional space
□ cell/compartment
○ space with hearth
▲ guard cell/room
△ large internal space-no hearth
reversed/open symbol for broch

■ open yard
● enclosure
□ first floor
○ scarcement level
☼ earth-house
⌒ stairs
---- unsure access

25. Access analysis. Each point represents the way in which a definable area within a site was used. Even superficially similar sites can produce different diagrams, so this analysis may clarify our understanding of the way in which space was used within them. (Reproduced with the kind permission of Dr S. Foster)

A similar but separate approach has been Todd Whitelaw's (1983) suggestion that physical distance in settlement layouts is representative of *social distance* – that is, of how closely connected in social terms were the individuals involved – showing (as have other scholars such as Simek, 1987) that settlement layout can still be used as a source for social archaeology in early prehistory.

Within buidings, the shape of rooms can be considered to promote or limit interaction, so that curvilinear rooms into which access is direct can be seen as having a greater 'communality' than rectangular rooms with porches and subdivisions. According to this theory, the latter type of rooms 'distance' one element of the population from the others by restricting interaction. The same basis can be applied to settlement analysis, such as the distribution of huts within an enclosure.

More straightforward, perhaps, is the evaluation of social rank or organisation through the application of resource-expenditure analysis to buildings. According to this view, the most costly buildings will be the most important, and so on. Another concept used in archaeology is to rank structures, consciously or unconsciously, according to *size-rank rule*. In this method the bigger a building, the higher is its rank. Similarly, in its most common application size-rank rule is applied to settlements on the same basis – the bigger the better (or rather, the bigger the socially superior) – and this can produce very complex interpretations when applied to whole settlement patterns. Archaeologists have also tried to identify areas used for specific forms of activity between and around structures and sites (*activity-areas*). These have usually been sought by relating the distribution of artefacts to features such as pits and post-holes.

Another approach is to consider the settlement-pattern itself (e.g. Chang 1968; Robbins 1966): the spatial relationships between settlements might be considered indicative of a specific form of social organisation; evidence might also be provided by the location of settlements in areas of differing resources, or with differing access to trade relationships.

Now that we have considered the main sources for social archaeology, I shall outline some of the themes which it has aimed to study. These encompass many levels of analysis and an extremely wide range of societies. Most societies construct political frameworks, including forms of land-holding and boundaries, and it is at this level that we shall begin, before looking at the archaeology of political structure itself.

Burial and land-tenure

Evidence of who owns or gains resources from land (*land-tenure*) can be reflected in burial on the land or close to it (for a recent discussion see Morris 1991). Burials may assert the rights of the kin of those buried, and may, therefore, form ceremonial or symbolic expressions of social position and of the claims of the burying population: such ceremonial or symbolic complexes are called *monuments*, and their construction is the province of a theory of *monumentality* (for a recent discussion see Bradley 1993). Such concepts have been very important in prehistoric archaeology, especially in Renfrew's work (e.g. Renfrew 1984), and found in historical archaeology in the work of Bonney (1972, 1976) and others on Anglo-Saxon England and Early Christian Ireland.

The observation of land rights through burial on land is often combined with burial in peripheral locations, marking the limits of territory, as possibly in Anglo-Saxon examples (for recent discussions see Goodier 1984; Reilly 1988), and certainly in early Christian Ireland (Charles-Edwards 1976). In prehistory, an interesting attempt to combine this view with environmental factors has been made by Spratt (1981), who defines Bronze-Age territories in this fashion.

Inscriptions offer even more potential for burials to contain information supporting the *legitimacy* of an individual or group to rule or own land. Inscriptions may directly refer to ownership or, as in Dark-Age Wales where genealogies were inscribed on stones, be used to assert land-tenure by relating burial and kinship to the landscape. Both uses of inscriptions assert the rights of the individual or kin to control land. These are the same claims which, in a pre-literate society, may have been represented by uninscribed monuments: 'land-charters in stone'.

Burial and collective identity

When burials are so structured (by the mixing of disarticulated bones, for example) as to confuse one individual with others, or collected into cemeteries, it is often supposed that a collective identity for contemporary society is asserted. In the former case the individuals themselves may be grouped together by the act of burial, possibly representing a denial of individuality, or an importance placed on group identity, in society itself. Such a procedure is facilitated by the *excarnation* (de-fleshing) of bodies before burial; this is achieved by *exposure* of the corpse to decay or animals. Concepts of excarnation, exposure and *collective burial* have been used in arguments concerning the place in society (*social identity*) of the individual in such disarticulated and mixed burials in the Neolithic period, as by Shanks and Tilley (1982). These scholars have also drawn attention to the way the bones in collective burials can become symbolically placed and sorted to reflect social and cognitive ideals or realities.

The archaeology of political structure

In discussing the work of Service we have already considered aspects of the political organisation of society. Political organisation expresses itself both consciously and unconsciously in terms of territories, boundaries, ideologies, institutions and specific forms of material culture.

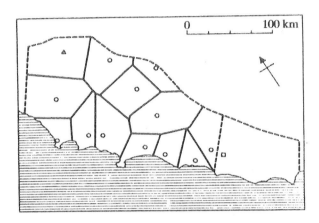

26. The early state module. This example is produced by applying this theory to ancient Etruria, Italy. (Reproduced with the kind permission of Professor Colin Renfrew)

State-formation and state-collapse

Most work on the archaeology of political organisation has concentrated on how political units come into existence, and especially how what Service would classify as 'states' emerge from pre-existing 'chiefdoms' (on chiefdoms themselves see Earle 1991; Drennan 1992; for an example, see Myhre 1987). Especially notable has been Renfrew's suggestion that there is a cross-cultural regularity in which states are built up from smaller territories sharing specific sizes and structures of organisation (Renfrew 1975). These smaller units, which he calls *early state modules*, have been disputed by other scholars (especially Fisher 1985), and this approach is no longer widely employed, with much recent work emphasising evolutionary trends or the detailed specifics of individual cases. Another characteristic of recent studies has been a move away from rigid classifications of societies into chiefdoms, states etc., toward more 'neutral' terms, such as *polity* (the highest level socio-political unit in any given situation), and complexity (where political units are ranked on a continuous scale from less to more complex (e.g. Tainter 1988; Chapman 1990). The definition of complexity itself has, however, proved exceptionally controversial since different scholars have seen different characteristics as significant measures of how complex any political unit or society was.

In the last decade there has also been a renewal of theoretical interest in the collapse of political units, especially those which might be called 'states'. The study of *state-collapse* has, therefore, joined *state-formation* as a central concern of the archaeology of political structure (e.g. Tainter 1988; Yoffee and Cowgill 1988). The other key concerns have been the identification of political centres and boundaries and of competition within, and between, political units.

The identification of political centres and territories

Surprisingly, archaeologists have engaged in only limited discussion of the identification of political centres and boundaries in prehistory (e.g. Renfrew 1984; de Montmollin 1989), the most sophisticated analyses being based upon forms of *locational analysis*. The distribution of sites or monuments in the landscape has been seen as a key to the distribution of political centres and frontiers. 'New Archaeologists' in the 1960s used *Thiessen polygons* (divisions decided by assessing the intermediate points between possible political or economic centres, or *central places*) to delineate the boundaries of territories dependent upon the centres involved. Archaeologists, geographers and social scientists have been extremely critical of this approach, known as *central place theory* or *CPT* (e.g. Grant 1986), but it can still be found in archaeology, in the work, for example, of Arnold (e.g. 1988).

Renfrew (Renfrew 1984; Renfrew and Cooke 1979) has introduced the concept of *dominance* into locational analysis, using this to assess the relationship between centres. Each centre need not, therefore, have a territory of its own, nor need centres have equally sized territories. Grant (1986) has modified this approach still further by introducing topographical features, such as rivers and coastlines, as possible constraints on political territories.

Another approach, more widely used among culture-historians, is to attempt to correlate the distribution of a specific site- or artefact-type, such as Iron-Age coins, with political territories (e.g. Sellwood 1980). The basis of this view was that production and/or distribution of the site- or artefact-type used was under political control and is unlikely to have been distributed outside the political unit concerned. A more subtle variant attempts to identify absences in the distribution of such artefacts across the landscape and so to recognise where another political unit was constraining that distribution. The use of *negative evidence* of this kind is, however, dangerous in all forms of archaeological argument, as new discoveries may alter distributions or statistical relationships. This is not to say that such arguments may not be employed, but it is necessary to be critical when doing so, and to be aware that only strong correlations of this sort are likely to endure in the face of new discoveries and the clarification of archaeological chronology.

Political reconstructions based upon artefact distributions have also incorporated natural features, such as rivers, mountains etc. as potential boundary lines, for example in Sellwood's (1980) consideration of Iron-Age tribal groupings based upon coin-evidence. The use of archaeological distributions as a source of information about past political units (*polities*) has been combined with other data such as linear earthworks. The evidence of contemporary written records which indicate that a political unit existed, but do not define extent, can also be taken into account, as can written sources deriving from the period immediately following, where the archaeological evidence is said to enable the retrospective projection of such political units into the earlier period. Such studies have been undertaken by, for example, Davies and Vierck (1974) and Burgess (1980).

Although archaeologists have generally felt uneasy about delineating political boundaries from material sources alone (e.g. Reece 1987), there have been instances, such as in the archaeology of the Iron-Age tribes mentioned above, when political units territorially delimited on this basis have found widespread acceptance in later study. Usually, however, archaeologists have been content to seek only political centres, and have generally done so by examining settlement or burial evidence. Most of the approaches used to do this have already been mentioned: size-rank rule and the ranking of structures and artefacts have, for example, been extremely widely used. In historical periods the use of written evidence or inscriptions has played a major part in archaeological attempts to recognise such sites or burials, for example in the discussions surrounding the Anglo-Saxon cemetery at Sutton Hoo, or the identification of *civitas* capitals in Roman Britain. In Chapter 2, the use of analogy between the form of such sites, or their location, and other ahistorical settlements or burials was mentioned, and this too has formed an important approach to the recognition of political centres in historical archaeology. An interesting alternative use of this evidence for prehistoric archaeology has been Clare's (1987) adoption of a historical analogy for henge monuments, comparing them on an archaeological basis with political centres identified by textual evidence in early historical Ireland.

Others have seen the 'continuity' of a political centre from one period to another, combined with hints from written evidence of the incorporation of archaic political units into later territorial organisation, as evidence that we can project back those political units to the preceding period. The classic instance of such an approach is the highly influential multiple-estate model (e.g. Jones 1971), which has been used to assert that Bronze-Age and later political units are recognisable from thirteenth-century and later written sources when these are correlated with earlier archaeological evidence. Although now discredited by several studies, the multiple estate model is a clear example of an attempt to use specific historical, geographical and archaeological evidence, together with the concept of continuity, to recognise political structure in prehistory.

Another view, based on *ecological determinism* – the theory that all human decisions are necessitated by relationships between human beings and the environment, even in detail – is that there are 'natural' and so constantly recurring political boundaries and centres. It might be, for example, that a small area of high quality soils capable of producing a much larger agricultural surplus is to be found in an otherwise relatively unproductive landscape. It could be argued that this will lead to the group occupying that area always having access to greater resources than those surrounding it, and so becoming pre-eminent. Political frontiers could equally be supposed to be 'naturally' determined by impassable or highly visible topographical features, such as rivers, mountains and the sea.

Isolation from neighbouring groups might also be seen as an important factor, and an ecological determinist might assert that a specific zone will, owing to its isolation, maintain a distinctive political identity. So, the archaeologist could seek this identity in a distinctive local, material culture. Processualist and post-processualist scholars have, however, been reluctant to adopt ecological determinism in the last twenty years, although such views were widespread in the 1960s and can still be found in contemporary archaeology. A major problem with the approach is that it does not seem to hold true in historical periods or in contemporary anthropological examples.

Alternatively, if we aim to seek evidence of political activity in the archaeological record, we might search for evidence not of territories or political foci but of political action. Two varieties of political action have been of special interest to archaeologists over the last generation – competition and warfare.

The archaeology of political competition and warfare

The political history of the last century has been characterised by both cooperation and competition, and there is no reason to suppose that the same was not true of, for example, Bronze-Age Europe. Political cooperation has not been much considered by archaeological theorists, but competition has been a major topic of study by theorists of all the major schools since the 1960s (e.g. Brumfiel and Fox forthcoming).

Competition can take two forms: non-violent and violent. Archaeologists have generally considered that both forms can be approached through the study of material data. The simplest way, perhaps, to compete non-violently is by greater resource-expenditure, or by copying the object of one's competition in such a way as to assert superiority or advantage. Such copying has been called *competitive emulation*. We frequently see these processes at work in modern western societies, when neighbours compete by doing what is colloquially called 'keeping up with the Joneses'. For instance, if family A has a garage built next to their house, family B will have a bigger garage built or, perhaps, a garage and a porch, but family A will counter this attempt to assert superiority by buying a larger or newer car and landscaping their garden, so that family B has not only to do all of these things in order to compete, but to do still more. Clearly such strategies can lead to a cycle of competition by acquisition, production and display (e.g. Bradley 1984). This type of competition by display and expenditure is essentially an additive process: each stage adds something rather than subtracting from what was there previously.

A common form of non-violent competition employing subtraction rather than addition is to compete by means of the consumption or destruction of wealth (e.g. Bradley 1986). This might be by feasting – eating up large quantities of a vital resource, food – or by gift-giving, or by the construction of monuments. Such activities constitute *competitive consumption* if they aim to assert superiority over a competitor. An alternative is *competitive destruction*, although this is often considered part of competitive consumption: in this strategy wealth is destroyed by breaking up artefacts, or placing them in graves, by dedicating resources or artefacts at temples, or depositing them in other places from which they cannot be recovered. Competition in this way works by asserting that the competitor has wealth to 'throw away' – which serves to show how much more they have than those with whom they compete.

Another way in which competition takes place is by the acquisition and manipulation of status symbols and of ceremonial: matters discussed elsewhere in this book. Political competition may take place in forms completely unrepresented in the archaeological record, such as written propaganda, the construction of elaborate family histories, or the patronage of poets and singers to produce works of art glorifying a ruling dynasty or élite, but involving no specific material culture unique to that activity.

Competition can become violent, and then it breaks out into warfare. Surprisingly, however, there has been little discussion of the theoretical basis for recognising warfare in archaeological sources (for anthropological discussions of the theory of warfare, see Venc 1984; Haas 1990), although the archaeology of warfare has been an important topic in Roman, Dark-Age Celtic and, more recently, Anglo-Saxon archaeology (e.g. Halsall 1989).

Bryony Coles (Orme 1981) has reminded archaeologists that warfare can be institutionalised as part of social and economic behaviour and such *endemic warfare* is attested in historical periods in Europe, e.g. early

27. **Archaeology and war.** A reconstruction of a Roman soldier fighting a Celtic Iron-Age warrior. (Photo: K.R. Dark)

Christian Ireland. There seems some reason to suppose that archaeologists have neglected the effect of warfare in past societies, perhaps because it is hard to reconstruct or from a tendency to romanticise prehistory.

As John Muke has pointed out, on anthropological grounds, a society can have many different types of warfare applicable to distinct circumstances (Muke, personal communications 1986-1991; unpublished Cambridge PhD dissertation 1992). He has also drawn attention to the fact that although there may be rules for war these can in some circumstances be broken, an observation also made in the case of early Christian Ireland, which, as we saw above, provides a historical European analogy (Binchy 1962).

Attempts at recognising warfare in the archaeological record have included Dixon's (1981) study of the distribution of arrowheads at Crickley Hill, and Dent's (1983) study of weapons and the evidence of wounds found on Iron-Age skeletons. In the first of these studies, flint arrowheads are found concentrated around the gate of a Neolithic enclosure, as if shot at defenders. Dixon interprets this as evidence for a battle in Neolithic Britain (Dixon, 1981). It is then argued that the arrowheads not only show us that warfare took place, but enable us to recover some details of the tactics employed.

No less interesting is the evidence of skeletons. Dent (1983) has used the pathological evidence of wounds and the presence of weapons in burials to establish both the existence and nature of deliberate wounding in Iron-Age Britain. The evidence afforded by both artefactual and skeletal studies can be very dramatic, as at Maiden Castle, Dorset, where an excavated skeleton had a Roman projectile point embedded in its spine. Even when there is no such close association between artefact and wound, it may be possible to connect a specific weapon, or pattern of use, with a distinctive type of wound, as in the case of Anglo-Saxon skeletons from Kent (Wenham 1989). These latter studies very clearly contribute to the reconstruction, not only of the type of weapons, but of the way in which they were used. In terms of the middle-range logic discussed in Chapter 2, they employ natural scientific reasoning in social archaeology.

Not all apparent defences need be connected with warfare, however. That settlements are enclosed by walls, earthen banks or ditches does not mean that they must be fortresses, for all these features might have been constructed for other reasons, such as to demonstrate social status, or to form religious boundaries or stock enclosures. Seemingly defensible positions might be chosen for settlements for non-military reasons: a hilltop could be selected to avoid periodic flooding, or in order to enable its occupants to view a symbolic location. The archaeologist must therefore define criteria by which defences, and defensible locations, can be isolated from those selected for non-military reasons, and plainly the less we know about other aspects of the society in question, the more difficult this will be.

Nor are all apparently military artefacts necessarily connected with war. To give an example, the metallurgical examination of early Anglo-Saxon swords has shown them to be so weak as to be useless as weapons (Tylecote and Gilmour 1986), while comparison of skeletal evidence and the weapons found in graves suggests that they were not all buried with warriors (Härke 1989, 1990, 1992). Such artefacts might, for example, have had a symbolic or ceremonial role.

As the previous example also shows, even in a society which we might assume to have been warlike (such as Anglo-Saxon England) it is unwise to assert that what seem to us weapons of war were necessarily employed for that function. This also applies to structures known from historical periods. For example, we generally assume that medieval castles were principally designed and used for military purposes, but many were intended to display and assert wealth and status rather than (or as well as) to protect it (Platt 1978, 174-7). A magnificent castle such as Bodiam can be seen (on the basis of both historical and archaeological evidence) to be 'an old soldier's dream house', perhaps set in landscaped grounds, with its design reflecting military tastes and ideals (Taylor *et al.* 1990). So symbolism may be used to explain what would otherwise seem 'obviously' to be military material culture.

28. **Fortress or ideal?** Bodiam Castle, Sussex. (Photo: British Crown Copyright/MOD)

Clearly, interesting problems arise when we attempt to recognise weapons, fortifications and warfare. This is, however, not an area in which debate has been fierce or much interest has been shown by theorists. This is in contrast to our next topic – gender.

Gender

Gender is the social concept of sex-roles and sexuality (for recent archaeological discussions, see Walde and Willows 1991; Conkey and Spector 1984; Gero and Conkey 1990; Ovrevik 1991; Claassen 1992; Bacus *et al.* 1993). The term 'gender' is used to differentiate these topics from biological sex, with which they may partly, or wholly, overlap. So, for example, there is no such thing as a biological group of eunuchs, but eunuchs – whose *gender* was chosen by, or for, them – were an essential element in, for example, Byzantine society.

In archaeology gender has been discussed mainly in the work of feminist scholars. They have seen social archaeology, and archaeology in general, as paying less than sufficient attention to women, or as reproducing contemporary sex-roles in the study of the past.

Gender studies in archaeology can also be seen as part of a broader debate in the social sciences and arts, concerning the role of women and classification of sex roles. In archaeology, discussions of gender have sought to recognise artefacts, structures and burials associated specifically with women, and to use these as sources to explore the status, exploitation, and other aspects of the 'social identity' of women in the past.

As examples, we may take Gibbs's (1987) study of women's graves in Scandinavia, where wealth, status and access to resources were correlated, and Scott's (1990, 1991) re-examination of the attitudes to women in the writing of the archaeology of the Roman period. Both of these studies attempt to recognise the way in which women are represented in the archaeological record.

Gender-based perspectives have spread into the wider archaeological community, so that non-feminist archaeologists may now consider gender, or the role of women, among their research topics. Although the institutional impact of gender-based and feminist archaeology has been strongest in the USA, the relationship between the feminist movement and gender-based archaeology has generated much interest in other countries, notably the UK. The debate has, for example, included discussions of whether women are more likely to innovate than men, of the control of resources by men, and of the representation of women in art. It has included a re-emphasis on the importance of kinship in social analysis and on reproduction and child-rearing, which are traditionally associated with women in Western eyes.

Not all archaeologists have received the gender debate well. Conflict has arisen in two main areas – that it is a separatist, or overly specific, way of studying society, and that it fails to integrate women's studies into the mainstream of archaeology. Consequently, by no means all of those interested in gender studies are 'feminist archaeologists'.

There can, however, be little doubt that, since it emerged in the 1980s, 'the gender debate' has been an important feature of archaeological theory. It has helped to highlight the archaeology of kinship and the role of women in the past, subjects often overlooked by scholars of the 1960s and earlier. The archaeology of children has also been a subject of recent theoretical interest, partly in connection with gender studies and feminist perspectives on the past. These have drawn attention to the relative neglect of studies of both children and of the old in social archaeology, although it would, perhaps, be misguided to suppose that the archaeology of women and children should be inextricably linked in the study of every society.

Children and the archaeology of caring

The concept of childhood is a cultural one: When does a child become an adult? Are the roles and dress of a child different from those of an adult? These are questions which archaeologists have found worthy of theoretical debate. Further, is there an age when children become 'human beings' in different societies? – even the most cursory reading of Classical literature shows that babies have not always been considered 'fully human' in all past cultures. Among those foremost in the study of the archaeology of children have been Scott (1990, 1991) and Crawford (1991). Watts (1989) has also considered these questions in relation to the archaeology of the Christian Church.

The approaches used by Scott and Crawford differ in as much as Scott attempts to understand the role of infants through the way in which they were 'used' by adult society – her study of infant burial stresses the 'use' of children in sacrifices; while Crawford attempts to recognise, from the comparison of skeletal ageing data and the employment of 'grave-goods', the age at which children were treated as adults. This, she suggests, represents their 'coming of age'. Using a retrospective argument, she compares this with the evidence of later written law codes concerning the age of maturity of children in the same society at a later date, and proposes a correlation between the two sources.

Watts (1989) has drawn attention to the differences in religious attitudes to children. She points out that only in Christian Romano-British contexts may we expect children to have received formal cemetery burial as though they were adults. This is with reference to the status of children as among the baptised, and so requiring appropriate burial. In Romano-British pagan religion, infants were not afforded conventional burial in the same way as adults, as Scott's work also confirms. Consequently, Watts's work highlights the potential for using an understanding of differing religious attitudes in the archaeology of children, and of using the archaeology of children to identify religious groups in Roman Britain.

These studies have begun to examine the range of arguments which will be needed if we are to write a social archaeology of children. It is interesting, however, that attitudes to children in all these cases can be recognised as a result of adult treatment of their bodies in religious contexts.

The examination of the social archaeology of children in relation to settlement sites is an even less well trodden pathway to the past, and while artefacts have been interpreted as children's toys (dolls etc.), without much consideration of their significance. Generally speaking children have been seen as identifiable in settlement contexts but peripheral to the main concerns of archaeology. It would be interesting to see whether artefactual evidence might enable us to identify areas where children slept, ate, or played both in relation to those used by adults and with regard to functional differences within settlements.

The archaeology of the old presents many of the same problems. The recognition of artefacts or areas on settlement sites specifically associated with old people, and the identification of age-related funerary practices both need to be considered. Even the burial evidence has only just begun to be examined. When do people become 'old'? Are they treated differently, or do they live in a different way? These are questions that need to be approached in archaeological analysis.

The similarities in the questions asked, and in the lack of study, have encouraged me to place children and the old together in this section. It must not be supposed, however, that this reflects the similarity of their status, nor, on the other hand, that we can overlook the care of children and of the very old in the same setting. Indeed, it would be possible to approach both subjects through an archaeology of caring, perhaps incorporating the study of the care of the infirm. Caring on the part of others has been recognised in the evidence provided by the burials of the physically or mentally disabled in conventional cemeteries, and is recognisable in their equally long, and apparently no more harsh, life than that of other adults in the same population. Where the body shows evidence of disability so extreme as to inhibit the ability to lead such a life unaided, care by others in the same community is strongly implied. Likewise, little has been done to study the integration of, or attitudes to, those less or more than conventionally tall or short into the community (although see Dangen 1990), though such individuals have been noted in archaeological contexts through the burial of their bodies in conventional cemeteries in a conventional way. Likewise, archaeological sources could, it might be supposed, be used in a study of discrimination, prejudice and lack of care – fields which have so far hardly been explored in archaeological theory, with the exception of the archaeology of slavery.

Slavery

Slavery seems to us an immoral and disgraceful way to treat another human being, but it is widely attested in anthropology and history, and our studies of the past must not neglect it. The identification of slaves through settlement evidence, the recognition of slave burials, and of artefacts associated with slaves, are all potential forms of evidence for recognising slavery in the archaeological record.

The identification of slavery on the grounds of artefactual evidence has been proposed in studies of so-called 'slave-chains' found in Early Christian Ireland (Hencken 1950). The ensuing archaeological debate – well-made chains for treasured dogs, high-status captives or hostages – shows a few of the attendant problems with using evidence of this sort (Scott 1978; Mytum 1992, 144). Moreover, the slave who sleeps on the household floor, owns no artefacts, is dressed in rags, and is casually disposed of in death (for instance, thrown in a nearby river), may leave no distinctive archaeological trace whatsoever.

The archaeology of slavery has been associated with historical, and also with Marxist, archaeology in Britain (notably Samson 1989, 1992, 1994). So too in the USA, scholars working in historical archaeology have usually been those most interested in slavery (e.g. Yentsch forthcoming). The slave plantations of the Caribbean and USA provide an obvious venue for its study, leading to fascinating work (e.g. Combes 1974; Schulyer 1980; Adams and Boling 1989; Pulsipher 1990). Such studies have shown that the recognition of slavery may be possible in archaeological contexts and that its examination can revise our views both of slavery within a society and of that society as a whole. Notable also in studies of slavery is the examination of the history of black Americans, a topic neglected by much historical archaeology in the USA until recently (see Deetz 1977, 138-54).

Other studies of the archaeology of slavery can be found, for instance, using evidence from ancient Egypt and Scandinavia, and it is notable that in all of these societies textual evidence leads to the acknowledgment that slavery existed. Could it be part of our idealisation or romanticisation of the prehistoric past that prehistorians have produced no discussion of slavery in Neolithic or Bronze-Age Europe? Or is this because slavery is considered unrecognisable in prehistoric archaeology? Or did slavery only come into existence with the formation of state societies?

The analysis of slavery can be a source for many wider discussions of, for example, class, race, exploitation, exchange and economics. But, as with the archaeology of other supposedly peripheral groups such as children, the archaeology of slaves (unlike the slaves themselves) is under-exploited.

It is, therefore, possible to consider the archaeology of many distinct social groups and to examine the social relationships between them. Archaeology has the potential to go beyond general consideration of social structures to discuss details of political and social organisation. Indeed social archaeology has an even wider scope, for it encompasses the study of the everyday life of past peoples. Attitudes and beliefs are considered in Chapter 5, but here it is worth examining two examples of how material evidence can be interpreted in such a way as to tell us about how people lived in the past: the archaeology of entertainment, and of appearance.

Archaeology and entertainment

Theoretical studies of the prehistoric archaeology of entertainment centre almost wholly on the study of past music: *palaeoethno-musicology*. This uses experimentation and anthropology to reconstruct the music of past societies by a detailed investigation of their instruments. Such studies face very considerable problems in recognising past musical instruments. There have been few theoretical studies of entertainment in historical archaeology, although the study of theatres, amphitheatres and other forms of 'entertainment' is a major element of Classical archaeology (e.g. Humphrey 1986; Golvin 1988).

While prehistorians have given less consideration to entertainment, reconstructions of prehistoric games have been attempted. Some have even felt able to re-introduce 'authentic' early historic games such as *Hneftafl* and *Tabula*.

If we are to identify board games (as with toys), however, we must assume that we can differentiate them from, for instance, tally-counting boards, and that we can be sure that dice were used in gaming, not in casting lots. Nor need all 'counters' be for gaming; they might be tickets, as in Roman theatres, or used for political purposes as in the case of the *ostraka* of Classical Athens, or be inlays or other decorations.

Nor has serious consideration usually been given to the theory of recognising and interpreting prehistoric sports, a study hardly mentioned in modern works. Here again, the theoretical imperative has been with historical, not prehistoric, archaeologists, where the study of Classical sport is an established area of enquiry.

The social archaeology of appearance

Archaeologists have generally considered that the most accessible aspect of the appearance of past peoples, other than their skeletal characteristics, is how they dressed. Archaeological sources for dress include artefacts such as brooches and pins, representations such as statues and paintings, and surviving parts of clothing or of hair (showing hair styles). These have all been used in recent studies. Generally it has been supposed that unburnt burials provide a plentiful and useful source for reconstructing past fashions in clothing, as elements of that clothing are often still seemingly in place (*in situ*) in the grave.

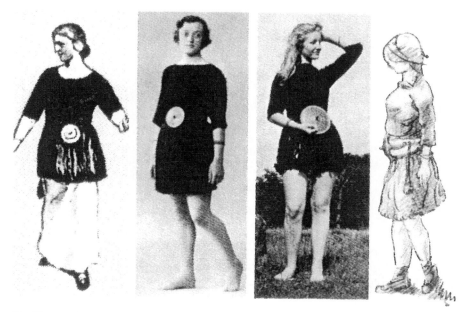

29. Alternative reconstructions of Bronze-Age Scandinavian dress. These have been made at different times since discovery, based on the same archaeological evidence. Note that differing social and cultural attitudes have produced different interpretations. (Reproduced with the kind permission of The National Museum of Denmark/W. Bruhn and Max Tilke: Das Kostumwerk)

Archaeologists have often aimed to reconstruct past styles of dress as an aim in itself, but some, such as Kaiser (unpublished TAG paper 1989), have proposed a far wider role for the archaeology of dress, employing it to recognise sub-cultures and other groupings in society. Kaiser draws on modern examples of the anthropology of dress-styles in an attempt to assess the archaeological significance of clothes. In her view, clothes are symbolic and express the identity of the wearer.

This approach was attempted by Clarke (1968, 400-1), who examined artistic representations of dress as evidence for tribal identities in Iron-Age Europe. Clarke saw dress as an expression of identity in a similar way to Kaiser's later, and more complex, consideration.

Vierck (1978), in a classic study, has adopted the same argument using burial data from Anglo-Saxon England. Vierck considered not only the evidence for dress itself, but how brooches were worn inside dress-conventions, as a means of understanding the cultural associations of the communities represented by the cemeteries.

The use of artistic data has been beset by problems of schematisation and the emulation of foreign or much earlier works of art, rendering apparent representations of contemporary dress uncertain. So, for instance, it is difficult to discern whether the material culture (including dress) depicted in Anglo-Saxon and Carolingian manuscripts is a reflection of the copying of Late Roman or Byzantine 'masters' (*exemplars*), or whether it represents artefacts and clothes in contemporary use at the period of the production of the manuscript (e.g. Carver 1986; Coupland 1990).

Another area where dress has been used to study society is in the identification of specific types of cloth, or weave, with specific cultures. The discovery of an apparently 'Romano-British' weave in preserved cloth from an Anglo-Saxon cemetery has been employed as evidence for continuity between the Anglo-Saxons and Romano-British local population (Sims-Williams 1990).

Cloth-production itself has recently been the subject of theoretical research. In very dry situations, such as the south-west USA, or in waterlogged deposits such as have been discovered in the Danish peat bogs, the preservation of cloth and other dress elements such as leather shoes enables more complex studies than on sites where the only dress-remains are metal brooches. It is sad, therefore, that such sources have not been explored more thoroughly by archaeologists. To date, most studies of dress, despite the above examples, have been of a descriptive nature.

These two examples, entertainment and appearance, illustrate the capacity for theoretical discussion of the reconstruction of aspects of the day-to-day lives of past populations. They also help to illustrate the potential for archaeology to inform us about many aspects of the past which may not immediately suggest themselves as accessible through study of its material remains.

Conclusion

Social archaeology is one of the main strands in modern archaeological research. It has, however, proved extremely controversial, with scholars using widely varying approaches and sometimes producing contrasting results from analysing the same material (for a well-known example see Fleming 1973; Renfrew 1973c). Post-processual scholars have observed that cognitive factors may 'mask' material representations of social reality, making the relationship between material culture and social organisation far from obvious (e.g. Miller 1985b). Despite these difficulties, the importance of social archaeology cannot be denied: all excavators have to consider the social dimension of the material recovered from their sites, and artefact analysis has to try to set the objects concerned in their social context. In field survey, studies of settlement patterns must, as we have seen, incorporate an understanding of these issues, while in the presentation of the material past to the public its social aspects form an important and instructive dimension with the potential to attract those who would not generally be interested in history or archaeology. Social archaeology has generally been carried out alongside and in conjunction with economic archaeology, and it is to this that we shall turn in the next chapter.

CHAPTER 5

Economic Archaeology

Economics is a subject which archaeologists have long felt competent to study (e.g. Clark 1952, 1989; Higgs 1972, 1975; Dennell 1983). As economics is mostly concerned with the production of material things and their subsequent consumption, it is hardly surprising that archaeologists have seen it as a suitable topic for investigation (for a recent attempt to do so, see Miller 1987).

Perhaps the simplest and most obvious theoretical approach to the archaeology of economies is to separate agricultural from non-agricultural production, industrial from pre-industrial, and coin-using from non-coin-using. While this seems obvious, it is a theoretical distinction made to divide the past into periods.

30. Hunting and gathering. A reconstruction of the Mesolithic site at Star Carr, Yorkshire. (Reproduced with the kind permission of the *Illustrated London News*)

It is conventional to characterise pre-farming communities as 'hunting and gathering' (on these, see Lee and De Vore 1968; Ingold 1983, 1991; Ingold *et al.* 1991; Bailey 1983; Davis and Reeves 1989) and to divide farmers into pastoralists (who keep animals), agriculturalists (who grow crops), and mixed farmers (who do both). Conventional, also, is the view that agriculture was a significant break in economics, leading to the development of a settled (*sedentary*) lifestyle, by the *domestication* (bringing into cultivation or farming) of crops and animals (for an introduction to the extensive literature on domestication and the transition to farming, see Harris 1977; Rindos 1984; Zvelbil and Rowley-Conwy 1984; Barker and Gamble 1985; Redding 1988; Harris and Hillman 1989; Miles *et al.* 1989; Gebauer and Price 1991).

The pre-industrial period is often characterised as having a *subsistence* economy (e.g. Earle and Christensen 1980), meaning that such economies produced only enough to support life. However, as a *surplus* in agricultural production is apparent at least from the Neolithic period onwards, others have questioned whether we can talk of subsistence economies at all.

The amount of agricultural (and other) surplus has been seen as recoverable either by calculating *crop-yields* (worked out using modern figures for yields by a specific plant, on a specific soil, in a specific climate, and under a defined agricultural regime) or by assessing the extent of storage of surplus in granaries or storage pits (e.g. Bradley 1978, 123). A more subtle argument has noted that, in order to support specialists such as metalworkers who do not take part in agricultural production, an economy must be producing a surplus (e.g. Hodges 1982, 130).

This argument can also be applied to the construction of large or labour-expensive projects such as hill-forts. People cannot produce food and do other work at the same time, so either their food must be produced by someone else (demonstrating that a surplus is being produced), or the amount of time required to produce food must be such that there is sufficient time left to build these works.

If all economic strategies can be divided between farming and non-farming, industrial and non-industrial, etc., so can they be divided in terms of their underlying aims. An *optimising* economic (or any other) strategy aims to produce the most it can – it aims at optimal production. A *meliorising* economy aims not at the most; it aims to 'do well'. A *sufficing* economy is an economy which aims for a sufficient amount of produce: it is the same in practice as a subsistence economy in that it aims to produce enough, but it can, unlike a subsistence economy, aim to produce enough not just for survival but for an elaborate system of exchange or a large number of non-producers.

Turning to non-agricultural economies (which need not be pre-agricultural): these too are capable of producing surplus food or materials. Hunter-gatherers can adopt strategies based on scavenging food already killed by other animals, and they can be based on hunting or foraging for plant foods. They can also employ fishing, or the collection of shellfish, and such strategies can support very stable communities and lead to a sedentary way of life, especially in coastal settings.

Most hunter-gatherers, however, as seen in the anthropology of modern communities, are *mobile*, following game or seeking resources according to the season of the year. These people use sites *seasonally* or occasionally rather than continuously, and this pattern may be sought in the archaeological record (Thomson 1939; Monks 1981; for an example, Weide 1969).

Not all farmers need be sedentary, nor need there be a firm division separating hunters and farmers (for recent views of this question, see Rowley-Conwy 1983; Zvelbil 1986; Gregg 1988; Williams 1988; Kent 1989; Harris and Hillman 1989). *Transhumance systems* are those which involve the movement of pastoralists and their herds as seasonal climate renders one area more favourable than another: for example, movement might be from lowland winter pasture to summer upland pasture (on herders, see Grigson and Brock 1984). This can be represented in settlement patterns by a network of lowland ('home') farms and far more transient upland huts (sometimes called *sheilings*).

Another form of mobile agricultural economy is *shifting agriculture.* In this system an area is sometimes farmed, sometimes abandoned, usually according to whether the soils have been drained of nutrients (are *exhausted*). Transhumance and shifting agriculture lead to agricultural economies that are neither fully sedentary nor completely mobile. Soil exhaustion can sometimes be averted by employing an area for different purposes in successive years: this is called *crop rotation*.

Completely different, and presenting huge archaeological problems, are the occasional exploitations of local resources by highly mobile *nomads* (e.g. Cribb 1991). The very brief duration of the settlements of these people and the flimsiness of the buildings they erect can lead to difficulties for the archaeologist, especially if they do not use the same site year after year.

It may be that one way of dividing up these differing economies is an evolutionary scheme: hunter-gatherers → pastoralists → agriculturalists, but this is not the only possible interpretation.

Early farming economies

Childe (1936) suggested that the transition to farming from hunting and gathering should be called a 'revolution' (on 'revolutions' in archaeology, see Van der Leeuw 1986), just as we call the transition from proto-industrial to industrial production the 'Industrial Revolution'. He named this transition the *Neolithic revolution*. Sherratt (1981, 1983) has since suggested that a later, but major, transition took place with the exploitation of products made from milk, and of the animals kept, which he called the *secondary products revolution*. These have been important concepts for the study of processes of transition from a hunter/gatherer to an agricultural economy.

Definition and chronology have, however, caused problems for both 'revolutions'. They now seem less sudden or uniform, and the secondary products revolution seems to have been close to, or even to have merged with, the more general transition to agricultural production.

Thomas has also questioned whether 'Neolithic' can be equated with 'farming' (Thomas 1991a) and stressed both the problems inherent in the definition of periods by their economic basis and the difficulties of assuming that economic and ideological, or social, change need be connected.

A similar point, on other grounds, has been emphasised in the work of Bradley (1978, 1984), who suggested that archaeologists have been keen to place importance on technology and economy because these topics are easily examined; as he puts it, in doing so 'they have chosen a very narrow personal mythology' (Bradley 1978, 3). Both scholars favour ideological and social aspects of the past over economics and technology, without denying the importance of economic or technological studies.

The result of these discussions has been to emphasise the problems of these concepts, and the term 'revolution' has been felt by some to relate too much to Childe's own Marxist outlook and to bear little relation to the gradual character of the development of agriculture. Although the concepts of Neolithic revolution and secondary products revolution have played a significant part in the theoretical development of Neolithic studies, it seems unlikely that they will continue to do so in the future.

Ecology and economy

Ecology is the study of the relationship between humans and the rest of the natural world (see Chapter 1). It is an obvious source of interest to economic archaeologists to examine how humanity relates to the natural world in economic terms (e.g. Sheridan and Bailey 1981). This can be seen in two ways: the implications of nature for humans and the implications of human action for the natural world.

Perhaps ecology has played an important role in economic studies of prehistory because of the biological background of environmental archaeologists, and of many prehistorians, or perhaps it is because prehistoric peoples are supposed to have been more 'natural'. Alternatively, it may be the relationship between the academic subjects of biology and early prehistoric archaeology (e.g. see Schaller and Lowther 1969; Evans 1975) and the amount of environmental evidence recorded in recent years that have made this approach of special interest to prehistorians such as Mellars (1976, 1985).

Ecology can help us to understand when seasonal resources are available (such as nuts or fruit), when animals will migrate and something of their patterns of migration: an approach used to effect at Tel Abu Hureyra (Hillman *et al.* 1990). If hunters are supposed to have followed a specific herd, or type of animal, then their patterns of movement may be recoverable by reconstructing the animal movements.

An alternative approach, suggested by Jones (1992), has been to employ the ecological concept of *food-webs*. These are the networks of inter-relationships between animals and other animals or plants as food. If people are fitted into this framework and studied according to ecological approaches such as *population dynamics*, *predator:prey relationships*, and *niches* – the small-scale environments in which they can survive – the concept of food-webs can be used both to study a community at a specific time and to look at how communities change.

In later periods a common approach has been to study the over-use of soils and the selection of specific locations for specific economic schemes. This latter approach, using ecological information about the relationships between soil-types, geology, animals and plants, communities and water-levels, has led to detailed studies of why some sites were chosen and others avoided. Combined with geomorphological concepts – erosion, for example – this is the basis of Butzer's (1982) ecological approach to the whole of archaeology.

Ecology has been important especially in processual archaeology and to the Higgsian school (e.g. Higgs 1972; Dolukhanov 1979; Jochim 1976; Bogucki 1989). Few archaeologists, however, understand ecology well enough to employ its concepts as a basis for their own research, and few have the biological training required to grasp its large and complex body of theory.

This brief summary can hardly do justice to the role of ecological studies in archaeology today, but it must be noted that the importance of ecology has been hotly disputed, for instance by Thomas (1988), who stresses the context of human action in relation to the environment. Thomas's comments have led to a debate between him and Mithen (Mithen 1991; Thomas 1991b), who favours an ecological approach. Thomas considers that the ecological view reduces early prehistoric archaeology to a 'cybernetic wasteland' in contrast to the past 'written' by 'socially-aware' and post-processual scholars of Neolithic studies. This debate is unresolved, but it goes to show the importance of ecology in understanding past economies. The use of ecological concepts in economic archaeology is, however, not restricted to those who adopt an ecological approach to explanation (see Chapter 6). It can accord with cognitive-processualism and culture-history, while it is a mainstay of functional-processualism.

Again, ecological approaches are widespread and not restricted to a specific school, although Marxist and post-processualist archaeologists have tended to play down ecological factors. Far more limited, but of great theoretical interest, have been what are, perhaps, the most detailed ecological studies undertaken by theoretically interested 'conventional' (as applied to 'environmental') archaeologists using *energy-flow models*.

Energy-flow models

An interesting application of ecological theory to archaeology has been the study of energy-flow. This consists of the examination and estimation of energy intake (by food) and expenditure (by action) in humans (e.g. Speth and Spielmann 1983). The amount of energy contained in relevant foodstuffs is calculated, the probability and energy-expenditure involved in acquiring them evaluated, and energy-requirements for a day of life for an individual or group estimated. Usually anthropology, biology and medicine provide the answers to most of these questions (e.g. see Pimental 1979).

Once the requirements and expenditures involved in a day have been discovered, computers can be used to help to simulate days, weeks, or years, and the results of the adoption of varying strategies. These can then be tested against the archaeological evidence.

An early and classic study of this type was by Odner (1972), who reinterpreted the economy of historical-period cave dwellers in Scandinavia. Recently, the same sort of approach, combined with decision-making analysis, has been adopted by Mithen (1990).

In its simplest form, the relations of energy expenditure and economic necessity underlie the *Law of least effort*, which holds that people will adopt the least energy-expending course of action to achieve their aims (e.g. Binford 1983a). This approach can be applied both to the acquisition of food and to other aspects of the economy.

Clearly, the more complex the range of economic decisions, the more irregular, or interdependent, the lifestyle of groups involved, and the greater the range of food-sources, types of energy-expenditure and forms of food acquisition available to them, the more complex energy expenditure models tend to be. It may be for this reason that, at present, they have not been applied to historical state societies such as those of the Roman and medieval worlds.

Some theories of post-neolithic economies

There are two principal theories of past economies: the *formalist*, in which modern economic theory is seen as applicable to past societies, and the *substantivist*, in which past economies are said to have operated on a different basis from modern economies.

Most archaeologists outside the USA use a substantivist interpretation, notably in response to the work of Renfrew (1972, 1975, 1977a) and Hodges (1978, 1979, 1982; Hodges *et al.* 1978). In the USA there have been some formalist studies, notably by Wells (1980).

Wells has suggested that modern economic theory, emphasising competition, entrepreneurs and cost-efficiency, applies equally to Iron-Age Europe. Such views are in contrast with two other perspectives, as well as with formalist economics — the Marxist view of the economy and the concept of the qualitative difference of pre-industrial economies.

Some scholars assert that the Industrial Revolution had a unique and completely transformative effect. An economic historian, Rostow (e.g. 1978), has attempted to isolate a very short timespan when 'take-off' in the economy (transforming it from low levels of industrial production to far greater levels) took place. Rostow's view would presuppose that the pre-industrial economy is not capable of analysis in the same way as the industrialised economy.

Taylor's view goes far beyond this, however, and is of much relevance to archaeologists. Drawing on earlier work, and especially studies by the economist N.D. Kondratieff, whose work has been independently used in archaeology by Going (1992), Taylor (1989) has noted that the pre-industrial economy, insofar as it can be quantitatively described, showed a consistent pattern of logistic growth and decline curves, while in the industrial economy *long-waves* of modal curves are visible (for an archaeological discussion of this, see Dark forthcoming). If this is true, then regular patterns of growth and decline in the pre-industrial economy can, in its broadest outlines, be reconstructed when considering complex societies, such as the Roman Empire or medieval Europe.

Marxist scholars have taken different views. They have generally followed Marx's classification of economic progress – as primitive, ancient, feudal, capitalist – and seen all economies as based on exploitation and conflict rather than co-operation.

These generalised opinions are supplemented by a vast array of economic concepts and methods, often drawn from outside archaeology. Those of two scholars, Wallerstein and Polanyi, have been especially widely used in archaeology.

The world systems model

Wallerstein's overview of the economies of complex societies is called the *world systems model* (1974). Although rather more subtle in detail, in outline it views the economy of peripheral areas (*periphery*) as linked to those of the (exploiting) economic *core*. Between 'core' and 'periphery' lies the 'semi-periphery' incorporating aspects of each. This *core-periphery model* has been widely employed in prehistoric and historical archaeology, notably in studies of the Classical world (e.g. Rowlands *et al.*

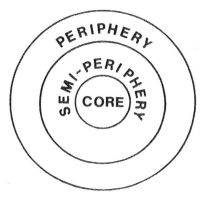

31. **The world-systems model** A simplified diagram

1987; Champion 1989; Woolf 1990). Incorporating both Marxist and systems theory elements, Wallerstein's approach has found many supporters in processual and Marxist archaeology.

Polanyi and economic theory

The leading substantivist theorist, Karl Polanyi, wrote about ancient economies (Polanyi *et al.* 1957; Polanyi 1963). Polanyi's scheme was originally devised as both classificatory and evolutionary, and envisaged stages: reciprocity, redistribution, and market economy.

Market economies are well-known to most of us. They encompass the competition between producers and suppliers in terms of prices. Such economies include our own and those of most medieval European societies.

The most difficult concepts in this scheme are those of reciprocal and redistributive economies, and it is worth discussing each of these in detail before considering the problem of trading-places themselves. These too have been considered in Polanyi's overview.

Reciprocity

Reciprocal exchange is when the transfer of materials, or services, is based on the requirement that each gift of materials or services is repaid by materials or services of equal, or greater, value. Consequently, a gift of, say, a cow, may be paid back by an identical gift or its equivalent (say, two pigs) according to an agreed set of conventions. Exchange in a reciprocal economy is often described as *gift-exchange*, and such systems are very widely spread in time and space.

Elements of a reciprocal economy can exist in other economic systems which are not principally reciprocal. An excellent example is the giving of Christmas presents in situations (such as a workplace) where this is

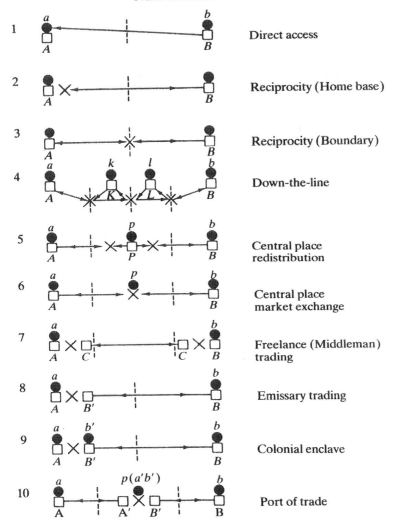

1   Direct access

2   Reciprocity (Home base)

3   Reciprocity (Boundary)

4   Down-the-line

5   Central place redistribution

6   Central place market exchange

7   Freelance (Middleman) trading

8   Emissary trading

9   Colonial enclave

10   Port of trade

32. Forms of exchange. Filled circles indicate the places of origin and receipt of a commodity. Squares A and B represent the individual at the source and the recipient. Circle p is a 'central place' and square P a 'central person'. Transactions are indicated by a cross and territorial boundaries by a broken line. (Reproduced with the kind permission of Professor Colin Renfrew)

based on convention. Each gift must be repaid by another of similar or greater value.

Reciprocal economies may employ the total range of resources and products for any type of exchange, or limit the use of materials or services which can be employed. In economies using only specific types of materials for specific types of exchange (such as exotic shells in marriage payments) we can describe these materials as *prestige goods*. A *prestige goods economy* is one employing such specialised reciprocal exchange.

The exchange of gifts in all reciprocal economies takes place within social conventions and as a part of social, as well as economic, relationships. That is, economics in such societies is part of the social framework and *vice versa*. Economies where this inter-linking of economy and society is found are sometimes referred to as *embedded*. They are found not only in prehistory and in anthropological situations, but also in historical circumstances, including the Greek and Roman worlds.

In a reciprocal economy the ability to manipulate others (by building up obligations) can be used to obtain or support social superiority or economic advantage. If a person or a group in society has access to greater resources or a larger number of products, or has a monopoly of access to a service or product, then they can use this in such a fashion. This is, of course, especially true in prestige goods economies.

A further possibility is that of acquiring a debt of resources or services, so that periods of shortage can be offset by demanding its repayment. Such a strategy is called *social storage* and can, for example, be an effective means of avoiding famine (O'Shea 1981b; on coping with famine, see also Halstead and O'Shea 1982, 1989).

Redistribution

Another economic type is the *redistributive economy*, which is based on the collection of resources or materials to a central point, or person, or group, and their distribution to others. Redistributive economies usually include some form of taxation or the collection of resources, but often exist alongside reciprocal systems.

Redistribution places economic and, potentially, social advantage in the hands of the redistributor. The central resources, especially food, can be both a valuable asset in avoiding famine or shortage and, in the wrong hands, a way of manipulating the population.

A special instance of this is the redistributive character of many early trading networks. The objects of trade are brought to a point controlled by the redistributor. Controlled access of this kind means that such products can be employed to further the political strategy of the controller of the point of access.

To give an example: if a medieval king has his court on the coast at the kingdom's only trading centre, and trade in overseas goods is forbidden by law outside that centre, then control of that centre controls legal access to the objects of trade. These can then be redistributed by the king, so that access to them enables him to engage in political relationships. An example of exactly this system is a well-documented situation in Late

Anglo-Saxon England, where royal control of trade and trading centres was strictly enforced (Hodges 1982).

Long-range trade

Archaeologists often write about trade, whether in prehistory or historical archaeology (Earle and Ericson 1977; Hodges 1982). Examples include the Neolithic axe-trade and the importation of Mediterranean goods into Dark-Age Britain. But the study of long-range trade presents problems of theory as well as the more obvious practical difficulties such as, for example, identifying its products.

The first problem is the conceptual difficulty of recognising trading-places. If a site is on the coast and has a concentration of overseas goods, it is often claimed that it was a trading place. But what *archaeological signature* should we expect from ports or fairs (Dark 1994b)? By this is meant, what distinctive archaeological characteristic, or combination of characteristics, will be needed to enable us to recognise such a site? There are coastal settlements rich in exotic items which were not trading-places, and coastal sites were, of course, frequently uninvolved in trade. Such centres may be, for instance, courts or monasteries, temples or fishing ports. Consequently, a coastal location or a concentration of exotic items cannot themselves be taken to be evidence of trading settlements. Although exotic artefacts at sites may suggest *indirect trade*, having arrived via another site rather than directly from their place of origin, this evidence does not enable us to identify the opposite, *direct trade*, where the artefacts have arrived from contact between the place of origin and the location in which they are found without intermediate locations being involved.

The identification of ports or trading-places cannot be based on proximity to a harbour alone, as this could be for non-trading purposes. To take two examples: the harbour at Whitesands Bay – one of the principal routes from Ireland to Britain in the Middle Ages – was used for pilgrimage, not trade, and the majority of such harbourside villages in medieval England were the domestic settlements of fisher-folk, and others, earning their living exploiting coastal resources other than trade.

However, we cannot suppose that all non-trading settlements received fewer of the products of trade than did trading ports. It is quite possible that high-status sites had far greater evidence of contact with a wider world in general terms than did low-status or trading communities.

A further problem is raised by the question of *seasonality*. Trading-places are not necessarily permanent settlements. In archaeological exacavation, one might be able to recognise seasonality in the stratigraphy of such a place, but without a stratigraphical control there are further problems.

The question of seasonality on any site is complicated by the question of food storage, because scholars have often attempted to use food remains to indicate the seasonal exploitation of local resources, as at Star Carr. That site does show variations in seasonally available food, but the question remains as to how much this represents stored produce.

One approach, used at Star Carr (Clark 1954, 1972; Day 1993), may be the use of natural materials (such as botanical remains) incorporated into archaeological deposits, to demonstrate seasonal use. If these show seasonal groups, we may claim that the site has been seasonally used. But this is of little use on 'dry' sites without well-preserved organic materials.

Places of exchange, which may or may not be the same as places involved in long-range trade, are also difficult to isolate in pre-monetary economies. The most common approach to this question has been to seek locations where people gathered, or may have gathered (such as ritual centres) and to compare the distribution of artefacts at or around these centres with that in the countryside as a whole.

Again, there are problems with differentiating the places of exchange from atypical, especially socially superior, settlements – they may, indeed, be the same sites. Alternatively, as with the ancient Greek agora (market), a specific physical setting may be used for the transaction of particular economic activities. The examination of markets and seasonal fair-sites is now well understood in, for instance, Viking-Age archaeology, and the recognition of specialised trading-places has been long established in, for example, Roman archaeology.

One widely used way of examining the question of recognising and interpreting trading sites has been the application of Polanyi's model of *ports of trade*. Confusingly, these are not simply trading ports.

Ports of trade

The underlying concept of 'ports of trade' is that trade is most likely to have taken place in politically neutral, and peripheral, situations (Polanyi 1963). Such places are used because of their locations to facilitate long-range exchange.

The concept of 'ports of trade' is most widely known in archaeology through Richard Hodges's *Dark Age Economics* (1982), which attempts to identify many such sites throughout Europe. Hodges notes that 'ports of trade' are frequently under political control and that their use is often seasonal.

Trade and exchange

Archaeologists often use the term *exchange* in preference to writing or talking about 'trade'. It might be assumed that all non-local artefacts result from trade between their producers and the population in the area in which they were found, but this is not the only possible explanation on general theoretical grounds. Even if we can identify the source of a specific type of artefact and establish that it is distant from the place of discovery, we have many options to consider.

An object might have been brought by traders, migrants, or spouses. It might have been given in 'payment' of non-economic dues, as in *symbolic exchange*, where symbolic artefacts are exchanged, or when the act of exchange is itself symbolic of social rather than economic relationships.

As we have seen, however, economic and social life cannot be separated in most, if any, societies. Social exchanges can be 'economic' in character, economic exchanges can be 'social' in character. Consequently, a simple distribution such as the discovery of artefact A in area B does not tell us that there was trade (economic exchange) between these areas. It can, if we discount migration, tell us that there was an exchange of artefacts between the areas. Such exchange may employ middle-men or entrepreneurs, and it need not be economic in rationale. Even migration itself can be seen as exchange in the replacement of, or addition to, one population group by another.

Nor need exchange go both ways between the producer (or group A) and the recipient (group B). Exchange can be one-way where relationships such as tribute are concerned, but even tributary relationships can be reciprocal.

These problems lead archaeological theorists to write about exchange when they cannot demonstrate that trade-relations are necessarily involved. Trade can be used as a term when the character of exchange can be demonstrated to be economic, for example in the exchange networks of the medieval North Sea.

But exchange need not be seen in material terms: people can be involved in exchange, as in the slave markets of the Classical world, or in migrations between areas such as occurred in the 1920s between Greece and Turkey. Non-material exchange, or exchange of symbolic material, has also attracted the attention of archaeologists.

Coinage and the mobilisation of wealth

Coins present theoretical problems generally absent from prehistory. The first is, of course, what is a 'coin'?

For us, coinage consists of round metal objects with designs and lettering on them, and pieces of paper also bearing designs and lettering which serve the same function. Historically, however, coinage has taken many forms. Shapes have varied, for example, from round to square, flat to dish-shaped, and solid to doughnut-like. Designs and lettering may or may not be present. Nor need coins be artefacts: they may be unmodified natural objects, such as shells. As we shall see, definitions based on function are also problematic, as coins may have many functions.

33. Coinage, but is it money? Iron-Age British coins. (Reproduced with the kind permission of Colchester Borough Council)

Casey has suggested an interesting solution: that a coin is an artefact used in exchange, distinguished by bearing an indication of its issuing institution or individual. This may take the form of a mint, king, or emperor's name, for instance, or the use of restricted materials controlled only by an individual or specific group could be taken as symbolic of the issuing body. Symbolism may also be present in designs, indicating who issued the coin: a heraldic device or picture – the sheaves of corn on Iron-Age British coinage – may serve this function (as argued by Koch 1987). The importance of this information is that the identity of the person or institution that issues a coin underpins its validity to be employed as coinage; in Casey's definition coinage is what is validated in this way.

Another problem is that of function. Coins can be used in regularised economic exchange, i.e. as *money*. But not all coins are 'money', for coins may be symbolic or ceremonial in their role. An example is the Indian coinage so worthless as to be of no use in exchange, but employed in symbolic acts of generosity to the poor. The presence of coinage alone does not therefore prove the existence of a monetary system (a system using 'money') nor that coins are part of an economic network.

Even if coins are used for an economic purpose, this may still be unconnected to their use for buying and selling. Classical Greek coins were used in an economic fashion, but this does not mean that they were necessarily part of a a two-way exchange network. Coins can be used in one-way payments, such as the exaction of tribute or taxes, in which coinage is closer to our understanding of 'token' than 'money'. Such coinage may be useless for everyday transactions, in the same way as prestige goods only serve specific roles. Coinage used only for specific (high-value) payments, but employed for exchange, has been called by Grierson (1978) *early money*. Such coinage is of no use in daily subsistence but contrasts with exotica used in ceremonial exchange, or *primitive valuables*, as George Dalton (1977) has called them. Such artefacts and prestige goods have as a characteristic, the restriction of the means of exchange to a specific range of artefacts in relation to a specific sort of exchange. That is, they operate within a narrow *sphere of exchange*. The sphere of exchange must, however, be differentiated from the zone in which contacts took place, which is called the *sphere of interaction* (Caldwell and Hall 1964). Other categories introduced by Dalton, and used in archaeology, are *primitive money*, which is used in peripheral market exchange, and early cash, used for paying fines or taxes as well as in market-based exchange.

When coinage is in use for exchange in a specific situation in time and place it is called *currency*. Again, by no means all coins are 'currency' and money is often 'currency' only in specific places. The English pound is (usually) currency in Britain but money in China, the Byzantine *solidus* is coinage in modern Britain but was currency in the Byzantine Empire (and beyond) in the Middle Ages. A coin can, therefore, cease to belong to currency, and an economy can cease to have money without ceasing to use coinage (it can 'demonetise').

Important, too, are the concepts of *face value* and *intrinsic value*. Face value is a form of *ascribed* value: an enhanced value is given to a (less valuable) specific type of artefact by a specific society. A British five pound note is worth far less than five pounds as raw material yet its ascribed value ('face value') is five pounds. Intrinsic value is the opposite: the value of an object when the face, or ascribed, value is discounted. Coins can have value (face or intrinsic value) in an economy, and many coins (all those with a face value) have face and intrinsic value together.

Of course, coins can have many functions. Most often we encounter coinage employed as money and/or currency, having a symbolic or ceremonial role, and being used as propaganda. Coinage, by carrying images or inscriptions, is an especially efficient propaganda tool in a monetary economy operating on a market basis. As everyone uses coinage and is liable to look at it, the images and text it 'contains' have the potential to reach the entire population. For example, it is likely that many of the inhabitants of the Roman Empire saw the emperor's face only, or most regularly, on coinage.

Coinage enables the storage of wealth and its transfer from one place or individual to another, and from one form to another, such as from livestock to land, very easily. The transfer of resources in this way (whether by coinage or other means), especially from the producer to the élite, is called *mobilisation*. Coinage facilitates the mobilisation of wealth because it facilitates the transfer of wealth.

Storing wealth through coinage is often achieved by means of collecting coins into groups (*hoards*), although other artefacts are also gathered in this way. Hoards have been the subject of theoretical debate: the reason for their deposition and the failure to retrieve them have been especialy scrutinised by archaeologists.

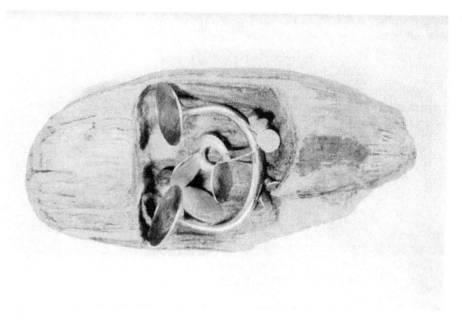

34. A hoard of valuables or a ritual deposit? Bronze-Age gold hoard in a wooden box from Killymoon, Ireland. (Reproduced with the kind permission of The National Museum of Ireland)

Hoarding and coin loss

Hoards are compiled for many reasons. They can be deposited to store wealth in times of uncertainty, or to destroy it. They can represent a collection of currency owned by an individual (a *purse hoard*, whether or not it was found inside a purse), or religious deposition of wealth (*votive hoards*) (on ritual hoarding, see Hines 1989). Some coin hoards are formed not by a single act but by the gradual addition of coins over a longer period, and these are called *coin accumulations* (see Aitchison

1988). When a hoard has been concealed, it may still be disturbed and the coins, at least partially, scattered – these are called *dispersed hoards*.

Context, if it is known, is obviously of much importance in deciding between these possibilities. A hoard inside a temple, and stratigraphically contemporary with its use, may, for example, be considered more likely to be a votive hoard than one found in a shop, assuming we can recognise a shop and a temple.

When hoards are deposited to store wealth, this may be in response to a threat or to social stress. Consequently, we might correlate hoarding with the geographical and chronological extent of that threat or stress. This has been widely used to study stress in the Roman and medieval worlds, and strongly supported by data from early modern England (Casey 1986).

Most coins are, of course, lost without being deposited in hoards or accumulations. Coin-loss can be approached through a series of concepts or questions. Casey (1986) proposes that it is proportionate to:

(i) volume issued
(ii) duration of use
(iii) value
(iv) size of coin

and has to be placed in the context of:

(v) political factors
(vi) economic factors

It is possible, as Casey has also observed, that the context of coin-loss may also be important in relation to questions such as how well lit and how clean a room is. If a coin falls to the floor in a dark and untidy room it is likely to be irretrievable, and this will increase the likelihood of coin loss.

Coin loss has also been approached in another way. The distribution of coin numbers over time, especially if 'calibrated' for rate of output of the coin, can be used to form a histogram (a graph showing quantities as bars of differing lengths). If the mints of coins are known, the varying proportions of the coins have been taken as an index of the intensity of trade between two or more areas. Coin histograms have also been seen as a way of differentiating between different types of site in the Roman Empire, as coin supply to, for example, military or official installations may have been different from coins supplied to civilian settlements, leading to differing patterns of coin-loss and so to different histograms for each type of site. There are, however, problems with each of these views.

Site-catchment analysis and resource allocation

The location of an archaeological site in its contemporary landscape has long been recognised as a source of evidence for its economy (e.g. Clark 1952). Access to land, water-supply, coastal resources and minerals are clearly factors in the selection of sites. Theoretical studies have attempted to go beyond this generalisation to define the resources available to a specific site. This has been approached in several ways.

Animal bones or seeds found on a site may help to define what local resources were used, and to provide an index of productivity. This raises questions of the importation of material and of exchange. Although these are sometimes answerable, this requires the careful collection and specialist studies of types of excavated material which were usually discarded by archaeologists working before the middle of this century. It is unsurprising, therefore, that scholars have inclined to the use of two other approaches.

The first is well-known in archaeology. Introduced by Eric Higgs (Vita-Finzi and Higgs 1970), *site-catchment analysis* depends upon the evaluation of natural resources within a travelling distance from the site under study. This is usually decided on anthropological grounds: the distance reached in a day's walk being most usually employed. This area, often depicted as a disc or radius around the site, is considered as the site's catchment area for resources.

Terrain, taboos and political factors, among others, can have an obvious effect upon the possible range of resources which were used, and distort the territory within walking distance from a circle into a more irregular shape. Critics of site-catchment analysis have doubted the validity of the approach altogether, because many of the factors which may have constrained the range of resources used are difficult or impossible to understand in most archaeological situations. The method has also been seen as affording only an indication of the possible range of resources, or as a key to examining possible cases of competition for resources or shared access to them.

The latter possibility – the sharing of resources – is usually considered in terms of *resource allocation*. This assumes that where important resources must be used by two neighbouring groups, they will reach an agreement over the allocation of those resources, so as to give each group an (often approximately equal) share in each resource. Such a strategy can be considered, alongside the use of territorial markers and political border-zones, as a *conflict-minimising device*, i.e. a means of limiting or preventing conflict between groups (e.g. Renfrew 1976; Mytum 1982). Some impressive and convincing examples of resource allocation can be found, for example, in the local political structure of medieval England (e.g. Sawyer 1976).

The logic of production and decision-making

Leroi-Gourhan (1943, 1945) and others (e.g. Krause 1990) have discussed not the theory of exchange or of the type of production, but the *logic of production*, sometimes called the *chaine opertoire*. If each step in a procedure producing something (whether an artefact or a non-material aspect of culture) is the result of a decision, then the sequence or network of decisions can be 'mapped' (e.g. Van der Leeuw and Pritchard 1984; Lemonnier 1993). They might potentially also be 'modelled' (i.e. simulated) in detail by mathematical or computerised means. Of course, a similar approach can be used to analyse decision-making concerning systems of acquiring and processing food or raw materials.

In historical archaeology, appeal might be made to studies of modern economic decision-making or of the historical evidence for medieval economic philosophies, e.g. Walter of Henley's handbook on estate management and *Yreave*, an Anglo-Saxon text on the same topic, which have been used to analyse archaeological data from medieval Britain (Alcock 1963, 37, and 1987, 34, 74, 85; Addyman 1976).

As Hodder (1992, 57-8) has pointed out, however, more potential for studies of the logic of production certainly exists than has yet been widely recognised. But a difficulty arises when prehistoric data are used, or where assumptions about economic behaviour underlie our understanding of the rationale behind such decisions. As ever, in using anthropological data to attempt a solution to such issues, questions of partial parallels and of comparability arise, leading to the danger of misinterpretation of only superficially similar economies by false analogy.

Specialisation

Specialisation, as the name suggests, is a concentration on a specific type of production, such as pottery-making or the rearing of a specific type of animal. Specialisation can include the production of subsistence products or the manufacture of non-essentials. Not all specialised production is of material artefacts; specialisation can include non-material products such as music.

Specialists may be located in a specific place, or move between employers who may offer subsistence or non-essential products for the services of the specialist. Specialists are frequently employed in patron-client relations, or may be independent within a market-economy. They may require their own sites, which have to be taken into consideration when analysing (for example) settlement evidence, and be connected with specific institutions.

When specialists move between patrons they are described as *peripatetic*. This is in contrast to the stability of *specialist production sites*

(sites specific to specialist activities which may or may not be the residences of specialists themselves). Specialist production sites require that specialists working at them supply their wares to surrounding areas or more distant markets.

In a detailed series of studies, archaeologists have examined the relationship between specialisation and social structure (D'Altoy and Earle 1985; Brumfiel and Earle 1987). As specialisation is frequently closely connected with the existence of élites, or groups with well-defined functions in society and/or economy, the social context of specialisation is of much interest.

A difference has been drawn (D'Altoy and Earle 1985) between *staple finance* – where a share, or tax, of subsistence products is redistributed to support specialisation – and *wealth finance* – where currency is used to pay state employees to specialise. Another view is that specialisation is a response to a variety of resources existing in especial abundance in a specific location, enabling its local economy to develop a specialised character. A *mutual benefit* model, in which each 'side' gains, is sometimes employed (e.g. in the study of livestock specialisation), while others have related specialisation to long-range trade.

Another way of approaching this question has been to seek a distinction

35. **Modes of production.** Was this Late Roman Oxfordshire ware the result of occasional pottery-making by farmers, or organised workshops aiming at regional markets? (Photo: S.P. Dark)

between *independent specialists* and those under the control of others (*attached specialists*), or to examine the relationship between specialisation and other economic activities: e.g. pottery-making and farming.

It must be stressed that specialisation, although frequently connected with the existence of élites and trade, does not require either, and that specialists within a society with both of these characteristics may be independent of them. Such specialists include village craftsmen and fishermen, for whom specialisation may form part of the local subsistence economy or serve to provide a service for that community.

The question of different types of production has been interestingly addressed by Peacock (1982), who has established a classificatory scheme for these. Although used by him to study Roman pottery manufacture, this has potential for wider application.

Modes of production

Peacock has defined eight types of production (or *modes of production*), developed in regard to the Roman world, but arguably relevant to all Neolithic and later situations.

(i) *Household production*
Production by members of the household for consumption by the household. Production is sporadic and secondary to other economic activities, having the role of a domestic chore. Little technology is employed.

(ii) *Household industry*
A term coined by van der Leeuw (1977) and developed by Peacock. Artisan production in van der Leeuw's view is limited to 'group use', but Peacock has disagreed with this aspect of the type. This is production for profit, but part-time and secondary in economic importance, and using *low technology*.

(iii) *Individual workshop*
Sporadic production, often in conjunction with farming, but of primary economic importance, and directed at markets.

(iv) *Nucleated workshops*
Clusters of type (iii) production sites resulting from the availability of labour, resources or markets. Longer production periods and high technology: technically accomplished and standardised. Often attracting entrepreneurial 'middle-men'.

(v) *The manufactory*
Conventionally, the proto-industrial production site. The producers are

gathered in a single place, although they can be under separate roofs. High technology is used but no machinery, and production is differentiated from the workshop level (iii and iv) by scale, the manufactory being larger. Specialisation of production into components is a characteristic of this type of production, and of the factory (vi), with each component specific to separate artisans who may be dispersed into a *dispersed manufactory* (or *domestic industry* in Marxist terms), or gathered together in a single location.

(vi) *The factory*
Distinguished by scale and the use of high technology and machinery, this also concentrates the specialised workforce on a single site. Factories are often claimed to have only existed in the modern period after the late eighteenth century and to be associated with the Industrial Revolution, but this is debatable. Peacock has indicated his willingness to credit factories in the Roman world, and I have argued for their existence in the fourth- and fifth-century eastern Mediterranean (Dark, forthcoming).

(vii) *Estate production*
'Household' production on an estate scale, i.e. within a specific unit of land-tenure, each estate producing sufficient for its own consumption. This often leads to exchange outside the estate.

(viii) *Military and other official production*
Production under official control for the use of government or the services. High technology and highly efficient production are usually found, as this is intended to be cost-effective.

Introducing the concepts of the manufactory and factory brings us to consider the question of industrialisation. While this is, of course, of little relevance to prehistoric archaeologists, scholars working on the medieval and modern period need a conceptual basis on which to discuss industrialised economies or those which show suggestions of industrialisation.

Proto-industrialisation and industrialisation

Archaeologists and historians have generally argued that the Industrial Revolution was a unique event. So far as we know, there has never been another industrial civilisation. This raises the important question of what we take to be industry, and what we define as an industrial revolution, because if we are unclear about these concepts the former assertion lacks validity: we cannot simply say that we know what an industrial revolution is when others may see the concept in quite different terms.

Happily, there is some degree of agreement between scholars over what constitutes an industrial economy. An industrial economy involves mass-production based on factories and inter-regional trade based on a monetary market economy. It also, especially, involves the application of technology to production and exchange, and the adoption of a 'scientific' logic of production, systematising this into repeatable stages. Such changes are associated with a sudden rapid increase in productivity and profit: what, as we have already seen, the economic historian Rostow calls the 'take-off'.

So far, this may seem obvious and commonplace, but it enables us to introduce the concept of *proto-industrialisation*. A proto-industrial economy is one in which production is centred on the smaller-scale manufactory. In the proto-industrial system there is no 'take-off', and regional markets are still favoured.

Characteristically, proto-industrial economies have their manufactories situated in rural settings, whereas industrial factories are often urban in location. The attributes of proto-industrialisation, therefore, include material and spatial elements which enable such economies to be identified on archaeological grounds alone.

The only application of the proto-industrial model to archaeological evidence has been in the study of the Roman and Byzantine economies, although it has been suggested that it might also be used to study the Late Anglo-Saxon and Viking-Age economies of Britain and Scandinavia (Dark forthcoming).

Most archaeologists, however, are concerned with pre-industrial economies or non-industrial aspects of economies. In such economies, social relations, as we have seen, are often reflected in economic relations, so it is important to consider some *socio-economic* concepts or institutions which have a wide applicability in interpreting material evidence. These link social structure, agricultural production and (often) specialisation.

Patronage, feudalism and render-systems

In complex societies, such as Iron-Age Europe or Classical Greece, the relations between social groups or classes can be formalised into *client:patron* relations. In such systems of *patronage*, important figures in the community (such as aristocrats) have 'hangers-on' (*clients*) who are dependent on their favour for subsistence or profit. Such systems depend upon the clients having a *patron* who can provide social or economic advantages in return for political, economic or military services. *Clientship* (the state of being a client) depends upon there being mutual gain perceived by the client and patron. This system occurs widely spread in time and space, and can take many precise and more or less formalised shapes.

The formalisation of clientship into a system of mutual reliance, in which each of a rigidly fixed order of classes owed to its immediate senior specific social, economic, and often religious services, is characterised in medieval Europe, and sometimes the Late Roman world, as a *feudal* system. *Feudalism* is the characteristic medieval mode of socio-economic organisation supporting knights and monks by the labour of peasants, but necessitating that the recipients of this support owed loyalty and economic dues to their superiors in the system, such as the king. This loyalty, often called *fealty*, was, in the feudal system, formalised into ceremonies and reflected in the spatial layout of society.

Unlike client:patron relations, people were born into feudal relations, and society was so ordered as to place them at its economic centre. This is dissimilar to societies operating systems of patronage, which seldom place these at the centre of their economies. Pre-feudal societies often seem to have operated a similar, non-voluntary, system of mutual claims to protection or services and dues in the form of *food renders* – where food was given to the social superior – or *service renders* – where services, such as labour to build houses, were due to a social superior. Like feudalism, *render-systems* are frequently central to the economy of the societies which exhibit them, and form a principal way in which services and resources are transferred from one person to another.

Historical archaeologists have usually been more interested in these topics than prehistorians, who have felt disinclined to postulate patronage, clientship or render-systems in the pre-literate past. However, there seems to me no reason why such concepts should not form an important part of our theoretical repertoire for examining many economies, including both those in later prehistory and our own, where client:patron relationships certainly exist and render-systems can be found.

The transference of labour and services, and their products, from one person to another is, of course, of even greater general relevance. The concept of mobilisation has already been mentioned, but archaeologists have attempted to develop theories to enable them to discuss the way in which such mobilisation occurs, and the character of both labour and services.

Labour and services

Labour can be defined as physical work or mental effort (*intellectual labour*, as it is sometimes called) which can be on one's own behalf or for another. If it is for another, we have to consider how labour or its products (the goods or foodstuffs produced) are capable of transfer through the economic system. The study of the transference of labour or *services* (i.e. non-material labour, or labour producing non-material or material products) through the economic system has especially, although far from exclusively, interested Marxist scholars because, in Marx's scheme, production and exchange were seen as underlying all social and ideological components of a culture.

The transference of goods and services is often considered by Marxists in terms of the *relations of production and exchange*, expressed in terms of *economic and social formations*. Recent anthropological and historical studies have refuted the classical Marxist view that relations of production and exchange underlie all other aspects of a culture, and this work has included studies by Marxists such as Godelier and Althusser, discounting the possibility that it derives from political bias against the Marxist view.

Most contemporary Marxist studies prefer to view the relationship between social and economic facets in more complex and reflexive terms. One does not need to be a Marxist, or to have Marxist sympathies, however, to understand that a conceptual framework for examining the mobilisation of labour and services, and relations of production and exchange, is closely related to our ability to interpret an economy.

Another concept to emerge from recent studies has been the theory of *commoditisation* (Hart 1983). This is, essentially, the point at which a specific item of labour or its product(s) can be bought and sold as a 'thing' or, in the terms used, a *commodity* (for an archaeological study, see Hodges 1989). Consequently, it would be mistaken to call a shell used in a 'prestige goods economy' a commodity; because it is not bought and sold. A can of baked beans in a modern supermarket is a commodity, because it can be bought and sold.

Marxist scholars have also been interested in the concept that time itself becomes commoditised, especially in industrial or capitalist economies. In such economies, wages for time or labour *commoditise* not only the products but labour and time itself. This, it has been argued, is a major difference from preceding economic attitudes to both time and labour.

Two further concepts are especially useful in discussing production and the mobilisation of wealth: exploitation and intensification. Needless to say, Marxists have emphasised the concept of exploitation as it is a central element in Marxist theory, although this concept has also been employed by non-Marxist scholars.

Exploitation and intensification

The term exploitation can be used in two distinctly different ways. It can mean the unjust removal of labour or products from one individual or group to another, or it can mean the removal of produce derived from a form of economic activity, especially farming. It is, therefore, possible to say that 'some Romans exploited slave labour', but one also frequently hears about the 'exploitation of the land', meaning that the land was farmed.

Tolstoy (1966) attempted to link exploitation in this second sense with the *intensification* of production. Intensification is an increase in the rate at which services or, especially, material products are produced. Intensification may be associated with new technology, a change in methods, or the exploitation of new areas, materials or sources. Intensification is, however, always connected with an increase in *productivity*, i.e. in the rate of production. Intensification is a useful concept in discussing economic change, whether the emergence of agriculture or the origins of industrialisation.

Conclusion

This diversity of archaeological theory in economic reconstruction might be interpreted in several ways. It could be said that theory favours economic issues because of the significance of Clark's work or that of Higgs; in other words, because such scholars laid a basis for theoretical studies of economic archaeology, it is a field in which conceptual developments have been especially advanced. Or we could see this as a reflection of the importance of biology (and thereby ecological theory) in the reconstruction of past economies (*palaeoeconomy*, to give it another, more clumsy, name). Whatever the reason, archaeologists have generally considered past economies an accessible subject for their analyses, and have seen economic factors as important in the study of the past.

CHAPTER 6

Cognitive Archaeology

Cognitive archaeology – the archaeology of mind, as Renfrew (1985a) has defined it – has grown in importance since its development by post-processualist and processualist scholars in the UK in the 1980s (e.g. Renfrew and Zubrow 1994). Foremost in this development have been Hodder and Renfrew. Culture-historians were deeply sceptical of the possibility of archaeologically reconstructing the beliefs and perceptions of past peoples, and cognitive studies did not play a central role in the 'New Archaeology' (for a 'New Archaeological' view, see Fritz 1978).

Cognitive archaeology includes a wide range of topics, encompassing all that is concerned with belief, thought, perception and decision-making. Religion and ritual can be considered here, as can symbolism and categorisation, and issues requiring the application of rules or concepts such as law, literacy, measurement and planning.

Renfrew (1985a, 1985b) has stressed that these topics are capable of being studied in a processualist manner, with testable hypotheses forming the basis of analysis, and he has proposed a new series of cross-cultural generalisations enabling the recognition of material evidence for religion. Most scholars working on cognitive prehistory have, however, been post-processualists, who have favoured more general 'theories of society' (what Binford [1983a] would call *social philosophy*), to support their work. In processualist studies, cognition in the past is usually supposed to reflect generalisations about cognition based on the present, and such an approach is, perhaps, close, in this, to the generalising theories of cognition used by post-processualists.

Yet post-processualists have proved resistant to the hypothesis that we can generalise about the content, rather than the basis, of cognition. They have seen all cognition as specific to its time and place, and to the individual, rather than ascribing cognitive similarities across cultures on any level above the conceptual structure of the mind. Consequently, an observation such as 'all people think alike' is said to be untrue by post-processualist writers (e.g. Shanks and Tilley 1987a), whereas the observation or hypothesis that 'we do not think like Romans' would be considered to be true. Cognitive archaeology lies at the heart of post-processualism and its concern for symbolism has encouraged a cognitive approach. Post-processual approaches to cognitive archaeology are non-generalising, as are those of many processualists (e.g. Hodder 1982d, 1991a, and 1992; Yengoyan 1985; Leone 1986; Gardin and Peebles 1992).

Processualists have been keener to assert similarities in human cognition and to examine the possibility of generalisation, without claiming that individuality is an illusion. Processualist studies have varied from the use of universals of cognition to extreme individualism, and this is also true of post-processualist analyses (for processual examples: Mithen 1991b; Morris 1993). Culture-historians have also covered the same range, while asserting that the ability to recognise cognition on the basis of archaeological evidence is minimal. This is, therefore, an area in which there are similarities between the major theoretical schools, and where there is also an especially high degree of controversy (although, for example, few would disagree with the observations of Coe 1978).

Processualist, post-processualist and culture-historical archaeologists have all been interested in the archaeology of religion and of ritual (e.g. Coe 1978; Leone 1982; Renfrew 1985b; Steinsland 1986). It has long been a joke in archaeology that if the function of a prehistoric artefact is

36. A monument to the problem of reconstructing prehistoric meaning? Stonehenge, Wiltshire. (Photo: S.P. Dark)

unknown, it is described as 'ritual'. This emphasises the serious point that, in order to recognise artefacts, structures or actions associated with religion or ritual, we must employ a reliable middle-range theory capable of doing so, unless we choose a relativist position and simply assert.

Religion, superstition and ritual

Religion can be defined in terms of belief and explanation. Religions are beliefs that explain the world and the individuals within it with reference to God or to gods, or to universal and absolute codes of action. They have the ability, therefore, to affect decision-making and action, and can require specific observances.

As Anthony Giddens (1992) and others have pointed out, there is no firm evidence that people in the past (even the quite recent past) were more (or less) 'religious' than today. Moreover, atheism (itself a religion) is not demonstrably more common in modern societies than in the past (Giddens 1989, 1992). Such conclusions can be supported for the last couple of centuries by statistical evidence.

Within a religion there may also be much variation between individual believers. Our own experience shows that believers of a state religion may adhere to a range of beliefs and observances; the Anglican communion is excellent evidence of this.

Nor is all ritual connected with God or gods. Folk-beliefs can produce non-religious ritual. Such ritual, unconnected with belief in God or gods, lacking explanation or a wider code of beliefs and lacking the other characteristics of religion, is *superstition* (see Dark 1993). Superstition is aimed at achieving a result not set within a religious or explanatory framework.

Nor is all ritual part of religion or superstition, as the USSR's May Day parade showed until recently – unless we consider Marxism a religion. There, an elaborate ceremonial carried out according to set patterns (i.e. a ritual) was conducted as part of a Marxist state ideology. We must be careful, therefore, in differentiating religion, superstition and ritual, and this is made even more complicated by the problem of recognising religion in the archaeological record.

Identifying religious artefacts

Much of the archaeological discussion concerning prehistoric religion has concentrated on attempting to recognise artefacts and structures associated with religion. Some objects, such as 'Venus-figurines' found on palaeolithic sites in France, have long been supposed to be connected with prehistoric religion. Prehistorians have also felt able to claim that some structures were temples, or otherwise used in prehistoric religious practice.

Special artefacts, assigned a religious significance in archaeological interpretation, have often been identified on the grounds of their unusual form, or from concentrations of similar artefacts in the same, or nearby, places. Artefacts with no obvious function in terms of economy, production etc., are those most frequently claimed to have an association with prehistoric religion, but this is plainly no more than speculation in most cases.

There have been few extensive accounts of how we may recognise structures associated with the religions of prehistory. This is the primary importance of Renfrew's book, *The Archaeology of Cult* (1985b), one of the few attempts to set out a conceptual basis for doing so.

There has been more discussion of the theory of interpreting artefacts as evidence for prehistoric religion. For instance, separate analyses by Ehrenberg (1980) and Bradley (1984, 1990) have examined the processes of deposition which brought so much elaborate Bronze-Age and Iron-Age metalwork to be found in British rivers such as the Thames.

The representation of artefacts in miniature has often been seen as a key to their ritual significance, and the same is true of miniature representations of people and animals. Consequently, small models and miniature objects found in 'temples' are usually considered *votive* (i.e. dedicated as part of religious ritual), but such objects might (as we saw in the last chapter) have been toys or ornaments; and plaques showing seemingly symbolic or naturalistic designs might be ornamental, or symbolic of other than religious matters – a plaque depicting a fierce dog might, for example, mean 'keep off the grass!' rather than having any religious symbolism.

When large, non-portable, sculptures in stone or wood occur in a building or other architectural setting, they present us with a choice between decoration and symbolism more usually considered archaeologically informative than the discussion of small portable items; for instance, a two metre high statue is probably less likely to be a toy than a small clay figurine. Archaeologists have frequently used preconceptions concerning the character of prehistoric religion to contribute to their interpretation of such artefacts; for example, placing importance on exaggerated sexual attributes if they consider that a fertility religion may have existed in the culture in question.

If a statue or other sculpture is prominently sited (say, at one end of a building) archaeologists might claim that the building is to be seen as a temple containing an idol. The probability of this can be said to increase when other statues, sculptures, or portable artefacts of a 'ritual' character (usually decided on the grounds so far mentioned) are found associated with it. But these criteria are not, in themselves, evidence that the building is a temple or the sculpture an idol, if they reflect no more than the preconceptions of the archaeologist proposing the interpretation. Such a building could be a domestic structure containing a work of art.

37. Archaeology and ritual. Excavated evidence suggests that the cellar in the foreground may have been used for ritual at Wortley Roman villa, Gloucestershire. (Photo: S.P. Dark)

Most scholars have felt special reluctance to interpret archaeological materials as evidence of prehistoric religion because of the pitfalls already mentioned. However, faced with deliberate deposits of human bodies, or unusually large assemblages of a single type of artefact, or with the deposition of artefacts in unusual locations, archaeologists have felt less reticent in proposing that these represent evidence of prehistoric religion. Such archaeological materials can be grouped as *special deposits*.

Special deposits: sacrifices and foundation-deposits

Special deposits present special problems. The *deliberate* nature of these deposits (e.g. a child burial beneath a house wall) may be apparent, but their ritual character may be uncertain. Even if the ritual character of the deposit is certain, there is the problem of discerning whether it represents religious, rather than non-religious, ceremonial.

This has been approached in several ways: by looking for evidence of religious artefacts or context, by the attempted recognition of associations (or patterning) within such deposits, and by studying the relationship between them and other features to assign them an interpretation.

The latter approach has recently been attempted by Scott in her study of child burial (1990, 1991). She has noted that the concentration of such burials in large groups, and their placing at kilns and beneath floors, consistently from site to site, suggests that the simple explanation – that they represent infanticide of unwanted children to control population – is unsatisfactory. She suggests, therefore, that these burials were being used ritually in connection with pagan beliefs about sacrifice.

'Sacrifice' has also been used to explain the deposition of human bodies in bogs in Bronze-Age Denmark (e.g. Glob 1969). These bodies often show indications of deliberate slaughter involving unusual modes of killing. Again, a ritual explanation is often offered, asserting that they are sacrifices, or executed criminals, or both. Deliberate killing is, therefore, often assumed to be evidence of sacrifice; however, deliberate killing takes place for many reasons, and the archaeologist has to find a way to distinguish between these reasons in order to interpret the deposit as representing a 'sacrifice'.

An instance in which we know the answer to this question serves as a warning to prehistorians seeking evidence of sacrifice in this way. The medieval graves of deliberately killed bodies at prehistoric or Anglo-Saxon burial mounds in England are known in many cases to represent the burial of criminals executed at gallows positioned on these barrows. They are not ritual executions, but expressions of the enforcement of law. Yet if they were found in a prehistoric context might they not be interpreted as ritual? Moreover, criminals might be executed in unusual ways as part of their punishment.

This example highlights the problem that the exceptional, or to us unusual, does not necessarily mean that the interpretation has to be ritual, still less that it must be framed in terms of religious ritual. Without doubt, however, ritual *can* produce unusual and exceptional deposits. Nor can we assume that, because a man, say, has been deliberately killed and deliberately deposited outside a conventional cemetery, he has been ritually executed: he may, for example, have been murdered and the body hidden.

Although these difficulties have been widely recognised, archaeologists have felt able to identify both sacrifices (the ritual killing of people or animals) and foundation deposits (the depositing of sacrifices, hoards or single artefacts, beneath or within structures, to attempt to comme- morate their foundation or to assign them greater fortune). Generally, each deposit interpreted in this way has been assessed on the specific grounds of its archaeological context, rather than in terms of an established body of theory concerning what constitutes evidence of ritual, or of prehistoric religion. Yet the same archaeologists would be shocked to discover equally idiosyncratic approaches to excavation methods, or methods of dating, themselves as much connected with theory as the interpretation of what we may consider evidence for religious ritual in prehistory (see Renfrew and Bahn 1991).

An excellent example is provided by the famous Anglo-Saxon cemetery at Sutton Hoo, England (Carver 1992b; see also Davidson 1992). There, burial mounds containing boats and/or cremations within metal containers are surrounded by a 'flat' (i.e. not mounded) cemetery of both young people and 'sacrifices'. The sacrifices are recognised because they are:

(i)   deliberately killed,
(ii)   buried with unusual artefacts (probably a plough in one case),
(iii) placed in atypical body positions,
(iv) situated on the edge of the mounds, as if associated with them.

This interpretation has been widely accepted by archaeologists, but it is questionable whether it overcomes the difficulties mentioned above concerning the recognition of such deposits as indicating prehistoric religion. Yet one cannot deny that both animal and human sacrifice occurred in the past, and foundation-deposits, albeit of a non-religious type, are still to be found in our own society.

When, and if, such special deposits can be identified in the archaeological record, they inform us of both the conscious and unconscious attitudes of those making the deposit, and even, perhaps, sometimes those of the sacrificial victim, if a volunteer. But the difficulties of identifying such deposits and of recognising evidence for prehistoric religion or superstition are considerable and controversial.

Religion, ritual and superstition often employ areas designated in special ways. Such zones also exist in non-religious (*secular*) situations, for instance, in areas of restricted access for political or economic reasons. The designation of these areas may be expressed in terms of physical or mental barriers between them and their surroundings. This topic has been the subject of much archaeological work during the last decade, resulting from the introduction, by post-processualist scholars, of the concept of *boundedness* into archaeological theory.

Boundedness

Boundedness is the construction of a conceptual barrier between two places or qualities, such as between sacred and profane, or between two legal states (Conkey 1982; Shanks and Tilley 1982). Boundedness can often be reflected in physical boundaries. Fleming (1982) pioneered the correlation of physical boundaries with conceptual boundaries, and this has now been developed into a wider consideration of the physical boundary as symbolic of the conceptual boundary, whether in terms of house-divisions, field-boundaries or settlement-enclosures, as by Bowden and McOrmish (1983), and Hingley (1984).

Others have applied 'boundedness' to art, and to the use of space for rubbish disposal or burial, as for instance by Conkey (1982). Such studies all have the essential and underlying belief that conceptual boundaries have their physical correlates and can, therefore, be recognised archaeologically. Boundedness has been the most attractive of the post-processualist concepts to many processualists, although it is not usually used in culture-historical analysis.

The principal problem with recognising that a conceptual barrier is symbolised by a physical barrier is, as so often, discerning that there is a specific link between the two. Usually this has been attempted on the basis that a physical barrier does not have an obvious function, as for instance, in terms of restraining stock or protecting the inhabitants of a site from enemies or wild animals.

In the archaeology of religion, boundedness has been recognised. In the archaeology of the Christian Church, the plans of churches and their surrounding enclosures can be seen to separate sacred from profane space, and it has also long been recognised that in Classical Greek paganism, sacred and profane space was differentiated. In Classical Greek religion this was between the *naos* (temple area) and the cult objects it contained, between the *naos* and the *temenos* (the 'temple enclosure') and between the *temenos* and the outside world.

It is harder, of course, to recognise a religious boundedness of this type in prehistoric contexts (for an interesting attempt to do so, see Richards and Thomas 1984).

Pollution

It is hardly surprising that anthropology shows that different peoples have different concepts of cleanliness or dirtiness, because we all know people who have different 'standards' of cleanliness from our own. These are often rooted in perceptions of what is considered 'clean' and 'dirty'.

Obviously, as so much of archaeology is concerned with people's 'rubbish', we have a direct interest, as archaeologists, in rubbish and, therefore, dirt (for a theoretical discussion of rubbish by a non-archaeologist, see Thompson 1979). Sommer (1990) has drawn attention to the importance of 'dirt-theory' (the anthropology and history of conventions of pollution and cleanliness) for archaeologists in relation to middle-range theory. Hodder (e.g. 1982c) has long advocated much more study of this question, as has Rathje (see Chapter 2) in America, who has developed the archaeological study of modern rubbish (or 'garbage').

Pollution can take many forms. Physical pollution is when physical 'dirt', such as excrement is involved. Ritual pollution is when the 'dirt' is of 'uncleanliness' derived from its place in religious understanding, such as the eating of pork for Jews and Moslems. Both types of cleanliness can be used in the classification of space and action, so that some places and acts are 'unclean', others 'clean'.

As archaeologists, we need to recognise when past populations have considered something unclean. It is well known that medieval Europeans threw human waste on urban streets, considered it healthy to have lice, and 'manly' not to bathe. Whereas we might feel that we know modern exponents of these values, there is no doubt that most modern Europeans do not act in this way. Their concepts of cleanliness are different.

Archaeologically, perhaps, the clearest widespread example is the view of Roman and Greek pagans that burial was ritually polluting. Burial was, therefore, prohibited from most settlement sites and, most of all, from religious sites, as the latter had to be kept strictly pure. But child burials do occur on settlement sites, suggesting that these were seen as a separate category (see Chapter 4).

In Christian Roman thought, burial is a sacred act and so the arrival of Christianity sees burial concentrating on religious sites, although it is still not usually found on settlement sites. But children were afforded 'conventional' Christian burial because attitudes to the baptised child were such that they were undifferentiated from baptised adults. So *attitudes* to religious purity and to pollution changed with religious change, and were reflected in the archaeological record (for the use of contrasting Christian and pagan attitudes to burial as a basis for an archaeological interpretation, see Dark 1994b).

The archaeological study of pollution is, then, a promising area for future research, as sources are common and (in historical societies) attitudes are often known from written evidence. However, the use of such approaches in prehistory is still in its infancy, and largely confined to post-processualist studies derived from the interest shown by Hodder and scholars who have studied with him (e.g. Moore 1982).

Church archaeology

The archaeology of the Christian Church is now a major field within archaeology in general, especially in Europe, Scandinavia and the Mediterranean, and has both its own theoretical basis and many important lessons for cognitive archaeology. It might be supposed that the archaeology of the Church would be theoretically simpler than that of prehistoric religion because of the wealth of information provided by written sources, the participation in Christianity by many of those undertaking Church archaeology, and the almost unequalled archaeological data-base provided by surviving buildings, monuments and religious sites. While many difficulties encountered in identifying prehistoric religion are overcome with ease in Church archaeology, other theoretical questions are raised. These questions highlight the aspects of potential study unrecognised in discussing prehistoric religion, making the archaeology of the Church a subject of especial interest in the overall theory of the archaeological study of religion.

38. Church archaeology. A medieval cathedral, St Alban's Abbey, built at, or close to, the site of a Roman-period martyrium. (Photo: K.R. Dark)

Identifying Christian churches and monasteries on archaeological grounds alone

Even if we understand the beliefs of a religion, the recognition of religious buildings associated with the religion can be difficult. Scholars have assumed that churches will:

   (i)   be rectangular,
   (ii)   be east-west in orientation,
  (iii)   have a cemetery or, at least, a single burial,
  (iv)   often have religious artefacts or one or more altars, and
   (v)   often be apsed or bipartite.

In fact, all of these criteria, while valid for the majority of buildings, are not true of every church.

In a recent theoretical study, Watts (1991) has tried to assign 'scores' to potential churches by constructing a list of attributes and considering which buildings show more or fewer of them. Watts considered that one can assign a probability as to whether any building was a church, although other scholars have employed other attributes, or placed more importance on the context in time and space wherein the building is found. Thus, an east-west building on the west of a monastic cloister is identified as a church, but not an east-west building in all other contexts.

Another related problem has been that of recognising monasteries in the archaeological record. As Rahtz (1974a) pointed out, monasteries are essentially settlements with churches, so how can we distinguish them from other settlements? Some have considered this an unanswerable problem, but an alternative view is to seek an answer in concepts such as boundedness, or attitudes to burial. If secular and religious space was strictly bounded, or burial was restricted to religious sites, then non-religious settlements can be differentiated from monasteries.

Alternatively, the recognition of monasteries and churches can rest upon how they fit into the landscape, or what sort of sites they were before the phase under consideration and after it. Consequently, combining these approaches, archaeologists have felt able to recognise churches and monasteries on archaeological grounds, e.g. where a possible church building has replaced a pagan temple and been succeeded by a later (more certainly identifiable) church; but it is a discussion which

39. The difficulty of recognising Christian burials. Neither alignment nor distinctive artefacts help us to decide between pagan and Christian late Roman burials. If identifying Christian burials in the Roman world has proved difficult, what are the theoretical implications for establishing the religion of those burials in other – for example prehistoric – graves? (Photo: K.R. Dark)

raises important questions of wider relevance in the archaeology of religion.

Many Christian churches are associated with burials. Again, it might be assumed that it would be easy to recognise Christian burials, but here, too, there are theoretical questions to be addressed.

Recognising Christian burials

Again, it is Watts (1991) who has most recently considered this question, and again she suggests that we might approach it by 'scoring' burials according to the number of attributes they have on a list derived both from considering Christian attitudes to burial and from historically-identified Christian burials.

The conventional approach to recognising Christian burials on archaeological grounds was often to concentrate on only one attribute: the orientation of the grave. It was believed that Christian graves were always east-west – but this assumption has since proved to be incorrect.

Rahtz (1978) has shown that Christian graves might, on archaeological grounds alone, have a variety of alignments. Christian graves could vary from east-west burial, and, on the other hand, non-Christian burials could adhere to an east-west alignment for various reasons such as to be aligned with the sun because they were of worshippers of a solar cult.

This led to the realisation that not all east-west burials were Christian, and not all Christian burials are east-west. A second important breakthrough was the realisation that the long held view that Christian burials never contain artefacts ('grave goods') is unfounded.

Not only do Christians often bury bodies dressed or in shrouds (leaving pins and dress fittings in the grave), but treasured possessions and other sentimental tokens placed in the grave can reflect familial and other emotions of love and respect. In practice, Christian graves where the religion of the person buried is otherwise historically attested are often found to be *accompanied* (i.e. have grave goods) in this way. In the Roman and Byzantine worlds, Christians are known to have been buried with artefacts in their graves, and medieval western Christians conventionally buried priests either with their chalice and paten (the cup and plate used in communion), or with a symbolic equivalent (for symbolism in medieval English burials see Butler 1987). But, again, not all priests' graves have either artefacts or, specifically, chalice and paten: they could not be identified in every case by symbolism alone.

Another possibility is that a Christian may, on religious grounds, choose to adopt a humble manner of dress or burial, and may deliberately choose unostentatious burial practices, poor quality clothes, or locations for burial usually considered low-status within society. This may also, of course, be found in the structures and artefacts connected both with individual Christians and with the Christian community.

When considering the archaeology of pagan religion, the use of symbolism and religious images as a means of recognising religion in the archaeological record was discussed. It has sometimes been supposed that religious symbols also provide a key to identifying the distribution of Christians within a past population, e.g. in Roman Britain (Thomas 1981). This is, however, also debatable on theoretical grounds (Thomas 1986; Dark 1994a).

Symbols, icons and iconography

In early Christianity, in the Byzantine world, and then again after the Reformation, many Christians did not, and do not, use symbols, or only use(d) a very restricted range of symbols, and then sometimes sparingly.

In these situations it is folly to seek symbols as a key to the identification and distribution of Christians in a community (Dark 1994a). The differences in the availability of symbols caused by wealth, the ability to produce them, cultural factors and status, all may also limit or prohibit the use of religious symbolism.

Thomas (1986) has observed that the implication of such an argument is that maps showing a distribution of religious symbols, or for that matter specific burial practices or building-types, show only the distribution of religious observance using them. Consequently, there is the theoretical implication that the distribution of symbols and artefacts is not a key to the distribution of a religion, and certainly not an adequate way of ascertaining the number and distribution of Christians in the past. The same critical argument can be applied to the evidence for the distribution of churches, as the use of house-churches (unrecognised in the archaeological record in most cases) by the early Christians until the fourth century would limit our ability to recognise the distribution of Christian religious buildings.

Another element of Christian religious symbolism also has interesting implications for cognitive archaeology. Byzantine Christians and modern Orthodox Christians made, and make, religious pictures called 'icons'. The modern observer usually considers icons to be stylised and extremely abstract, but there is written evidence showing that Byzantines saw icons as naturalistic pictures. That is, the Byzantine perception of naturalism in religious art was very different from our own. This is an important and well attested example of the differing perceptions of past peoples, for it shows that naturalism and symbolism may be defined in other terms in the past from those seemingly obvious today.

Relics and pilgrimage

The archaeology of relics and of pilgrimage are both extensively studied subjects and of interest to non-specialists because of the theoretical questions they raise (for an introduction to the archaeology of this subject see Stopford 1994). Relics are artefacts assigned importance on a religious basis. Not only, for example, was the saint's body (the *corporeal relics*) considered important but so too were artefacts associated with the saint and *secondary relics* – objects which had touched the corporeal relics.

Relics can be contained in specific buildings or structures inside buildings (*shrines*), or in portable containers (unsurprisingly, *portable shrines*). Such shrines attracted, and still do attract, travellers motivated by religious intention (pilgrims), who often follow specific routes of symbolic or religious significance (*pilgrim routes*). A specific type of shrine is the *martyrium*, or martyr's shrine, for all martyrs may be considered saints.

This digression into the practice and terminology of relics and pilgrimage is necessary to give the vocabulary and conceptual basis to discuss an interesting theoretical matter. How, even when we know these practices took place in the past, can we recognise a relic, its shrine, a pilgrim route, or a martyrium? Can we, moreover, use theory to give us a further understanding of what pilgrimage meant in order to discuss it more adequately?

The concept of *liminality* has been used to examine religious travel as a symbolic state of being 'in between' (Turner and Turner 1978). *Liminal* situations are those incapable of a binary classification – like being at the threshold of a house, or on the way between Point A and Point B. Pilgrimage was seen as a liminal state between secular and religious, and between perceived religious impurity and purity, as well as between the starting point of the pilgrim's journey and the place of pilgrimage. This concept has been valuable in stressing the importance of travel in pilgrimage and the significance of the journey, as well as of its destination.

The anthropology of pilgrimage in the modern world has included ethnoarchaeological examination of its associated artefacts. Because we can study aspects of modern pilgrimage, unlike medieval pilgrims' routes and practices, this may be used to help us to understand medieval pilgrimage. Obviously, change may have occurred, but there are many continuities visible in the material record, compared with historical sources and the archaeology of medieval pilgrimage.

The use of ethnoarchaeology to study pilgrimage has much potential in building up a rounded picture of the relationship between material and non-material culture, and for middle-range theory. There are, however, only a couple of studies, including that by Rahtz and Watts, on this interesting avenue of research (Rahtz and Watts 1986).

Most archaeological studies of relics and of the cult of saints have concentrated on the question of recognising shrines containing relics in the archaeological record. Studies have examined relic-containers (reliquaries) and shrines, and have drawn attention to the possibility of recognising the burial of relics in pits beneath church altars. Outside such useful sealed assemblages, relics may be unidentifiable, or not survive in the archaeological record. The identification of Christian relics by reference to these sealed contexts has interesting general implications – without a key to recognising the significance of these contexts how could we reconstruct the widespread cult of relics in the Middle Ages on archaeological grounds?

The difficulty of recognising relics has already been mentioned in Chapters 2 and 4, and the identification of non-corporeal relics seems an even more complex theoretical question. A non-corporeal relic could be no more than soil from the ground close to a shrine. Yet relics were perceived as of special significance throughout the medieval world.

The saints' and martyrs' graves at surviving shrines and martyria have also been the subject of theoretical debate. If these are located in highly distinctive circumstances – notably within saints' chapels or under altars – isolated, and elaborated by symbolism (such as 'whitening' of the graves with chalk, lime, or gypsum, or the construction of shrine-structures above them), they are visible in archaeological examination. But they might be simple, unadorned burials. We can, however, recognise even these graves as *focal* (forming the focus of burial), and observe that cemeteries form around them. In both cases, importance can be identified by considering their symbolism and context.

Likewise, the formation of paths to graves, and paving of assembly zones around them, enable their recognition as foci of importance in the cemetery. An example of such a grave identified on archaeological grounds alone may be at Cannington, where a path leads to a grave set within a paved area and distinguished by a carved stone within an otherwise somewhat undifferentiated cemetery (Rahtz forthcoming). This again emphasises the importance of symbolism and context and the significance of the treatment of the grave in the archaeology of the cult of saints, and so is of interest in the theory of cemetery archaeology in general.

The archaeology of religion is probably the most extensively studied aspect of cognitive archaeology. Another important aspect of this field is the archaeology of individuals: the decisions they make and the ways in which they communicate about, and classify, the world around them.

The archaeology of the individual

Undergraduates studying archaeology at university are often taught that the individual is not a topic for archaeological analysis. This is plainly untrue, as a great deal has been written on the subject.

In addition to the study of artistic, and other, representations (e.g. Bailey 1994), individuals can be studied through the artefacts they

40. The remains of a prehistoric individual. The Lindow man, a partially-preserved human body from Cheshire. (Photo: The British Museum)

produce or their skeletons (e.g. Brothwell 1963; Wells 1964; Brothwell and Sandieson 1967; Hill and Gunn 1977), and individuals have been recognised in the specialised work of craftsmen. Pathology can reconstruct details of the life of the skeleton being studied: diseases, types of work undertaken and wounds endured, whether a woman has given birth, and the age and health of the person at death. Together with inscriptions or symbolic decoration, this information can be used to write a 'life-history' of the individual, even if the details included are not those usually found in biographies, or necessarily those which we, as archaeologists, would most like to know.

We may take as an example a burial of an Anglo-Saxon, found at Banstead Common (Barfoot and Price Williams 1976). This is not the grave of a historically known individual. The burial, dated to the seventh or eighth century AD on the grounds of objects deposited in the grave, is of a tall (probably 6′ 4″) heavily built male in his twenties or thirties. His burial beneath a mound suggests high social status (see Shepherd 1979) and his grave goods support this view. He was buried with a spear and shield and suffered from a skeletal abnormality caused by excessive horse-riding. His clothes, of which fragments were preserved, were of high quality and he wore leather boots which – in view of the skeletal evidence – might be riding boots. In the context of what is known about Anglo-Saxon England from other sources, not relating directly to this individual, the excavator interpreted this evidence as indicating that the grave was that of a warrior. That is, we can retrieve information about the life of this individual from archaeological sources alone, which does not merely reflect the generalised circumstances of the social and economic context of the burial being studied.

Exceptional circumstances, where we may recognise a well-documented individual in a richly-evidenced archaeological record, enable us to make even more sophisticated contributions to the archaeology of individuals. At Vergina, northern Greece, the uninscribed tomb of a Hellenistic aristocrat was examined. Datable to the end of Philip of Macedon's reign, the wealth and style of the tomb suggested royalty, and it was proposed that it could be the tomb of a member of the Macedonian royal dynasty – the family of Alexander the Great and Philip of Macedon (Prag 1984; Prag *et al.* 1984). When the abnormalities of the skull of this burial were examined by a pathologist, they were shown to indicate a distinctive and very unusual wound. This wound was paralleled by a modern injury inflicted upon a construction worker in a freak accident in which he was hit by a metal rod falling from a high building. This was comparable with an injury known to have been sustained by Philip of Macedon during the siege of a walled town, when an arrow shot from the walls hit him in the face, blinding him in one eye. The combination of the dating evidence, suggestions of royalty provided by the type and contents of the tomb, its location, and the evidence provided by pathology, has led to the interpretation of the burial as that of Philip of Macedon. This, in turn, has the potential for adding further details to the life-history of this historically-known figure by the analysis of the tomb and its contents.

Other studies of the archaeology of individuals have attempted to show that individuality itself was represented in different terms in the past. These studies by post-processualists have, however, met with scepticism from most archaeologists, and have not been a major part of archaeological studies of the individual. More widespread have been attempts to approach individuality and cognition through the study of decision-making.

Decision-making

Artefacts, structures and material traces of human activities are, in part, the products of human decision-making. The artefacts we recover have been designed by, and embody concepts belonging to, past people. Some of these are easily visible when we can recognise that there was a range of options of which only a small number have been chosen by the past manufacturer (e.g. Taçon 1991). Artefacts can also show evidence of more

41. **Decision-making.** How can we discover the choices involved in building this Roman-period hut group at Din Lligwy (Anglesey)? (Photo: S.P. Dark)

general concepts, such as symmetry, or perspective-depictions in art (e.g. Washburn 1983). In this respect, consistent recurrence may be a useful tool in understanding past decision-making concepts: if a single stone axe is symmetrical and made of blue stone it may not be significant, even if blue stone is rare in the vicinity, but if one finds that very many hand-axes are symmetrical and made out of the same type of rare stone, then one might assign greater significance to these factors.

This question of the assignation of significance to specific characteristics is, of course, a universal problem in archaeological reasoning, but it becomes more acute in cognitive archaeology. We have to find some way — whether by predecided results of an earlier empirical study, or on theoretical grounds — of assigning cognitive significance to visible attributes of the archaeological record. We have to ask, 'How can we know what people thought was important?'

Simulation of patterns of decision-making or of the results of decisions made has been used as a way of discerning past cognition which avoids having to move from artefacts or deposits to past decisions in an empirical fashion. Other scholars have felt able to use social or anthropological hypotheses of how decisions are made to move from hypothesis concerning cognition to archaeological data. Both of these approaches have been incorporated in the recent attempt by Mithen

(1990) to use mathematics to simulate the results of alternative strategies in prehistory.

An alternative approach has been to analyse the way in which designs were executed (*style*) or the structure of designs – often alongside design grammars – and to discuss how artefacts or symbols were consciously recombined to form symbolic systems, an approach favoured especially by post-processualist scholars. Their understanding of decision-making, in its relationship to the individual and to cognition, is frequently different from that so far outlined because it concentrates on decision-making as the subconscious working-out of *deep structures* in the human mind, or on a theory of *symbolic representation* whereby the structures of perception and communication found in art, or decoration, or symbolism, represent the world around us as we schematise it (e.g. Fischer 1961). It may be that such concepts fail to see the decision-making individual as an originator and, at least to some extent, free agent, in the choices made.

Much attention has also been focused on *skeuomorphism* – the rendering of functional characteristics in a medium in which they have lost their function, e.g. the simulated 'weave' sometimes found on solid plastic 'baskets' in modern supermarkets. It is argued that this informs us of past perceptions, because if importance had not been attached to the characteristic rendered in this manner, then its simulation would have been pointless.

Closely related to discussions of decision-making is the issue of the ability to choose. Some scholars have felt that so central to human choice are the effects of environment, biological make-up, or psychology, that humans are not free to decide. That is, human cognition is *determined* by other factors, e.g. by the environment. The alternative is to suppose that people can, at least to some extent, make free decisions: *free-will*. This debate has ancient origins and is often combined with the debate between materialist interpretations of history – where material issues underlie all others and *idealist* interpretation in which ideas lie at the heart of all aspects of culture.

In archaeology there are, as we shall discuss more fully in Chapter 7, many *deterministic* theories of change. In these theories individual decisions are *pre-determined* and as such simply the 'froth' – so to speak – on the sea of determining factors. Free-will has been recently defended in modern social theory, and to some extent in archaeology, by Giddens and his school.

To Giddens (1984) total free-will does not exist, but neither are people pawns in a game played by determining factors. In his theory of the individual and action (*structuration theory*), he sees people as 'conscious strategic actors' who are knowledgeable about the material and social world in which they live. They are not wholly determined by social and natural factors, but make their choices within codes of action (*structures*), whether consciously or subconsciously. They are, therefore, not wholly free either. Environmental and other constraints, such as uncrossable rivers, mountains etc., are also limiting structures upon their action. But the same structures that constrain action also 'enable' action to take place – that is, there is a paradox: structures both constrain and enable action. This, called by Giddens the *duality of structure*, has been of much interest to archaeologists within both processual and especially post-processual studies.

Giddens's idea has been greatly misunderstood in much archaeological debate, being considered structuralist, post-structuralist, relativist, or Marxist; all claims which Giddens himself has been at pains to deny (e.g. Giddens 1984 and 1987). As the disclaiming passages have been ignored by archaeological theorists and the secondary sources, rather than Giddens's writings, have most often been quoted by archaeologists, these have been overlooked in recent archaeological discussions of his work.

In archaeological terms we might see structuration as a useful approach to discussing the role of individuals in society in general, and in cognitive archaeology in particular. If we take an artefact, such as a decorated pot, the manufacturer has usually a number of choices partially, but not wholly, constrained by cultural and practical considerations (i.e. by experience or tradition) but can make decisions based, for example, on judgment or aesthetic emotions. The potter may assess advantages to be gained from specific design modifications, or attempt to fulfil pre-decided requirements, that are themselves enacted through, and constrained by, cultural and practical factors: in Giddens's terminology, structures. That is, we can easily apply this concept of structure in an analysis of the relationships between cognition, individualism, constraints and the archaeological materials available to us. Consequently, although decision-making in itself may be a valuable clue to past cognition, it requires a theoretical context in order for that source of information to be used.

Interestingly, while Giddens stresses that individuals have intentions (*intentionality*) he also stresses that the results of action can have unintended consequences. This may be a useful perspective on, for example, the design of artefacts and/or structures.

Another area of cognition which archaeologists have attempted to explore has been the way in which past people communicated about and measured the world in which they lived. This has produced an archaeology of language, literacy and measurement, and of past concepts of time and place.

Language, literacy and identity

Language, if defined as a means of information exchange, is always, of course, non-material when spoken, and only transformed into material form by its symbolic expression in writing or 'decoration' (e.g. Braithwaite

1982; Weissner 1983; David *et al.* 1988). So it is hardly surprising that archaeologists have felt reticent about the possibility of studying past language through material remains, and that Renfrew's recent attempt to study language-change (especially Renfrew 1987) through material evidence has prompted a heated controversy. Archaeological approaches to language, including Renfrew's, have taken two forms: general theory about the relationship of language to other (archaeologically identifiable) non-material characteristics, such as ethnic identity, or an economic institution, or by seeing language as symbolically expressed in terms of signs or 'structural deposits'. Renfrew, as Childe before him, chooses the former option: language is linked to archaeological evidence – by observing culture-change we can observe language-change (Renfrew 1987).

Language closely relates to two aspects of cognition, fields not themselves wholly linguistic – literacy and identity. Literacy requires language, but by no means all societies are literate (although none lack language). These non-literate societies are often called *pre-literate*, although there are problems with this term as it implies a sequence which is sometimes absent, for literate and 'pre-literate' societies can co-exist in the same period or literacy may be lost.

It is probable that language and literacy will become more active fields of study in cognitive archaeology, but currently there is little other than the studies of material culture as a *symbolic text*, i.e. encoding meaning as does writing, to supplement the above examples.

Language also has a close relationship to identity, and some, such as Renfrew, relate language and identity very closely. This has been a theory common in, for example, Celtic and Anglo-Saxon archaeology since long before the 1960s. Here, the correlation between a specific archaeological assemblage (e.g. Anglo-Saxon cemeteries), a linguistic identity (the speakers of Old English), and a cultural identity (the Anglo-Saxons) has been long accepted. Currently this question is the topic of a major continuing study by Hines and has attracted more debate. In this case it is necessary to explain the disappearance of a Celtic language and a 'Celtic' native identity in eastern England in a period of little more than two centuries, but it is hard to adduce sufficient population movement totally to replace the native Celtic speakers. This has led to a split between those who propose the continuity of the local population on archaeological or historical grounds, and those who adduce discontinuity on linguistic grounds.

Whether language and identity are tied together is itself a debatable question. If so, can we use this to recognise either or both in the archaeological record? The problem of the spread of languages beyond populations sharing the identity implied by that language – English is the obvious example – shows that language and identity are not always linked in a one-to-one relationship.

Group identity in past societies is usually sought in archaeology through shared characteristics, such as artefact or architectural types. These, archaeologists claim, even after the widespread abandonment of Childe's concept of culture, enable the identification of what Carver has called a *commonality* (a commonly perceived identity) among the users (Carver 1989). Some may well see such a concept as very close to Childe's 'culture' although those sharing a commonality need not be a single 'people' in Childe's sense, so there is a difference.

Archaeological perspectives on the archaeology of language and the recognition of identity have produced little agreement. There has been a greater measure of consensus concerning the possibility of recognising deliberate planning and measurement on archaeological grounds.

Metrology and planning

Metrology is the study of measurement. This can be the measurement of time (e.g. archaeologically through the study of early timepieces, calendars, etc.), of space (e.g. by discovering past systems of measurement), and of size or mass (e.g. by examining weights and scales). These can, as Renfrew has pointed out, be used as sources for past cognition (Renfrew 1985a; Renfrew and Bahn 1991, 350-2).

Metrological studies have included attempts to use building or monument dimensions to demonstrate the use of a standard unit of length in their layout, as by Hope-Taylor and recently by Huggins (Hope-Taylor 1979; Huggins 1991; see also Fernie 1991; Marshall and Marshall 1991; Bettess 1991). While these scholars have used examples from historical archaeology, Thom (1967) proposed that prehistoric megalithic monuments provided evidence of a series of standard measurements used in their layout, but this has met with widespread scepticism.

Huggins has pointed out the similarity of a hypothetical unit derived from the detailed analysis of the dimensions of Anglo-Saxon buildings to 'traditional' units of length used in north-west Europe in modern times (Huggins 1991). Hope-Taylor went further than simple metrics and hoped to show the organising principles (the *site geometry*) of the layout of the Anglo-Saxon royal complex at Yeavering (Hope-Taylor 1979). He was able to show that some underlying geometric rules (chevron-layout for instance), were used in planning the settlement, and so to demonstrate that deliberate planning had taken place.

The issue of planning is another area of cognitive studies in archaeology. In analysing sites such as Iron-Age hill-forts and late Anglo-Saxon towns, metrological studies have shown that roads or buildings were laid out according to a plan, although this need not have been a drawing or set of written instructions (Biddle and Hill 1971; Biddle 1975; Guilbert 1975). The recognition of a plan behind a settlement layout can be taken as evidence of the planner's intentions, and so constitute evidence of cognition.

Prehistorians have made less use of such approaches. Almost as controversial as the work of Thom, but perhaps more widely supported, is that of Marshak (1972a, 1972b, 1975, 1991), who has attempted to interpret apparently non-random symbols in palaeolithic 'art' as the earliest known calendar. Marshak's approach has been to search for regularities in the patterning of symbols and compare these with astronomical information.

These examples illustrate that while metrology holds much potential as a source for past cognition, it is an area characterised by controversy and dispute, especially when metrological studies have been undertaken on prehistoric data. Less controversy has derived from studies of planned settlements, and it is notable that Biddle and Hope-Taylor's models of planning have been widely adopted. If anyone were to doubt the relevance of settlement planning to cognition, the anthropological example of the Dogon homestead is often cited as a demonstration of its potential and its relevance to cognition.

Not only is the Dogon homestead planned, but its layout represents a 'map' of the cognitive world of the Dogon (Hodder 1982b; Lane 1987). Each element of the settlement has its symbolic equivalent in their world view.

A similar argument in archaeology on the borders of symbolic analysis and the analysis of planning, is the suggestion by Hodder that similarities between Neolithic tombs and settlement-sites on Orkney show that tomb 'meant' house in the Orcadian Neolithic. Hodder's (1984) approach is, therefore, that of drawing detailed comparison in form (*formal comparison*) between one type of site and another, so as to demonstrate that one was a symbol of the other (*symbolic equivalence*).

Such arguments are closely linked to studies of artefact symbolism and the analysis of site plans, and therefore to social archaeology. Again, as with so many aspects of cognitive prehistory, it cannot be claimed that Hodder's views are widely supported (even by Hodder 1992).

Measurement extends not only to distance, but to time. Even if we cannot dig up past systems of measurement, we can still try to understand how varying concepts of time may affect the archaeological materials which we try to explain.

Time and timescales

The timescale upon which analysis is undertaken is important to many types of archaeological question (e.g. Gosden 1994), and analysis incorporating varying timescales, which Bailey (1981, 1983, 1987; see also Gamble 1987; Fletcher 1992) has referred to as *time perspectivism*, is often proposed because different events or processes may act, or be visible, only on different timescales.

The archaeological visibility of ritual, for instance, Bradley (1991) has argued, is enhanced by the length of 'ritual time' – extending beyond a single generation – and, therefore, more in accordance with the clarity of archaeological timescales than are short-term events. The relationship of the timescales used by the archaeologist and those of past peoples may also be important when, for example, the division of chronological periods into discrete phases hinders our recognition of phenomena such as continuity from one phase to another. If only very short phases are examined in isolation, underlying processes of long-term change may not be recognised.

As different processes, or aspects of the past, may only be recognisable on a specific scale of analysis, it seems reasonable to study the past on many different scales of time and space (for a recent attempt to study time in prehistory, see Mizoguchi 1993). Archaeologists have attempted to do so since the 1960s, and Clarke's study of Glastonbury was one of the first cases to be examined in this way (Clarke 1972). This concept of the integration of many scales of time and space has been called the *multi-scalar* approach. Each time-span, or spatial zone, examined is seen within an overall perspective as a level of analysis, each of which is possibly, but not certainly, intricately related.

If the people whom we study had different concepts of time from our own, this may have led to actions which, although seemingly irrational to us, would be clearly understandable if one were capable of perceiving the past timescales employed. This raises the question of how to assess past concepts of time.

Modern Westerners often think and plan in days, months, years, or decades, but this does not mean that people always did so in the past. It is impossible to give a sweeping generalisation such as that past peoples planned according to longer timescales, as they might equally have planned according to much shorter timescales than those which we employ. Except where historical texts inform us of past attitudes, archaeology is our principal source for past perceptions of time. The design of projects (the pyramids are a famous example) which would take long periods of time to complete, may assist us in recognising the timescales employed on archaeological grounds alone, but few studies have attempted to recognise characteristics of this type.

Moreover, not all concepts of time attested by anthropological studies agree on the character of time itself. To some, time might seem a dimension through which movement is possible, to others time is a cycle, repeating itself, and others might differ over whether the past or the future exists independently. Yet others would say time is the sum of contemporary (or contemporary and past) action. The future is the sum of the implications of the present for what will happen next. Again, although such arguments may, at first, seem obtuse and irrelevant, upon our concept of time will, it is argued, hang the way in which we interpret and explain the past and its relationship to the present. On past concepts of time may depend many of the issues which we would hope to study through cognitive, social and economic archaeology.

There have been few archaeological studies attempting to approach the theoretical problems raised so far in regard to time itself. While archaeologists have been aware that such questions may be important to their interpretations, the principal approach so far adduced has been to

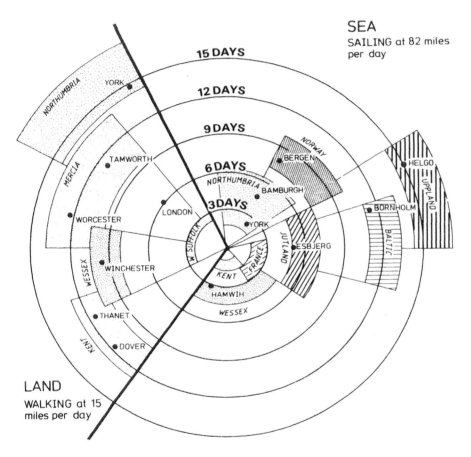

42. Time:distance geography. Travelling times between Ipswich (Suffolk) and neighbouring locations in Britain and north-west Europe. Note that, by this calculation, in terms of time:distance, Bergen (Norway) is closer to Ipswich than is Worcester (England). (Reproduced with the kind permission of Professor Martin Carver)

employ an examination of travelling times alongside past technology to attempt to evaluate the relationship between past perceptions of time and space.

This solution to the understanding of past timescales has been based on the use of travel times to generate *time-distance* maps. These maps distort what we consider geographical reality (e.g. 'Essex is close to Kent') by the calculation or estimation of the time taken to make various journeys. The proximity of areas to one another is then mapped according to the time taken to move between them.

The classic early application of this approach in archaeology was by Clarke (1972b) in his study of Glastonbury Lake village, mentioned earlier in this chapter. Recently, it has been employed by Carver (1990) to assess sailing-times across the North Sea to Britain and *vice versa*, in comparison with sailing times between the south-east coast of Britain and other parts of the island. These place East Anglia closer to northern continental Europe than to Midland England. This, Carver has argued, places Anglo-Saxon East Anglia more accurately in its geographical context than does a modern perspective on its geography.

Technology can be used to calibrate these methods of estimating time-distance maps, if, by the study of communications, the time taken for information to be transmitted (rather than simply travelling times), is used to recalculate the time-distance map for a site or area. For instance, a radio-signal will distort time-distance in a different way from that caused by use of a motor-car. Time-distance mapping can be made even more sophisticated if differing access to forms of communication and technology is incorporated within the approach, as this means that a number of levels of time-distance might exist within a single society in a specific location. This also means that we cannot estimate, for example, a standard medieval time-distance equation, applicable in every situation, because this may be different for separate social groups (e.g. kings or impoverished hill-farmers) and in different areas or topographical settings.

Time-distance mapping is a specific and complex approach and the establishment of past perspectives of time and distance is likely to involve complex argument. Its study has, however, hardly begun.

Conclusion

Cognitive archaeology is, perhaps, the newest sub-discipline within archaeological theory, and it is representative of the potential of this exciting new field that so much work has already been undertaken on it. It is reasonable to suppose that as the number of scholars working on cognitive aspects of the subject increases, and in view of the amount already achieved, this will be a major area of theoretical archaeology in the next decade.

CHAPTER 7

Explaining Cultural Change

Change obviously occurred in the past, as it continues to take place today: if it did not, the present would be identical to the past. Every archaeologist is aware that change has occurred, for the artefacts and other remains of the past are dissimilar in many respects to those of the present. Only the relativist can deny this observation.

In this chapter, I shall refer to change in past societies as 'cultural change', using the term 'culture' in a broad sense, to differentiate this from change in the natural environment.

Yet we must define very carefully what we mean by change, and consider how we are to explain it, if that is our aim. Some archaeologists, of the culture-historical school, may say that the explanation of cultural

43. **The reality of change.** Apart from these ruins at Wroxeter (Shropshire), the area of what was a large Roman town is now farmland. (Photo: S.P. Dark)

change is impossible, or irrelevant, but most archaeologists consider the explanation of change important to their subject.

People have been trying to explain cultural change for a very long time – at least since Classical Greece – producing a large number of pre-modern explanations (examples in Mango 1963; Ussher 1969; Hunter 1973; Phillips 1974). These were in turn replaced by 'scientific' explanations in the seventeenth to the nineteenth centuries, and eventually by explanations proposed by archaeologists working in the nineteenth and twentieth centuries (Walters 1934; Hunter 1971; Daniel and Renfrew 1988). Here, it will only be possible to consider a few of the most widely used recent perspectives on this subject to be found in archaeology.

There are problems concerning the explanation of cultural change, general to many theoretical viewpoints. Do we see change as coming from within a culture (*endogenous*), or from outside (*exogenous*)? Do we think that a single factor causes change (*monocausal explanation*) or that many factors act in combination (*multi-causal explanation*)? Are some situations, e.g. islands, where outside contact might be supposed to be limited, especially useful for discerning the causes of change (Evans 1973)?

Over what timescale do we examine change, and is this the same for all types of change, e.g. change in dress-fashions and economic institutions? Other problems of scale must be considered: whether we group together all change from the individual within his or her lifetime to the nation over centuries, or from the single bronze pin-type to the metalworking tradition within a culture; or do different aspects of any culture change at different rates or for different reasons? All these questions must be addressed by a theory of explanation.

Some scholars have suggested that change on specific scales occurs over certain timespans: political ideologies change over centuries, but fashions over decades. Others see a close relationship between change over one scale of time or space and change in all, or many, of the others. This view is a multiscalar approach.

Another debate exists between scholars who feel that every change must be explained in its own time and place (that explanation must be specific only to that time and place) and those who feel able to generalise between two or more such situations. Generalisation is a very controversial issue in explanation (e.g. see Cherry 1978; Hodder 1992), both in archaeology and in other disciplines, and scholars favouring it are divided between those who argue for *generalisations*, and those who hold that *laws of cultural dynamics* can be formed by recognising the universal explanations of cultural change (for an attempt to form such a 'law', see Binford 1971). It is important to differentiate between generalisations and laws of cultural dynamics and between patterning and explanation (e.g. Flannery 1972), since, increasingly, while arguing for the former processual archaeologists have discarded the latter (see Renfrew and

Bahn 1991). A law of cultural dynamics might take the form 'if A and B then C', while a generalisation might run 'if A and B then usually C unless other factors are present'.

Explanation in terms of laws of cultural dynamics was very popular with the early processualists of the 'New Archaeology' (e.g. Read and LeBlanc 1978). 'New Archaeologists' supposed that explanations of this type made archaeology more 'scientific' because they were similar to laws of natural science such as 'gravity', but such generalisations frequently proved trivial, or what Flannery (1973) called *Mickey Mouse Laws*. Processualist writers have recently tended to favour generalisations rather than cultural laws, but Bell (1992) has emphasised that the proposal of universals, although incapable of testing, is valuable for the development of archaeological reasoning. As Bell points out, we can never know if a universal is true in archaeology, because (as yet unknown) evidence might show it to be incorrect.

Culture-historians and post-processualist scholars have obviously favoured explanations which do not make use of universals or generalisations, although structuralists (who believe that the way to understand human behaviour lies in universals of cognition) are 'universalists' when it comes to explanation. Both of these schools prefer explanations specific to the time and place, unrepeatable in any alternative time and space. Such explanations are called *historically-specific*, and give rise to the view that 'history never repeats itself'. Every event is 'entire unto itself' and unreproduceable.

Contrast can also be found in the application of mathematical approaches to the explanation of culture-change. There are many mathematical techniques which enable 'predictions' about how a society will change over time to be worked out. The simplest is to construct a 'picture' of how a society works as a flow-diagram, representing a single year, month, week or day in the 'life' of that society, and to run it on a computer for a set number of simulated years – say for a 'century'. The effects of the simulated time on the reconstructed society can then be measured, enabling us to see how, and potentially why, it has changed over that 'time'. Such studies are an aspect of *computer simulation*, which we have already met in economic reconstruction. They are exemplified by the work of Doran (e.g. 1982), and Zubrow (e.g. 1975), who has used a *carrying capacity* model to examine cultural change. It is clearly preferable if the simulation is capable of generating archaeological 'expectations' which may be recognised in the real-life evidence. For instance, if the simulation shows that after a century towns have got larger but rural settlement has ceased to exist, this is a pattern which field archaeology might be able to recognise (e.g. Irwin *et al.* 1990).

Another form of mathematical approach is to employ mathematical concepts in archaeological explanation. There have been four examples where this has been especially important in the development of archaeological theory: the 'wave of advance' model, systems theory, catastrophe theory, and the use of non-linear dynamics.

The wave of advance model

In order to explain the transition from hunting and gathering to farming, Ammerman and Cavalli-Sforza (1979) proposed a mathematical model (the *wave of advance* model) showing how continual random movement results in the gradual spread of a characteristic across space. They suggested that, when compared to archaeological data, this explained the spread of agriculture as directionless and random, rather than by purposeful migration. This random movement, known as a wave of advance, was not derived from observing archaeological data but from a mathematical procedure used to simulate the spread of a characteristic in biology.

Systems theory

Systems theory has also been used to explain cultural change (e.g. Clarke 1968; Flannery 1968; Renfrew 1972, 1973a, and 1984; Plog 1975), having been introduced into the 'New Archaeology' in the 1960s. It proposes that the total (the *system*), in our case 'a culture', is comprised of many parts (*sub-systems*). In archaeology these may be economy, social organisation, psychology, environment and religion, etc., each interacting with all the others to a greater or lesser degree. These interactions can be measured by examining *feedback* between the sub-systems. Feedback consists of inputs promoting stability or change. That promoting stability is called *negative feedback*, that promoting change *positive feedback*. When a system changes from one set of relationships between the sub-systems and another, each successive set of relationships are taken together to form the *trajectory* of the system. If, however, there is no change in the relationship between the sub-systems, the system is said to be *homeostatic* (staying the same).

In systems theory, the total system is geared towards equilibrium, and will balance its sub-systems so as to achieve this. It is possible to define many kinds of equilibrium, some including dynamic change within the system, others total stability.

Systems theory was an important way of explaining cultural change in the 'New Archaeology', alongside evolutionary and ecological approaches (e.g. Clarke 1968; Flannery 1968; Renfrew 1972; Plog 1974). It was considerably modified, especially by Renfrew (see Renfrew 1984; Renfrew and Bahn 1991, 411-12, 420-2), making a conceptual framework rather than a mathematical procedure for analysis (when it is used in this form it is called 'systems-thinking').

Two specific qualities of systems are of special interest in explaining change: the *multiplier effect* and the concept of *hypercoherence* (Flannery 1972). The basis of both of these is simple to understand. The multiplier effect (see Renfrew 1984) operates when change in one sub-system promotes change in another (or others), which in turn promotes further change in the original sub-system. Change is, therefore, 'multiplied' by this process. Hypercoherence occurs when the stability of a system depends upon the maintenance of an exact relationship between its constituent parts. That is, the parts are so integrated with each other that change in any of them will lead to sudden change in them all. This has proved an important concept in understanding the collapse of complex societies.

Systems theory affords an opportunity to build explanations based on endogenous change. It is also a convenient way of thinking about inter-relationships between what might at first seem unrelated aspects of, for example, a society or economy. Obviously, every sub-system does not affect every other in every culture in such a way as to modify it, and systems concepts have often been found more useful than the mathematical application of hard-and-fast systems-based explanations. Post-processualists have criticised systems theory for being functionalist, i.e. for claiming that culture serves a function in relation to society, usually regulatory in some way. There is, however, no reason why concepts from systems thinking should imply a functionalist outlook, and systems need not be used only within explanations stressing equilibrium or adaptation.

Post-processualists have also considered that systems theory has left little space for individuals, cognition and symbolic behaviour. Consequently, systems theory has tended to be seen as 'old-fashioned' and outmoded by most archaeological theorists who are post-processualist in outlook. Even most processualists would not claim to depend on systems theory to explain cultural change. Systems thinking, however, retains a central role in many processualist explanations, even if it is not explicitly stated as such.

Catastrophe theory

As systems theory waned, a new mathematical theory of change gained ground in processualist writing (Renfrew 1979a, 1984; Zeeman 1982). This is *catastrophe theory*. Although it requires some complex mathematics, the basis of catastrophe theory is very simple: that a build-up of minor factors promoting change can suddenly overload the system (to put it in 'systems' terms) and cause rapid collapse, before a new level of stability is reached. It is simply the old story about the last straw breaking the camel's back, put into mathematical terms.

Catastrophe theory has been shown to have very wide application outside archaeology. It is certainly capable of modelling rapid decline in many spheres of life, even stock-market collapse! In archaeology, it has mainly been linked to the work of Renfrew (1979a, 1984), who has shown it to have the potential to explain rapid cultural collapse and sudden changes in innovation.

Renfrew has produced a catastrophe theory model of the collapse of state societies which has achieved widespread acclaim and seems to have a broad applicability. Although there are historical and archaeological problems which make this model unlikely to be a full explanation of the situations in which it has been used, it has probably been the most influential mathematical model in archaeology since systems theory was introduced. This is especially true of historical archaeology, where there has been perhaps the most interest in Renfrew's approach (discussed in Dark forthcoming).

Other scholars – perhaps intimidated by the complexity of the mathematical basis of catastrophe theory, attracted by the rise of post-processualism at about the same time as Renfrew proposed this model – have not used catastrophe theory to explain change. It has been conspicuously absent from explanations of prehistoric change after Renfrew's own work.

Non-linear dynamics

The most recent development in the application of mathematical concepts to archaeological explanation has been the use of *non-linear dynamics* to attempt to explain change. Non-linear dynamics, sometimes called *chaos theory* (after one aspect of the field), is founded on the assumption that the initial state of a system is crucial to its development, and that a complex pattern of interrelationships exists between factors, so that seemingly unrelated factors can cause major fluctuations. For this reason, seemingly random patterns can be shown to exhibit regularities, and highly unstable and irregular development can be modelled. Usually combined with computer simulation, and sometimes referred to as 'dynamical modelling', few studies of this type have yet been published that are relevant to archaeologists (but see Segraves 1982; Allen 1982; Dendrinos and Sonis 1990). Applications in history and geography have indicated the potential of this approach. It is, however, too early in the application of non-linear dynamics to archaeology to assess its impact on archaeological explanation.

Non-mathematical approaches to explanation

Of course, by far the majority of archaeological explanations do not employ mathematical concepts, at least not explicitly. Most culture-historians and post-processualists consider such concepts inappropriate to archaeological explanations. Among processualists too there are many alternative approaches to explaining change.

Archaeological explanations of change can be grouped under five headings: evolutionary, biological, Marxist, historically specific, and individualist (or cognitive). Another major division exists between explanations which allow for freedom of choice and those which are determinist in character. Determinists argue that there is no freedom of choice: a non-human factor – such as climate, geography, or economic relations – determines or necessitates the way culture changes.

Cultural evolution

The view that societies evolve like organisms is about as old as the theory of evolution itself (for some more recent views, see Friedman and Rowlands 1978; Dunnell 1980; Mithen 1989; Spencer 1990; Yoffee 1993; Kosse 1994). Evolution is usually seen as occurring by gradual change over time in response to outside pressures, or as a result of internal stimuli which cause such pressures from within. The process of change is generally explained by *adaptation* to changed circumstances, and the general direction of change is considered progressive (e.g. the approach of Martin and Plogg 1973). This *progress paradigm*, often found in evolutionary approaches, has a long history of its own and is sufficiently embedded in modern Western thought as to become part of many concepts of change.

Evolutionary approaches to cultural change have been particularly associated with mathematical models of change (such as systems models) and with ecological explanations, but they are not themselves based on either mathematical concepts or ecological relationships in every case. However, it is perhaps unsurprising that evolutionary explanation has been closely connected in archaeology with both systems models and ecological theory, as evolution, systems theory and ecology are closely linked in other disciplines – notably, of course, biology (e.g. by Bordes 1971).

Recent approaches employing cultural evolution have included Flannery and Marcus's cognitive-processual study *The Cloud People*, which has the telling sub-title *Divergent Evolution of the Zapotec and Mixtec Civilisations* (1983), a work often used as an epitome of processualist models of explanation. This work is especially important in that it shows that evolutionary approaches need not involve the rejection of cognitive archaeology.

Few would doubt that cultural evolution was characteristic of the 'New Archaeology' of the 1960s, as in the work of Binford and of Plog. To many 'New Archaeologists', cultural evolution seemed to hold the answer, alongside an ecological approach, to explaining cultural transformation.

Cultural evolution has been rejected by post-processualists on the grounds of being deterministic, *mechanistic* (i.e. treating human culture as if mechanical), *dehumanising* (denying the humanity of the people it studies), and functionalist: processualists have also had their doubts about this approach (e.g. Daly 1978; Shennan 1993). While all these charges are capable of substantiation with regard to 'New Archaeological' cultural evolutionary explanation, Flannery and Marcus's work indicates that cultural evolution does not necessitate any such attitudes. Despite this, many post-processualists have considered these aspects intrinsic to the use of such concepts, and cultural evolutionary explanation today seems somewhat 'old fashioned', as does systems theory, to many archaeological theorists.

Cultural evolution can, therefore, be seen as a characteristic processualist explanation of change, mostly found in the functional-processualist school where it has been closely linked to processualist uses of ecological theory, systems theory and mathematical models of explanation. It is still widely found among functional-processualist writers, especially in the USA (for a European example, Kristiansen 1991), but seldom in modern culture-historical writing or in post-processualist explanations.

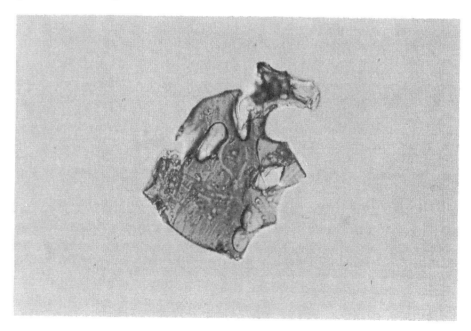

44. Environmental explanation. Volcanic eruptions produced dust clouds leading to crop failure and famine, so potentially having wide-ranging impacts. The photograph shows a piece of this dust (tephra) from the Orkney islands. (Photo: S.P. Dark)

Biological approaches

While evolution is in origin a biological concept, more directly biological approaches to explaining cultural change have often been adopted by archaeologists. The most widespread has been an ecological approach, usually either environmental or demographic, but sociobiology has also occasionally been used in this way (e.g. Dunnell 1980; Shennan 1991).

Environmental explanation

Environmental explanations have usually been either determinist or combined with some other form of explanation. Environmental determinists believe that some aspects of the environment (or several together) determine all human cultural change. That is, free-will (the ability consciously to choose) is an illusion and all action and thought is a product of human relationships with the environment in the past or present, i.e. of ecological relationships.

Environmental determinists are sometimes known as ecological determinists or, if they claim that environment determines by means of adaptation or natural selection, their approach is called an *ecological evolutionary* view (e.g. Gall and Saxe 1977). Such views may place precedence on plant or animal resources or on factors such as rainfall, terrain, sea-level, climate or land-quality. To many, ecological determinism is not the result of a single factor: it is the whole environment which causes cultural change (e.g. Kottak 1972; Welinder 1975, 1977, 1979, and 1983). They stress the connection between cultural and ecological change and seek to correlate the two chronologically and specifically in order to link them in terms of cause and effect (make a *causal link*). Such an approach, using the whole of the environment as explanation, is often called a *holistic* view. Recently, Jones (1992) has attempted to formalise such an approach in the use of the concept of food-webs: the relationship between animals and plants in terms of food resources. By locating past peoples in the food-web they can be related to ecological processes of change, which can in turn be used to explain cultural change.

An ecological evolutionary approach, and environmental determinism, were key aspects of the 'New Archaeology' in the 1960s, and persist in modern processualist studies. But ecological approaches and environmental determinism have a far longer history, even in archaeology, going back to the work of scholars such as Fox.

Today, ecological approaches to explanation are less favoured by processualist scholars, especially cognitive-processualists such as Renfrew, but the importance of ecological factors playing a part in (but not determining) cultural change is recognised by many archaeologists (Zubrow 1975).

Ecological determinism is still to be found in some functional-processualist studies, such as the work of Barker (1981). Ecological approaches have, however, had a subtler, but noticeable, role in culture-historical explanations. An example of the latter is the standard explanation of the Anglo-Saxon migration to England given by culture-historians, as the result, at least in part, of the flooding of the northern European lowlands (e.g. Hawkes 1989). Post-processualists have strongly opposed ecological explanation – unsurprisingly, given its often anti-individualist and determinist basis and strong connection with the 'New Archaeology' (e.g. Thomas 1988).

Demographic change

Changes in the number, health or distribution of people in the landscape have also been used to account for change. Often this has been linked to ecological or technological explanations, as in Wittfogel's famous 'hydraulic hypothesis' for the origin of state societies (Wittfogel 1957). Explanation, in Wittfogel's view, lay in the development of irrigation and water-movement strategies capable of supporting larger populations in a single location.

The more usual use of demographic explanation has also seen society as an adaptation to larger, or smaller, population numbers. So if the population rises, the institutions and settlements it supports will be larger – thus, it is argued, bringing about cultural change.

Another view is to adduce gradual decrease in the fertility of the population brought about through pollution, lifestyle or social organisation (e.g. Jones 1979). As the population declines, so social organisation, again, is supposed to adapt to it.

Alternatively, sudden decline can be argued to have been caused by drought (e.g. Bryson *et al.* 1974) or disease, as in Wacher's (1974, 414-22) well-known interpretation of the end of Roman towns. Wacher argued that Roman towns, as population concentrations, were disproportionately affected by plagues, which caused their numbers to decrease both because fear of disease caused an exodus of their residents and because of the death of the remaining populace. So, it is adduced, towns were no longer viable as settlements and disappeared from the landscape.

Another interpretation, of a similar form, is the explanation for social mobility reflected in archaeological sites by reference to the Black Death (on this see Platt 1978, 91-137). Because the plague killed off a disproportionate number of people in specific classes or locations, the survivors could take advantage of the gaps it produced in the range of available services and specialists in society, and in the settlement pattern.

Similar explanations are often employed to explain rises in the number of fortified sites, attributing these to social stress caused by depopulation, or plague, or disorder in a stressed society. The absence of settlement sites of a specific period – such as the late Bronze Age in Europe – has been explained by sudden demographic decline (Burgess 1985, 1989). This decline may be linked to ecological factors such as crop failure, brought about as a result of volcanic dust veils, as in Baillie's recent interpretation (Baillie 1989, 1992, 1994; Baillie and Munro 1988). This serves to emphasise that demographic change is closely linked as a form of explanation to ecological approaches.

Once the most common type of demographic explanation, but now seldom found, is explanation by reference to the migrations of peoples. Closely connected with the culture-historical school and with the concepts of diffusion and of the 'archaeological culture', this is now favoured by few processualist or post-processualist scholars as a way of explaining cultural change.

Some 'New Archaeologists' in the 1960s and 1970s hoped to use demography in a deterministic and law-like way to understand social change, but (perhaps because of this) it is an argument that is seldom used today in post-processualist studies. But demographic factors are occasionally assigned significance in post-processual archaeology, as in Parker-Pearson's (1984) interpretation of change in prehistoric Denmark.

Archaeologists have also used forms of explanation originating from outside archaeology and derived from the writing of history (*historiography*): the Annaliste approach and Marxism. Both of these schools are to

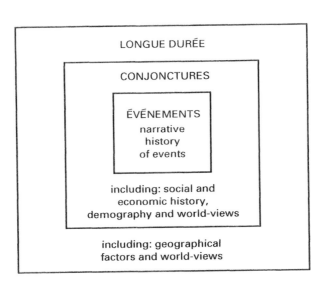

45. Time-scales used in the Annales school of explanation (see p. 180).

be found among historians, and both are based on theories of history rather than mathematics or biology.

Annales historiography and archaeology

Archaeologists have only recently become interested in the Annales school of historiography (Schnapp 1981; Lewthwaite 1987, 1988; Skeates 1990; Bintliff 1991; Knapp 1992). Annales historians, called *Annalistes*, have distinctive and important views on the study of the past. Scholars such as Braudel and contributors to the French journal *Annales*, which gives the school its name, stress the significance of studying differing processes on differing scales, both in time and place. Yet they go further to suggest that different processes operate on different scales and different sorts of explanation are applicable to them. In Braudel's view, there are three main levels: *événements*, short-term events such as those of political or military history; *conjonctures*, middle-term processes or factors, whether cognitive, social or economic; and the *longue durée*, long-term processes deriving from ecological factors, for example, and the history of world-views (*mentalities*). Bintliff has urged archaeologists to employ Annales historiography in their explanations, and there has developed a distinctive archaeological Annaliste perspective (e.g. Bintliff 1991; Knapp 1992), which has incorporated both processualists such as Lewthwaite and post-processualists such as Moreland (1992). An alternative use of Annales historiography by archaeologists has been Hodder's (1987b) *long-term history*, a post-processual approach based on the *longue durée*, studying continuities, regularities and change over long timespans, and large-scale processes such as acculturation.

By stressing a multiscalar approach and the importance of cognition alongside other factors in explanation, and by re-emphasising the role that modern historiography can play in archaeology, Annalistes have contributed much to recent theoretical archaeology. Interestingly, Annaliste perspectives have been shared by scholars from both the processual and post-processual schools.

Marxist explanations

In classical Marxism, change is explained as the outcome of underlying forces of production and exchange. These may be seen as determining social and political changes because, in a Marxist analysis, all non-economic aspects of society constitute a *superstructure* supported by, and representing, the economic relations of production and exchange. Because such economic relations are never equal, Marxist studies stress inequality, class-conflict and especially *contradictions* between the relations of production and of the distribution of wealth. These are seen as crucial factors or mechanisms in the process of change. Marxism sees history as having a discernable 'plot' or 'aim'.

Such deterministic views would be discounted as *vulgar Marxism* or *vulgar materialism* by many modern European and American Marxists. They suggest a *post-Marxist* or *Marxian* analysis in which Marx's theory is modified by the addition of social and anthropological theories such as structuralism or relativism, and are usually not in favour of a determinist view.

In archaeology, classical Marxism has been championed by scholars such as Roskams and Saunders (see Saunders forthcoming), who are strongly opposed to post-Marxist and post-processualist theories of change. They stress the closeness of their Marxist analysis to political Marxism: the Marxist-Leninist (Marxist ideology as formulated by Lenin or *Marxist-Leninism*) doctrine of the Soviet revolution. These scholars stress their opposition to the later *Stalinist* (i.e. authoritarian and intolerant) state ideology of the former Soviet Union.

Post-Marxist or Marxian scholars frequently simply refer to their own work as Marxist, and such opinions have played a major role in post-processualist archaeology. Examples include the well-known analyses undertaken by Friedman and Rowlands (1978), and Frankenstein and Rowlands (1978), who introduced the view to archaeology, and the volume edited by Spriggs (1984), and can be found in the post-processualist 'orthodoxy' (if such a term can be used of a relativistic and pluralistic school) of Shanks and Tilley (1987a, 1987b) and Hodder (1986, 1992). Less explicit post-Marxist views of change, deriving from *structural Marxism*, the combination of structuralist and Marxist theories often associated with Althusser (1977) and Godelier (1977), are found in Bradley's work (e.g. 1984), while the school of archaeology and anthropology based at University College London ('UCL') has made frequent use of the structural Marxist view in the works of its members, such as Rowlands, Bender and Thorpe (e.g. Bender 1978; Rowlands 1982, 1984, 1986, 1987; Gledhill 1984; Thorpe 1984; Thorpe and Richards 1984; Miller *et al.* 1989). Strongly associated with the *archaeological* tradition of Marxism, and unlike classical Marxism, is the reference to the social context of knowledge and a tendency toward a relativist viewpoint. Childe himself was, of course, a classical Marxist, and his modern successor, Trigger, has developed his views, somewhat independently of this school. Nevertheless, classical Marxism as viewed by Childe (1949) had some similarity with the structural Marxist approach of the 'UCL school'. Trigger (1978, 1989), the most severe contemporary critic of the 'New Archaeology' from a Marxist stance, has stressed the importance of social and intellectual history in the evaluation of archaeological theory in general and explanations in particular. In Trigger's opinion, Marxist analyses, in origin classical Marxism but with some later additions, form a starting point for the explanation of cultural change as they did in Childe's work (Trigger 1978, 1981, 1982, 1984a, 1985a, 1985b, 1985c, 1989).

The diversity of views within the Marxist tradition of archaeological explanation means that the term 'Marxist' gives, in itself, little clue as to the nature of an explanation being offered: a Marxist analysis can range from the firmly positivist to the completely relativist, from determinism to *historical particularism*, from an explanation grounded in economics and technology to one based on cognition, and from one close to the former ideology of eastern European and present Chinese governments (for the role of archaeology in Soviet Russia and communist China, see, e.g. Trigger 1989, 175-7, 212-41), to one without a stated political allegiance. It is, therefore, not enough to say that an explanation is 'Marxist' to give an account of it; one needs to say in what way it is Marxist, or what Marxism itself means in the context of that explanation. A starting point for such an approach might be the useful 'check-list' of attributes given by the sociologist Anthony Giddens for evaluating the extent to which a study, claiming to be Marxist, may be considered so (Giddens 1981).

This diffuse range of approaches has provoked a widespread reaction, even by sympathetic archaeologists, to deny the label 'Marxist' for their analyses. Alcock (1987, 3), to cite a prominent example, has, after mentioning his early interest in Marxist archaeology, stated that 'Marxism implies no more than a firm grasp of the obvious', because he considers that contemporary Marxists 'have so far diluted the theoretical content of their writings'. If this is true, it may be unhelpful to place too much importance upon the self-assigned label 'Marxist' given by scholars to their own work.

Despite this, Marxism remains a widely employed form of explanation, even in the 1980s and early 1990s when it appeared that, as Bintliff (1991) has pointed out, its (apparent) followers were deserting it in their millions world-wide. An alternative to structural Marxism is, of course, to drop the Marxist element completely and to employ explanations based on structuralist concepts alone.

Structuralist explanations

In structuralism, as we have already seen, it is supposed that universal *deep structures* exist in human cognition (Gellner 1982). These reflect themselves in the classification of, and conceptual framework for, the world around us, especially through the establishment of *binary oppositions*: light and dark, fire and water, hot and cold, up and down. Structuralism is not used in archaeology to explain change on its own, as it is a theory concerned with differences within a single timespan (*synchronic* differences). The two most explicitly structuralist analyses are, perhaps, those which have concerned vernacular architecture in Britain and America, proposed by Glassie and Johnson (Glassie 1975; Johnson 1986, 1990, 1993).

Johnson, in his study of the late and post-medieval English house, has suggested that structural change is a reflection of cultural change, on the basis of a structuralist analysis. Johnson combined such a perspective with a post-Marxist approach to the importance of social and economic relations in the explanation of change, so that even his view represents structuralism used within a broad interpretative framework.

Johnson's approach is strongly derivative of Glassie's work in the USA. Almost certainly the clearest structuralist analysis of change yet undertaken in archaeology, and the most durable in surviving criticism, Glassie's (1975) work has shown that a shift of attitudes to space is recognisable in American vernacular architecture. He has used the changing social and cognitive context as a way of explaining architectural change, so that even his analysis explains change partly in social terms, rather than wholly in terms of the conceptual structures of the mind. As Hodder (1992) has pointed out, such a view is less useful in prehistory, where the cognitive and social context is hard (or impossible) to discern, aside from the analysis of further archaeological data, itself requiring a framework for interpretation.

Structuralist analyses of the type Glassie has attempted are, therefore, less 'structuralist explanations' than social or cognitive factors using structuralist concepts of cognition and its reflection in the material world. Structuralism remains little used as an explanation of cultural change in prehistory, where there is always the difficulty of recognising the relevant contextual data.

Consequently, it has been approaches based on structuralism, or on perspectives which modify it (*post-structuralism*), which have played an important role in explaining change in post-processualist archaeology (convenient summaries of the archaeological use of structuralism and post-structuralism are provided by Hodder 1982b, 1982d, 1986; Shanks and Tilley 1987a, 1987b; Tilley 1989c; Bapty and Yates 1991). These approaches have been derived from the writings of a number of social and literary theorists outside archaeology, such as Foucault, Derrida, Bourdieu, Saussure and Barthes. Post-structuralist archaeologists, as they sometimes style themselves, have also tended to incorporate Giddens's early work in their approach, perhaps under the mistaken belief that he is himself a post-structuralist (on the misunderstanding of Giddens's theory in archaeology, see Chapter 6), and have also used a version of Collingwood's 'question and answer' approach (Hodder 1992).

Post-structuralist theorists and archaeological explanation

An essential part of the post-structuralist approach is that post-structuralist theorists do not attempt to form a limited or coherent body of theory (e.g. Deetz 1983; Hodder 1986, 1992; Bapty and Yates 1991). They represent numerous writers examining themes arising from the application and development of structuralist positions.

The five scholars listed above (Foucault, Derrida, Bourdieu, Saussure and Barthes) are among those most frequently cited by post-processual archaeologists. Foucault (1972, 1977, 1986, 1988) has emphasised the concepts of *power* and *discourse* (for archaeological applications see Barrett 1988; Hodder 1992). By 'power', Foucault meant the ability to act positively or negatively, and by 'discourse' the internalised relations of communication permitted within a field of activity, whether in the past or the present. An example of this is the forms of argument which would be acceptable within the field of 'classical archaeology'.

In archaeology, Barrett (1988) has attempted to define specific areas, or 'fields', of 'discourse' in Foucault's sense, in which separate forms of communication or activity are conducted, although, arguably, this is already implicit within the theory of discourse. Foucault has also claimed that individuality is a modern concept connected with wider issues of discourse and power, which must be seen in their social and historical contexts.

Derrida (1976, 1978, 1981a, 1981b, 1987) aims to disassemble 'structure' in both the past and the present – in his terms, to *deconstruct* it. Understanding, in Derrida's view, comes through this process, and he places special importance on *difference* – the 'space' between something which is perceived and its mental or linguistic symbol. To Derrida, a key for understanding this is his concept of *iteration*: by which he means repetition.

The work of Bourdieu has also been important in post-processual thinking in archaeology (especially Bourdieu 1977). He has suggested a 'theory of practice' in which attention would be given to the difference between observation and interpretation and participation (see Hodder 1986, 1992). Bourdieu developed the concept of *habitus*, or the structuring principles capable of generating strategies and enabling the individual to cope with unexpected situations. To Bourdieu, habitus is a logic of practice and a body of knowledge relevant to it; it is unconscious and incapable of being reduced to a set of rules. Habitus lies at the basis of behavioural regularity because of the situation of the individual in society, and is transmitted by participation from generation to generation, both structuring action and being changed by it. A major attraction to archaeologists has been that Bourdieu relates habitus to material culture: for him, because habitus is learnt through participation in culture (*enculturation*), including in the material world, it is possible to speak of 'the mind borne of the world of objects' (Bourdieu, 1977, 91).

Saussure (1959), writing from the viewpoint of linguistic theory, emphasised the *signifier* as distinct from the *signified*. The signifier is the symbol or word for the signified; for example, the word 'axe' and the axe itself. Saussure stresses the arbitrariness of the relationship between the signifer and signified. Only context can reveal this relationship, while the practical working out of language (*parole*) and its grammatical structures (*langue*) stand in a reflexive relationship. To Saussure, *synchronic* analysis is more important than that through time (*diachronic* analysis). Foucault, on the other hand, stresses development, which he understands in terms of *genealogies*, or patterns of relationship through time.

Other linguistic concepts have played an important part in the development of post-structuralist theory in archaeology. For example, Barthes's (1977) work, stressing the contrast between the 'obvious' meaning of language (*denotation*), and its ideological meaning (*connotation*), has been employed to suggest that the 'text' which, it will be recalled, in post-processualist archaeology (following Ricoeur 1971) is understood to be the archaeological material, is open to multiple readings of equal validity. It also distances the author from the text, so that the author's understanding of what is written is no more true than that of the reader. In archaeological terms, one way of 'reading the past' is as true as any other. Likewise, Saussure's work has encouraged the search for symbolism and the examination of the relationship between symbols and their use.

Post-processualist archaeologists have also been interested in the theoretical products of the so-called 'Frankfurt School', who developed what is referred to as *critical theory* (e.g. Leone *et al.* 1987; Shanks and Tilley 1987a; Hodder 1986, 174-80, 1992; for a sceptical view, see Graves 1991). Vincent (1982), outside post-processual archaeology, has independently developed this stance. Similar to many of the scholars so far mentioned in this section, 'critical theorists' hold that all knowledge is historically constrained and subjective. They claim that research within existing frameworks has a 'reactionary' character, supporting the systems of domination in society. 'Critical theory' sees such frameworks in terms of an 'ideology of control' used for maintaining dominance in the contemporary world, and it seeks to break away from them through understanding what has been concealed in order to control society: what 'critical theorists' call a *hermeneutic* approach. As used in archaeology, 'critical theory' places importance on the social and political context of knowledge and asserts that science attempts to impose control on society. It shares with many other schools of post-structuralist thought the view that all knowledge is value-laden (i.e. expresses the values of those interpreting the past or the present), and that the representation of the past is ideological.

Post-structuralist interpretations share at least some of the following views: that the present and the past stand at a distance from the observer; the relativity of individuality, perception and expression; and the political content of action, analysis, communication and the means by which these are achieved. Such approaches can be made to fit either a post-Marxist or a relativist standpoint, or concepts derived from some of these theories can be used in a 'literary theory' of archaeological explanation, seeing material culture and its change as representing a changing material text. Most scholars employing such theories have, therefore, stressed that no single explanation or interpretation is possible. They have argued that there is no restricted range of ways to analyse material – in their view this 'opens up' material culture to simultaneous, even contradictory, interpretations. It is the task of archaeologists to interpret change, as much as it is their task to interpret any other aspect of material culture, but no single interpretation, or even single approach to interpretation, is 'correct'. Explanation is reduced to a discussion of possible explanatory methods, political critique, or a personalised process specific to each 'reader' of the material record. Hodder has suggested that the text produced by an archaeologist itself stands separate from that archaeologist's own interpretation, while proposing to introduce a self-conscious style of writing adopting a personalised and rhetorical tone.

Such views have, in general, met with a very critical reaction from scholars outside the post-processual movement. Younger scholars, such as Tarlow, who have tried to use literary theory in archaeology, have themselves been keen to distance their work from the extremes of this approach. It is also frequently pointed out by processualists that very few detailed and extensive studies have attempted to employ post-structuralist analyses in archaeological explanation. The synchronic nature of many of these approaches does not encourage such analyses, but recently book-length studies by Hodder (1990); Thomas (1991a) and Barrett (1994) have been published. Post-processualist writers have countered such criticisms by polemic, stressing the 'reactionary' character of their opponents and pointing to the relationship between the 'archaeological establishment' and viewpoints critical of their (supposedly radical) opinions. They have also stressed the generation gap which separates most post-processualists from many of their processualist critics, although by no means all their critics are 'reactionary', part of the archaeological establishment, or belong to an older generation (Bell 1990). It is, therefore, worth looking at an example of how post-processualist explanations can be formulated using post-structuralist theory. It seems appropriate to use one of the longest and most detailed studies of this school, produced by the archaeologist usually credited with its foundation, Ian Hodder.

Hodder has attempted to employ a post-structuralist approach to explaining the origins of the Neolithic period in Europe. To do so he has introduced two concepts, *domus* and *agrios* (Hodder 1990). The domus encompasses the world of the home, the controlled and the cultivated. The agrios, conversely, is the outside, the wild or savage. Hodder intends these terms to be broad and loose in their meaning, in accordance with his overall approach. Hodder's text also reflects his approach: it is personalised in its tone, self-critical and rhetorical. Hodder is keen to express doubt, to incorporate gender relations in his explanation, and to stress the ambiguity of the material record, in accordance with views widely expressed by post-processual scholars. In practice, Hodder shows how he can illustrate the use of the concept of domus, the taking into the world of the house and home of the uncultivated exterior, to explain the emergence of Neolithic culture. Instead of concentrating on the domestication of animals and plants, he tries to show how the agrios was itself 'domesticated' – that is, brought into the world of the domus. A series of case studies is presented in which evidence of burials, structures, artefacts and settlements is interpreted within this theme. In 'reading' material culture in this way, Hodder wishes to stress symbolic and cognitive changes rather than economic or technological developments. The resulting text is very different from what might be produced by, for example, a culture-historical or classical Marxist view and, of course, contrasts with a processualist explanation.

Other post-structuralist archaeologists have attempted to use Kuhn's concept of *paradigm-shift* (see Chapter 1) as a way of explaining change. Change is seen as a change between cognitive structures, as it is in Hodder's view, although here these are explained in terms of historical particularism. There are, of course, scholars who favour historical particularism as a mode of explanation independent of all other approaches, and this has, as already mentioned, been strongly associated with the culture-historical school.

Historical particularism and contextual explanation

Historical particularism, that using historically specific explanation (sometimes called culture-historical explanation), is explanation in terms of the immediate circumstances contemporary with, and preceding, the event to be explained (e.g. Piggot 1965). For this reason it is sometimes referred to as 'historical' explanation, but this seems to me a misleading and confusing term, suggesting a connection with written sources or with a concern for sequence, aspects of explanation common to many, for example cognitive processualist, approaches.

Popular among both culture-historians and post-processualists, historically specific explanation is claimed as a correlate of the universal distinctiveness (and location within a specific set of cultural and temporal circumstances) of each event. All history is, therefore, made up of events which can only be explained in relation to their situation in time and space. No other form of explanation is adequate.

Examples are plentiful in recent culture-historical studies. Hawkes (1986) and Higham (1992) use this approach to explain the Anglo-Saxon conquest of central southern England, and Frere (1987) adopts it in discussing Roman Britain. A closely-related approach is Hodder's contextual archaeology, where this discusses change (see Chapter 2). In contextual archaeology, the explanation of change is as 'a fuller type of description': i.e. the more detailed description of the circumstances of the context account for change.

Processualist scholars tend not to favour historically-specific explanation or a contextual approach even as an element in otherwise generalising explanations (an example of the reaction is Flannery 1967). Some scholars in this school do employ historical-specifics to explain individual action or short-term change, but the use of historically-specific explanation is not generally part of processual explanations of long-term or large-scale change.

The attraction of particularistic explanation to post-processualists is obvious: it avoids generalisation and determinism, it stresses the individuality and plurality of events, and it is easily compatible with relativism. Every event is unknown because each event is different. The past was always different from the present, so analogy by ethnographic generalisation can never inform us about the past, only about the observed event, and even then there are problems of preconception and perception. Perhaps, say such scholars, the only events we truly understand are those in which we participate, and we may not even understand them.

Processualists, too, have been interested in the role of the individual in

46. **Individuals and change.** This well at Chedworth Roman villa (Gloucestershire) was used in pagan religion but later Christianised, as symbols carved on the stone slabs surrounding it show. Here, individual actions and changes in beliefs brought about a different use of the same feature. (Photo: S.P. Dark)

the explanation of change. We saw in Chapter 6 that the archaeology of the individual has a long history in processualist theory. Since the 1970s, whether in conjunction with mathematical or ecological approaches, or as part of an independent view, individualistic explanation has played a major part in processualist thought. Although it has often been supposed that this derives from post-processualist theory, its origins lie in the 'New Archaeology' of the 1960s and 1970s, from which both it and post-processualism can be said to have originated. When criticising processualist approaches, post-processualists have tended to overlook this school of explanation, even though it is now central to Renfrew's cognitive-processual approach.

Individualist approaches to explanation

The 'great man' approach to explaining change is often criticised by archaeologists. Apart from the possible objection to the use of the term 'man', the concept that 'great' people have a decisive effect on cultural change is frequently disputed by Marxist, cultural evolutionary, ecological and other archaeological theorists. Yet some leading theorists, such as Hodges (1989), have stressed the importance of specific innovators or political/religious leaders.

Few would doubt that some figures in the past continue to play a role in society and ideology, and the concept that individuals can effect long-term change is to be differentiated from the concept that all change is explicable in such a way. The latter approach (the 'great man' theory) can be contrasted with an individualistic approach to explanation in which people can bring about change, or individuals (not necessarily with political, or other, rank) can have an effect on the course, or process, of change. Ideology can, of course, also motivate individuals (for an important study using ideology in a cognitive-processual explanation, see Hedeager 1992b). Closely related to this individualist approach is the view that society cannot be considered a separate entity from the individuals comprising it. Therefore, all social change involves change enacted through individuals, and consequently the possibility for individualistic causes of that change has to be admitted.

Obviously, classical Marxists or structuralists might disagree with this point of view, as do ecological determinists – although there is less disagreement about the role of the individual among the latter. Yet individualist explanations play a part in processual, post-processual, and culture-historical archaeology, and increasingly few archaeologists would discount the role of the individual in the explanation of change.

Individualistic explanations have generally included analysis of decision-making or innovation, because these seem the most obvious ways in which individuals can bring about or change events. Modern ecological theory, for example, allows for individualistic action within ecological or evolutionary explanations (e.g. Mithen 1989).

Outside an ecological approach, individualistic explanation has been combined with elements drawn from structuration theory and information exchange theory (for which see below) to explain widespread, near-simultaneous change. As already mentioned, other (individualist) analyses include work by Hodges (1982) and Renfrew (1984), who use individual choice and innovation in systems theory and economic archaeology contexts. Flannery and Marcus (1983) have employed an individualistic approach alongside cultural evolution in their work.

As a viewpoint held by several younger scholars, and common to most of the principal theoretical schools, this approach may play a larger role in the future development of archaeological explanation than at present. It is also, interestingly, an area in which archaeology seems to be at the forefront of theoretical development.

Information-exchange

Very closely related to individualistic explanation has been the study of information-exchange as a means of explaining cultural change. Following early leads in the 'New Archaeology' (e.g. Rathje 1975; Wobst 1977), it is van der Leeuw (1981a, 1981b, 1982, 1983; van der Leeuw and Torrence 1989) who has 'set the agenda' in this field of theoretical writing.

Van der Leeuw has used organisational and social psychological theory to develop his own model of the transfer of information (*information flow*) through social structures. In his model, he views the scale of society as closely related to information-exchange networks, so that the greater the scale of a society the more efficient and complex the information-exchange network needs to be. Using this perspective, he has proposed a *vortex model*, explaining cultural change in these terms, the resulting diagrams of the flow of information giving the model its name.

Information-exchange has been employed to explain social collapse through inadequacies in information-flow. It has also been used in the theory of *peer-polity interaction* to explain the emergence of similar cultural forms in adjacent areas following contact between similar political groups (Renfrew and Cherry 1986).

These views have recently been developed alongside individualistic explanation into the *macrodynamic model* (Dark forthcoming). In this explanatory framework, information-exchange, including interaction is seen as important in the process of long-term change, and the rate of change is argued to be proportional to the rate of interaction. While the process of change can be modelled in this way, short-term change and events are unable to be modelled, being *contingent*: that is, they are dependent upon historically specific circumstances.

Cyclical change

A significant element of the macrodynamic approach, and a major concern of cognitive processual archaeologists in general, has been the recognition of cycles, or recurrent patterns, of change in the past and present. To the Annaliste scholar this has been encompassed within the theory of *conjonctures*, while others have suggested economic long-waves or models integrating decision-making and information exchange to produce regularities of this sort (for a review of recent work, see Dark forthcoming). This approach is shared by Marxist and evolutionary perspectives (e.g. Parker Pearson 1984; Kristiansen 1991) from which standpoints scholars have attempted to recognise cycles of change, while mathematical and ecological approaches have also been used in this way. The identification of cyclical change is common to many of the schools of explanation so far mentioned, constituting an important common ground between otherwise conflicting theoretical approaches.

Diffusion and invasion

There are, then, many possible ways of explaining change which have been employed in archaeology since the 1960s. Many of these approaches have been used in conjunction with one another, and elements of many others have been utilised by scholars taking different approaches. To conclude this chapter I shall return to a frequent theme of theoretical debate over the last thirty years: what role we assign to migration, innovation and acculturation in the explanation of cultural change.

In a *diffusionist* explanation, cultural change is said to occur because a characteristic has been transferred from one area to another (e.g. Rouse 1972). This may occur as a result of migration (a *migrationist* explanation) bringing a group of people into an area previously occupied by another group, or because of contact between groups, spreading out knowledge across space (see Adams *et al.* 1978). The latter has many obvious analogies – gas diffusion in air, or ink in water.

Diffusion formed the principal means of explanation among culture-historians before the 1960s. Renfrew (1973b) dealt the theory a serious blow by exposing its weaknesses compared to new data available from radiocarbon dating. Whereas diffusionist explanations supposed a gradual spread from a core area and, therefore, that the earliest instances of a given attribute would be in its originating 'core', Renfrew (1973b) showed that new dating evidence disagreed with this interpretation in regard to key case-studies in prehistory.

The 'New Archaeologists' totally rejected diffusion as a means of explaining culture-change. Nevertheless, this concept continues to be used (for a recent debate on the topic, see Kristiansen 1989; Damm 1991; Champion 1990).

47. Diffusion and culture change. Diffusion was once used to explain the distribution and similarity of megaliths such as this at Trethevy Quoit (Cornwall). (Photo: S.P. Dark)

A somewhat related view is the use of invasion as an explanation of cultural transformation. This is most clearly seen in historical archaeology both in Europe and elsewhere. The Romans, Anglo-Saxons, Vikings and Normans are all claimed to have transformed British culture, and in America the European 'invasion' of South America is seen as transforming local culture there. Such instances may be difficult or impossible to refute, but what of invasions in prehistory?

Whereas prehistorians of the culture-historical school talked of invasions alongside migrations and diffusion, this concept, too, is now out of fashion, and even those post-processualists, who might hope to return to much of culture-historical reasoning, have ceased to talk about invasion. Obviously, invasion may be hard to differentiate from peaceful migration, and both are certainly 'catch-all' terms incorporating many different processes. But the fate of invasion as a form of explanation has, if anything, been even more abrupt and total in its removal from the writing of prehistory than has diffusion, and it is uncertain whether it should have been so totally jettisoned.

Innovation

The immediate successor to diffusion as a widespread explanation of change was often *independent innovation*. This is simply the concept that people in different places, at different times, can, without contact, invent the same things. Especially associated with Renfrew (1973b), independent innovation was noted by him to have occurred in relation to megaliths and monumental complexes on islands, and in relation to metallurgy in Europe and the Mediterranean. To demonstrate independent innovation most convincingly, Renfrew has sought to show how it occurred in locations incapable of contemporary contact.

F   *Discontinuity and Long-Term Change*

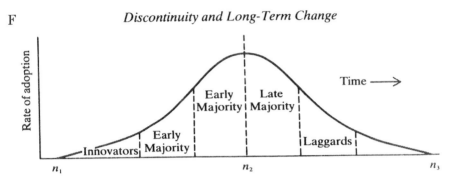

48. **Innovation theory.** Expected pattern of adoption of an innovation over time. (Reproduced with the kind permission of Professor Colin Renfrew)

The independent innovation model has become the dominant concept of explanation in prehistory, but has made little headway in historical archaeology. To take an interesting case study: John Manley (1987) has built upon Aileen Fox's (1976) work to show that Iron-Age hill-forts in Europe were closely paralleled by contact-period hill-forts in New Zealand, and social similarities also existed between the Iron-Age British Celts and contact-period Maoris. Obviously, what would in European terms be Iron-Age contact between the two areas is absurd, so that independent innovation must explain the similarities found in such diverse areas.

The concept of independent innovation is now widely accepted in archaeology, but it has been stressed that it does not preclude other forms of innovation, or other explanations of change. Renfrew himself has suggested many alternatives (e.g. Renfrew 1984).

This is, then, one of the few theoretical concepts which has not come under severe attack in recent years. It is also a key element in much processualist explanation.

Spratt (e.g. 1989), and Renfrew (1984) have introduced *innovation theory* into archaeology, while *critical-path analysis* had already been applied by Clarke (1968). Recently, work by several scholars (collected together in van der Leeuw and Torrence 1989) has realised the greater potential implicit in innovation theory, introducing concepts of risk and experimentation, as well as considering contexts in which innovation can occur accidentally.

Innovation has, then, been a central concept in archaeological explanation since the 1970s, and continues to be so. Recent developments include extending innovation theory to cover *soft cultural forms* (such as social organisation) as well as *hard cultural forms* (such as new types of artefacts), and the greater use of mathematical models, such as catastrophe theory and non-linear dynamics.

Acculturation

Recently much attention has been focussed on the concept of *acculturation* (e.g. Brandt and Slofstra 1983; Parrington and Widerman 1986). Acculturation is culture change which occurs when one group adopts the culture of another group, among whom it lives. So, when a native Briton adopted Roman ways, or a Roman Briton living in Anglo-Saxon England adopted Anglo-Saxon ways, this is called acculturation.

Archaeologically, acculturation has been recognised in burial contexts, as at Wasperton (Cleary 1989, 201-2) where a Romano-British cemetery was replaced by an Anglo-Saxon cemetery on the same site, but the Anglo-Saxon cemetery was characterised by the adoption or continuation of Romano-British burial customs in 'Anglo-Saxon' burials, and of 'Anglo-Saxon' burial customs in burials in the Romano-British style. Consequently, seen as a sequence through time, this cemetery can be claimed to represent an 'acculturating' population.

Acculturation is a useful tool for discussing colonial or migrant societies, and for examining change alongside interpretations involving collapse, rapid transformation, invasion or diffusion. Nevertheless, acculturation does represent a sort of internal 'diffusion' within a society, involving specific cultural concepts and attributes, and a form of information-exchange (van der Leeuw 1983). This process has been harder to identify in settlement studies, but is widely recognised – albeit implicitly – as the way in which *romanisation* (the adoption of Roman ways by non-Romans) occurred in the Roman Empire.

Also implicit in acculturation is the concept of 'strong' and 'weak' cultures or customs. This sees some cultural attributes as having a greater potential for endurance in circumstances of competition and stress than others. Such attributes with a high potential for endurance are considered 'strong', those with a low endurance potential, 'weak'. This characterisation can be disputed on various grounds: some would see it as associated with political or cultural élitism or imperialism, others would consider that it is merely a reflection of our own perception of the 'strengths' and 'weaknesses' of past cultures, and yet others would regard it as a circular argument (if a characteristic does not survive it is 'weak', so it did not survive because it was 'weak', etc.). It is probably fair to say that, unlike acculturation, this concept has found little support among modern theorists.

Conclusion

No area of theoretical debate has been as hotly disputed as the explanation of culture change. All the major theoretical schools have been associated with a specific range of approaches to this subject. While these approaches contrast greatly and are frequently incompatible, there are many overlaps and some agreement about what it is important to explain.

Conclusion

In this overview I have only been able to mention a few of the main themes of theoretical archaeology. Demographic studies, the analysis of style, of technology, of urbanism, and of the public presentation and management of archaeology and its sources, have all been other important topics of contemporary theoretical archaeology, considered here only in passing, if at all.

To me, however, there seem to be five broad themes which have emerged while writing this book, and which, without ending on too biased a note, may be worth mentioning, if only as a basis for further debate.

(i) Theory is central to all archaeological methods and practice. It establishes the field of enquiry and the approaches of archaeologists. It forms the logic for, and affects the language used in, archaeology .

(ii) Theoretical contributions are not restricted to British and American prehistorians. Scholars of many nations and subject areas have made important contributions to the available body of theory and to its discussion: the contribution made by historical archaeologists, in particular, has been underestimated.

(iii) Although theoretical schools do exist with distinctive characteristics, many of which are contradictory, much is shared between them.

(iv) Theoretical concepts used in archaeology have often originated outside the 'core areas' of theoretical archaeology, or archaeological research, rather than within them. Modern archaeological theory frequently derives from, and is part of, theoretical themes extending past the 1960s into the nineteenth century, and across disciplinary boundaries into the social and natural sciences.

(v) The 'New Archaeology' was important for intensifying theoretical debate in archaeology and introducing a new interest in the process of explanation. The continuing nature of this debate has maintained the vigour of theoretical research.

These observations show the value of theoretical archaeology and may, I hope, encourage further theoretical work. If this book has left you feeling that you have a clearer understanding of what archaeological theory consists of, and why it is important to all archaeologists, I have achieved my aim.

Glossary

Absolute dates. Those which fix events or material culture in relation to calendar years.

Accompanied burials. Those which have artefacts included with them.

Access analysis. A method of architectural study that places importance upon the location of entrances and the flow of movement through buildings or settlements.

Acculturation. The adoption by one group of the culture of another, especially the adoption by those under the rule or domination of another group, of the culture of the ruling or dominant group.

Activity-areas. Parts of a site or landscape in which specific tasks take place, or which have special functions.

Adaptation. Change to accommodate changed circumstances.

Ad hominem. Literally, 'to the man' (the feminine would be, *ad feminam*): a judgement or evaluation based on an assessment of the individual offering an opinion or the author of a piece of work, rather than an assessment of that opinion or work on the grounds of logic, method, theory or fact, etc.

Agrios. In Hodder's terminology, the world of the wild outside. Contrasts with domus (see below).

Analogy. Comparison or metaphor.

Annalistes. Those who favour the Annales approach (see p. 180).

Applied archaeology. Archaeological methods used in the solution of problems in the modern world.

Arbitrary classification. Grouping things according to the judgement of the observer without an explicitly stated set of methods, or the application of mathematics. Also known as 'intuitive classification'.

Arbitrary stratigraphy. This is a logical impossibility: the term is used to mean the erroneous view that horizontal slices through a site approximate to chronological divisions.

Archaeological signature. Characteristics by which a something can be recognised in the archaeological record.

Ascribed value. The assignation of value on the grounds of cultural perception.

Assemblages. Groups of things found together.

Attached specialist. Craftsman or other skilled individual in the entourage of, or dependent upon, a socially superior patron or patrons.

Attributes. Traits or characteristics.

Binary oppositions. In structuralist analysis, things which are precise opposites.

Boundedness. The construction of limits between different qualities or areas, either in culture or material culture, on the grounds of cognition or cultural perception.

CPT = central place theory (see below).

C-transforms. Changes to material culture resulting from cultural factors, especially those affecting the representation of culture and material culture in the archaeological record.

Calibration. The assessment of the reliability of one set of information, or chronology, with reference to another which is considered more reliable.

Carrying capacity. Limit of what is supportable in a specific ecological or economic situation.

Catastrophe theory. A mathematical theory of sudden change.

Causal link. Connection between two or more events or processes, suggesting that one results from another.

Central places. Administrative or economic centres with dependent hinterlands.

Central place theory. A specific set of concepts developed in geography, concerning the relationship between central places in the landscape.

Chaine opertoire. The sequence or logic of production (see logic of production, below).

Chaos theory. Forms part of non-linear dynamics and is often used to stand for this. A mathematical theory of change.

Cladistic classification. A mathematical theory of taxonomy introduced into archaeology from biology.

Classical Marxism: see Marxist-Leninism.

Client: patron relations. Support of individuals (clients) by wealthier or socially superior individuals (patrons), often in return for loyalty or services.

Clients. Those dependent upon a patron in client:patron relations.

Clientship. The quality of being a client, or the system of client:patron relations.

Cognitive-processualists. Those who hold that the archaeologist must seek explanation and process using testable hypotheses, but who place importance upon the individual and cognition (including beliefs), in explanation and process.

Coin accumulations. Groups of coins resulting from a process of piecemeal addition rather than a single major deposition.

Collective burial. The deposition of bodies or parts of bodies in a single grave or burial place.

Commoditisation. Transformation into a commodity.

Commoditise. Make into a commodity.

Commodity. Something which can be bought or sold.

Commonality. Shared identity.

Competitive consumption. Acquisition or use in such a way as to display status, usually by exceeding that of others.

Competitive destruction. Deposition or other forms of removing artefacts from circulation, so as to show status.

Competitive emulation. Copying in order to demonstrate status.

Computer simulation. Use of computer program to copy cultural or natural events or processes, so as to establish likely outcomes.

Concordance. Testing by the mutual compatability of hypotheses or observations.

Conflict-minimising device. Something designed to reduce the likelihood of hostility or dispute.

Conjonctures. In Annaliste analysis, medium-term processes of change.

Connotation. In post-structuralist or post-modernist analysis, the ideological meaning of language.

Contextual approach. Testing by concordance (see above) with reference to other aspects of contemporary material culture.

Contingent. Depending upon specific circumstances, rather than general processes.

Contradictions. In Marxist analysis, contrasts promoting or constraining change. Especially those between relations of production and exchange.

Core. In world-systems analysis, the ruling or dominant zone which exploits the surrounding periphery.

Core-periphery model. Basis of world-systems analysis, a theory of the relationship between the exploiting core and exploited periphery.

Corporeal relics. Parts of the human body of saints venerated in, for example, the medieval and modern Roman Catholic church.

Corroborated. In refutationist testing, that which has survived a test in which it could have been refuted.

Critical path analysis. Examination of the sequence of events producing the separate components or elements of an invention or change.

Critical theory. Also called 'the Frankfurt School': a Marxist and post-modernist viewpoint which sees all scholarly activity as supporting the established political order.

Crop rotation. Use of parts of the landscape in a sequence, so as to avoid soil-exhaustion or other forms of land degradation.

Crop yields. The amount of useful product resulting from the cultivation of a specific crop in a given location.

Cross-dating. Formation of a sequence of relationships between assemblages in order to date those containing no intrinsically datable objects by reference to those that do.

Culture. Today, usually used to stand for all ideological, social, artistic and economic aspects of a society. Before the 1970s, generally used to mean assemblages recurring together at several sites, and supposed to be equivalent to population groups. The term 'archaeological culture' is also used to refer to the latter meaning.

Culture-historical. Approach stressing description and empirical testing, rather than explanation and process.

Currency. Coinage used in the exchange system of a specific area.

Data. Information. Note: *data* is a plural; see also *datum*, below.

Dating by association. Key approach of cross-dating, involving the assignation of a date to an otherwise undatable object, by its occurrence in an assemblage containing a datable object. Although usually applied to artefacts, this can be used to date structures and burials.

Datum. Singular of data, meaning a piece of information. Also used to mean a fixed point.

Deconstruct. In post-modernist analysis, to apply the theory of deconstruction. This is a relativistic critical procedure.

Deductive-nomological approach. The theory that the only valid explanation is in the form of universal laws. Testing, in order to form these laws, is by the formal method of a sequence: hypothesis → testable proposition → test against independent body of data.

Deep structures. In structuralist analysis, the basis for all perception and classification in the human mind.

Demonetise. To cease to use as money.

Dendrochronology. Dating using annual growth rings in wood.

Dendrograms. Tree-like diagrams showing relationships, such as a classification system.

Denotation. In post-modernist analysis, the literal or functional meaning of language.

Depositional factors. Circumstances leading to the formation of the archaeological record.

Descriptivist. Seeking only to describe, rather than to interpret or explain.

Determined (cognition or action). Necessitated by previous events or processes.

Deterministic. Processes or rules necessitating a specific outcome.

Diachronic. Through time.

Diagenesis. Change, such as decay, before burial or deposition.

Difference. In post-modernist analysis, the relationship between something which is perceived and its mental or linguistic representation.

Diffusionist. Placing importance on the spread of a characteristic from a single point of origin, in order to explain change. Usually connected with culture-historical archaeology.

Direct comparisons. Identification of similarities between one thing and another which are made in terms of specific points of alikeness, rather than metaphor or analogy.

Direct historical approach. Projection of an anthropologically described situation into an earlier period, on the grounds that the same population and culture existed in the same area at that time.

Direct trade. Contact involving exchange between one group and another without 'middle-men' or other intermediaries.

Discourse. In post-modernist analysis, usually, the internal conventions of discussion or presentation within a specific field or type of expression.

Dispersed hoards. Groups of objects once collected together and deposited as a hoard, but recovered following post-depositional separation into smaller groups or individual artefacts.

Dispersed manufactory. A system of proto-industrial manufacture based at workshops not centred at one location

Domestication. Use for farming or cultivation (of animals or crops), or taking into the world of the home, or 'taming'.

Dominance. Exercise of superiority or control of one individual, group, place, or polity, over one or more others.

Domus. In Hodder's usage, the world of the home, the cultivated, tamed, or controlled. The opposite of agrios.

Duality of structure. Giddens's term for the ability of codes of action and other 'structures' (in his terms) both to constrain individual choice and action, and to enable it.

Early cash. Money used for paying fines or taxes, as well as in market-based exchange.

Early money. Coinage used exclusively for specific high-value payments involved in exchange.

Early state module. Political unit seen as 'building block' in state-formation and considered to be always of similar size wherever it occurred (see also state-formation).

Ecological determinism. The view that relationships between humanity and the natural world control all human action.

Ecological evolutionary view. The application of biological evolution to human society and culture. This sees change as explicable in terms of relationships between humanity and the natural world, but does not view these as determining human cognition, society, etc.

Economic and social formations. Term for the relationships seen in Marxist theory between society and economy, and especially between relations of production and exchange.

Empirical. Relating to data, or to the world perceived to be external by the analyst.

Empiricism. Drawing inferences or conclusions from observations about data. Moving from observation to hypothesis or interpretation, rather than from hypothesis to testing against data.

Enculturation. The absorption or adoption of culture, usually by participation.

Endemic warfare. War which is accepted by a society as part of its conventional relationships, forming a constant part of these relationships.

Endogenous (change). Transformation from within (e.g. from within a society).

Energy expenditure. The amount of effort or quantifiable physical energy required to achieve a specific task.

Energy-flow models. Representations of the movement of energy through a biological or cultural system, e.g. by measuring energy uptake from food and expenditure through effort.

Energy input. The amount of energy expended or taken in a task.

Ethno-archaeology. Anthropological description made for the purposes of assisting archaeological interpretation.

Événements. In Annaliste theory, short-term events in which the individual can play a significant part.

Excarnation. De-fleshing of the body in mortuary practice, e.g. by exposure to animals and decay.

Exchange. Transfer of materials, or non-material culture, from one individual or group to another.

Exemplar. Basis from which copies are made.

Exhausted (soils). Drained of nutrients required to support plant growth.

Exogenous (change). Transformation originating from outside, e.g. transformation originating outside a society.

Explicitness. Clarity or description of specifics.

Exposure (of body). Placing of body, in mortuary practice, so as to facilitate decay.

Face value. A form of ascribed value, where an object used as money is worth a predesignated amount unrelated to the value of the material and labour involved in its acquisition or manufacture.

Fealty. Loyalty owed to a superior in a feudal system.

Feedback. Reflex of action or input producing stability or change (see also negative feedback and positive feedback).

Feudal. A system of ranked social relationships dependent upon rigidly enforced links of loyalty and service, forming the basis of the social structure of medieval European kingdoms.

Feudalism. The system of feudal relationships.

Focal graves. Burials attracting groups of other burials, clustered around them, often so as to be distinct from other aspects of cemetery layout.

Food-web. Relationships between plants and animals, based on the food requirements of each.

Formal classification. Grouping according to form or shape.

Formal comparison. Analogy according to form or shape.

Formalist economics. The projection of modern economic theory into the pre-modern past.

Formation processes. Factors involved in originating the archaeological record, whether before or after its deposition in the ground.

Fossilised. Used in archaeological theory to mean 'kept unchanged'.

Free will. Ability to act according to intention, without uncontrollable constraint.

Functional classification. Grouping according to use.

Functionalism. Theoretical view that utility must be the basis of all explanation.

Functional-processualists. Major school stressing explanation and the processes of change, and employing functionalism and evolution as means of explanation. Strongly associated with attempts to make archaeology a natural science, and to explain by reference to universal laws.

Genealogies. Relationships of descent, whether biological or metaphorical through time.

Generalisations. Interpretations held to have a widespead applicability, while not necessarily being universal.

Gift-exchange. Social or economic system in which services or artefacts of similar value are transferred in return for each other.

H-D approach = hypothetico-deductive approach (see below).

Habitus. According to Bourdieu, knowledge used in forming strategies and in coping with unexpected situations.

Hard cultural forms. Artefacts or material culture products.

Hermeneutic. In critical theory, the discovery of what has been hidden in order to control society.

Historical particularism. Theory that events and processes are unique both in time and space, placing emphasis on the short-term and on detailed local sequences.

Historically-specific. The explanation of change in terms of short-term and localised events.

Historiography. How history is written.

Hoards. Groups of artefacts kept or deposited together.

Holistic. Taking all factors into consideration. Used especially of taking both human and natural factors into consideration.

Homeostatic. Self-stabilising.

Hypercoherence. Over interdependence of constituent elements: for instance, of an economy. Hypocoherence usually leads to collapse when one aspect of the network of dependence fails.

Hypothetico-deductive approach. Logic for test which leads from hypothesis to testable suggestion (proposition), to comparison between the proposition and data. Seen by many as the only true scientific procedure for validating hypotheses, especially in the 'New Archaeology'.

Idealist. In Marxist theory, the view that action and culture derive from cognition rather than as a response to the relations of production and exchange in the material world. Philosophers use 'idealist' in a different sense to mean the view that existence is dependent upon belief.

Independent innovation. Discovery of same or similar thing (such as metallurgy) in different places or at different times without contact between them.

Independent specialist. Artisan outside the control of patron or social élite.

Indirect (comparisons). Analogy by generalisation, implication, metaphor or in overall terms rather than specific details.

Indirect trade. Economic exchange via a 'middle-man' or entrepreneur.

Information flow. The movement of data (true or false) through a system.

Innovation theory. Widely employed model of adoption, popularity, decline and rejection of a technological development or fashion.

In situ. In place.

Intellectual labour. Work involving mental rather than physical effort.

Intensification. Increased rate of production.

Intentionality. Having reason to act.

Interfaces. Boundaries between stratigraphical units. Also used of other boundaries outside archaeological stratigraphy.

Interpretation from within. Understanding by participants, for example by those involved in an action or event.

Intervisibility. Ability of two or more places to be seen from each other.

Intra-site analysis. Study or interpretation of evidence from within a single site, for example the distribution of pottery at a settlement.

Intrinsic value. Worth deriving from materials comprising an object or from the labour used to acquire or produce it.

Intuitive classification. Grouping according to the opinion of the analyst rather than that based upon mathematical procedures.

Iteration. Repetition assigning meaning to an action.

Land-tenure. The holding of territory.

Langue. Grammatical structures of language.

Laws of cultural dynamics. Rules relating to change in human society or economy held to be universally true.

Law of least effort. Rule that humans will expend the minimum energy to achieve any task.

Legitimacy. The right to hold a specific position in society, economy, law or land tenure.

Liminal. On the border of, or between two distinct qualities or places.

Liminality. Being in between, or on the border of, two states.

Locational analysis. Study of distribution, especially in landscape. Sometimes applied specifically to central place theory and related concepts.

Logicism. Framework of analysis stressing the construction and reasoning of archaeological analysis and interpretations.

Logic of production. Analysis of steps involved in manufacture or acquisition of artefacts or raw materials used in their fabrication.

Long-term history. Post-processualist understanding of the *longue durée* usually stressing continuities.

Long waves. Recurrent patterns of economic growth and decline identified by the economist N.D. Kondratieff.

Longue durée. In Annaliste terminology, the long term in which environment and world-views or widespread ideologies play a role in change.

Macrodynamics. Theory of change stressing relationship between the individual and long-term change.

Manufactory. Proto-industrial production site employing a compartmentalised sequence of manufacture.

Martyrium. Burial place of Christian martyr.

Marxian. Founded on Marx's interpretations. Often used of structural Marxism.

Marxist-Leninism. Classical Marxism as modified by Lenin, official government ideology of former Soviet Union.

Material culture correlates. Reflexes or implications in material terms of cognitive or social characteristics.

Materiality. The quality of being material.

Matrices. Mathematically, sets of data or networks. In archaeology also used to mean networks of stratigraphical relationships.

Meaningfully constructed text. Written or material production showing deliberate structure or purposeful construction.

Mechanistic. Like a machine.

Meliorising (strategy). Producing a successful, but not optimal, result.

Mentalities. In Annaliste terminology, world-views or widespread ideologies.

Metrology. The science of measurement.

Mickey Mouse laws. Over simple or simplistic, supposedly universal, rules.

Middle-range theory. Logic linking material data and its interpretation.

Migrationist. Placing importance upon the movement of population as a means of explaining change.

Minimalist. Making little or no interpretation.

Mobile community. Population group moving from place to place.

Mobilisation. The transfer of resources, especially from the producer to the élite.

Model. Idealised representation of reality.

Modes of production. Types of economic activity grouped according to scale and character.

Modified. Used in stratigraphy to mean a deposit which has been changed by depositional or, especially, post-depositional, factors.

Money. Coins employed in regularised economic exchange, rather than having only a symbolic or ceremonial purpose.

Monocausal (explanation). Explaining by reference to a single factor.

Monothetic classification. Grouping according to the presence or absence of a single shared characteristic

Monuments. Sites showing ceremonial or symbolic expressions of social position and ownership.

Monumentality. The quality of being a monument, or the use of monuments in a political or social strategy.

Multi-causal (explanation). Explaining by reference to many factors.

Multi-scalar approach. Examination of a problem or explanation on many levels of scale.

Multiple-working hypotheses. The use of several models simultaneously as options for testing against data.

Multiplier effect. In systems theory a feedback process where change in one sub-system causes change, usually growth or an increase in scale, in another.

Mutual benefit model. Relationship in which each participant gains.

N-transforms. Natural changes occurring in depositional or post-depositional modification of archaeological materials.

Negative evidence. Use of absence as part of argument or interpretation, for instance the absence of a pottery type from a geographical area.

Negative feedback. In systems theory input from one sub-system to another promoting stability rather than change.

Niches. Ecological contexts suitable for a specific species.

Nomads. Population groups who constantly move from one area to another.

Non-linear dynamics. A mathematical theory of change.

Numerical cladistics. Mathematical theory of classification employing set theory as a basis for grouping and employing numbers to represent attributes used in classification.

Numerical taxonomy. The use of numerical mathematics (rather than, for example, set theory) as a basis for grouping and establishing relationships between groups in classification.

Objective. Without interpretation and uncoloured by the views of the analyst.

Optimising (strategy). Seeking the best or most.

Palaeoeconomy. Study of past economics.

Palaeo-ethno-musicology. Study of past music.

Paradigms. Overall views.

Paradigm-shift. Change in paradigms.

Parole. In post-structuralist theory the working out of practice of language.

Particularism. Study of, or emphasis on, details.

Patron. Sponsor of client.

Patronage. System of having patrons.

Pattern cladists. Those favouring cladistic classification who view the resulting groups or sets as representing networks of relationship rather than sequences before the addition of other chronological data.

Peer-polity interaction. Theory of change emphasising contact between similar political units.

Peripatetic. Mobile, moving from place to place.

Periphery. In world systems analysis, territories exploited by the core both surrounding and economically dependent upon it.

Pilgrim routes. Standardised journeys made by pilgrims, often along specific roads or seaways.

Pluralism. Simultaneous existence of many, often mutually incompatible, views.

Pluralistic. System based on pluralism.

Polities. Political units or groups, especially those of large scale.

Polythetic classification. Grouping according to characteristics only some of which need to be held in common by each individual in the group.

Pollution. Uncleanliness, used both of dirt and of ritual uncleanliness.

Population dynamics. Change in numbers, age and sex structure, health and distribution of human groups.

Portable shrines. Containers for relics capable of being carried from place to place.

Ports of trade. In Polanyi's economic theory, neutral trading places situated on the borders of, or between, political units.

Positive feedback. In systems theory, input from one sub-system to another promoting change.

Positivism. Philosophical position that only that which is testable is true, and/or that all hypotheses are capable of being tested.

Post-depositional factors. Causes of modification of material evidence after deposition, such as animal burrowing and root disturbance.

Post-Marxist. Theories, often post-structuralist in character, which although relating to the work of Marx, are claimed to supersede it.

Post-modernist. Theoretical school stressing subjectivity, diversity and relativism.

Post-structuralist. Approach derived from, or superseding, that of structuralism.

Power. The ability to act, or control.

Predator: prey relationship. In ecological theory the relationship between one type of animal (the predator) and another (the prey) which forms a source of its food. A sizeable body of ecological theory exists about the relationship between predators and their prey.

Predetermined. Processes or events the outcome of which is decided before they begin.

Pre-literate. Before the use of writing.

Prestige goods. Items assigned special importance and restricted to specific types of exchange, in which it is impossible to participate without them.

Prestige goods economy. Economic system incorporating the use of prestige goods as a major element within it.

Primitive communism. Opinion that early (especially Neolithic and pre-Neolithic) societies were egalitarian.

Primitive money. Money used in exchange at peripheral markets.

Primitive valuables. Exotic items used in ceremonial exchange.

Probablistic. Based upon probability.

Productivity. Amount able to be produced.

Progress paradigm. Theory that all change eventually results in improvement or progress.

Proto-industrialisation. Economic system which exhibits many characteristics of industrialisation and may be industrialising, but has not had an industrial revolution and is not fully industrial.

Purse hoards. A group of coins forming currrency belonging to a specific individual, regardless of whether it is found within a purse.

Ranking. Social division according to individual status.

Reciprocal exchange. In Polanyi's economic theory, a system based on the giving and receiving of services or gifts of equal value.

Redistributive economy. In Polanyi's economic theory, a system based on the collection of resources and their distribution by a central individual or organisation.

Refutationist. Philosophical view that while it is impossible to prove a hypothesis, it is possible to disprove it.

Relations of production and exchange. In Marxist theory, the relationship between different parts of the economic system.

Relativists. Those who believe that it is impossible to test any hypothesis.

Relative dates. Dating based on chronological relationships instead of calendar years.

Renders. Provision of services or materials to social superior.

Render systems. Economic systems based on renders.

Residuality. The occurrence of material of an earlier date than the deposits in which it is found, in a context where this derives from disturbance of earlier layers.

Resource allocation. The partition or division of natural or material resources.

Resource expenditure. The quantity of resources required in production, or the input of resources into a task.

Romanisation. The adoption of Roman ways or material culture.

Sealed. In stratigraphical theory, a deposit unable to be modified so as to contain later material.

Seasonally. According to seasons of the year.

Seasonality. Activity or movement dependent upon the season of the year.

Secondary products revolution. Initial use of milk products.

Secondary relics. Objects which have touched corporeal relics of a saint, according to medieval and modern Roman Catholic doctrine.

Secular. Non-religious.

Sedentary. Remaining in one place throughout the year.

Segmentary (society). Having differentiation between roles and specialisms, but little or no ranking or other 'vertical' social stratification.

Semi-periphery. In world systems analysis, an intermediate zone between the core and periphery sharing characteristics of both.

Service renders. Duties owed to social superior in a render system.

Services. Assistance, duties, work, or other non-material aspects transferred in a social or economic system.

Settlement patterns. Distribution of occupation sites in the landscape, sometimes used to refer to distribution of all, or all non-mortuary, sites in the landscape.

Shape grammars. Standardised, usually geometric, codes for describing outlines, patterns, designs, decoration etc.

Shifting agriculture. Farming in which production moves location in response to depletion of soil nutrients.

Shrines. Structures used for religious observance, often employed to mean structures smaller than those designated temples, or churches. Also used for structures containing relics of saints, often within major medieval churches.

Signified. In post-structuralist theory, that which is designated by a specific term or phrase.

Signifier. In post-structuralist theory, the symbol or word designating the signified.

Site-catchment analysis. Form of locational study attempting to define the area exploited by the occupants of a site.

Site geometry. Planning involved in the layout of a settlement or other site.

Size-rank rule. Method of assigning status or importance by placing sites or artefacts in increasing order of size. The largest is assumed to be the highest status or most important.

Skeuomorphism. Representation of the functional characteristics of one type of artefact in a non-functional context on another type of artefact.

Social distance. Metaphorical expression of social relationships representing difference of, for example, rank in terms of space.

Social identity. Role or place in society.

Social philosophy. Philosophy of society; sociological philosophy.

Social storage. In a reciprocal economy, the accumulation of indebtedness by the giving of unrepaid gifts. At times of economic crises this debt is recovered to avert hardship, while it can also be used at other times to political or social advantage.

Social stress. Pressure on society resulting from, for example, warfare, economic crises, climate change or political collapse.

Socio-economic. Social and economic, or the relationship between society and economy.

Soft cultural forms. Non-material aspects of culture, such as social structure.

Source criticism. Analysis and evaluation of the value of data as evidence.

Specialist production sites. Locations, often settlements, primarily involved in crafts or other manufacturing activities. Especially those of artisans.

Sphere of exchange. Range of types of exchange for which an artefact may be employed as a means of exchange.

Sphere of interaction. Geographical zone throughout which contacts took place.

Stalinist. Relating to the Marxist theories and political activities of Stalin and the government headed by him in the former USSR.

Staple finance. Redistribution of part of subsistence production to support specialists.

State-collapse. The decline and cessation of political units considered to be 'states'.

State-formation. The origin of political units considered to be 'states'.

Stratigraphy. The study of stratification.

Structuralism. Theory of cognition stressing the importance of the structure of perception.

Structural Marxism. Combination of structuralist or post-structuralist theory and Marxism stressing the importance of ideology in pre-capitalist societies.

Structuration (theory). Theory of analysis and change viewing action as both constrained and assisted by codes of action (structures) and constraints deriving from cognitive, social, economic and environmental factors and contexts.

Structured the record. Resulted in non-random patterning, e.g. in archaeological deposits or distributions.

Structures. In structuration theory, codes of action and other cognitive, social, economic and environmental factors, which both restrict and facilitate action.

Style. The manner of execution, for example of a design.

Subjective. Involving interpretation deriving from the views of the analyst.

Subsistence economy. Production adequate to support life without producing a surplus.

Substantivist economics. Theory that pre-modern economies operated differently from modern economies.

Substructure. In Classical Marxist theory, economic foundations of non-economic life: for instance, of social organisation or change.

Sub-systems. In systems theory, the constituent parts of a system which form units of analysis in themselves: such as social organisation, economy, technology or environment.

Sufficing (strategy). Economic or other system aiming to produce sufficient, rather than an excess.

Superstition. Ritual aimed at procuring advantage or avoiding disadvantage, but not forming a broader code of living and not requiring a wider set of related beliefs.

Superstructure. In Classical Marxist theory, the non-economic reflex of economic foundations.

Surplus. Excess to requirements: for example, food production excess to the needs of the group involved in it.

Symbolic equivalence. Use of metaphor in which one thing symbolises another, e.g. a depiction of an artefact may be seen as equivalent to that artefact.

Symbolic exchange. The transfer of symbolic artefacts. Also used for exchange, which itself is symbolic.

Symbolic representation. Use of symbolism to indicate a quality, such as social identity.

Symbolic text. Structured use of symbolism to communicate information.

Synchronic. At the same time.

System. In systems theory, the unit of analysis comprising the total number of sub-systems.

Systems theory. Viewpoint, mathematical in basis, stressing analysis of the total number of components in any situation and the relationships between these.

Systems-thinking. Use of concepts from systems theory, without the formal use of systems theory or its mathematical basis.

Terminus ante quem. The last date at which a specific event could have occurred or a specific artefact could have been made.

Terminus post quem. The first date at which a specific event could have occurred or a specific artefact could have been made. In stratigraphy, usually the date of the latest sealed find in a deposit.

Theory-laden. Incorporating a theoretical component.

Thiessen polygons. Geometric shapes defining the territories appertaining to specific sites in central place theory.

Three-age system. Division of the (especially prehistoric) past into Stone, Bronze and Iron Ages.

Time-distance maps. Mapping of geographical relationships according to the time required to travel between the points involved.

Time perspectivism. Analysis using several time scales.

Traits. Characteristics or attributes.

Trajectory. Overall change or development through time.

Transhumance. Movement of agricultural or other production in response to varying environmental circumstances or seasons.

Typological conservatism. Unchanging form of a type of artefact, as a result of deliberate choice on the part of the producers.

Typology. Study of types, or grouping according to types.

Unsealed. In stratigraphical theory, a deposit capable of containing material later in date than itself.

Validation. Demonstration that a hypothesis is corroborated or given value.

Value-laden. Incorporating moral or other values.

Variables. Characteristics which may vary.

Vortex model. Information-flow model of change in complexity.

Votive hoards. Groups of artefacts deposited for religious or ritual reasons.

Vulgar Marxism. Structural Marxist term for the simplistic application of Marxist theory.

Vulgar materialism. Simplistic adherence to the Marxist superstructural-substructural theory.

Wave of advance model. Mathematical theory of the gradual spread of a characteristic.

Wealth finance. Use of currency by state to pay specialists.

World systems model. Theory of economic relationships in which an exploited periphery is economically dependent upon an exploiting core area (see also core-periphery).

Bibliography

Adams, M. 1991, 'A logic of archaeological inference', *Journal of Theoretical Archaeology* 2, 1-11

Adams, W.H. and Boling, S.J. 1989, 'Status and ceramics for planters and slaves on three Georgia coastal plantations', *Historical Archaeology* 23, 69-96

Adams, W.Y. 1983, 'The archaeologist as detective', in D.W. Lathrap and J. Davison (eds), *Variations in Anthropology* (Urbana)

————— 1988, 'Archaeological classification: theory versus practice', *Antiquity* 61, 40-56

————— and Adams, E.W. 1991, *Archaeological Typology and Practical Reality* (Cambridge)

—————, van Gerven, D.P. and Levy, R.S. 1978, 'The retreat from migrationism', *Annual Review of Anthropology* 7, 483-532

Addyman, P. 1976, 'Archaeology and Anglo-Saxon society', in G. Sieveking *et al.* (eds), *Problems in Economic and Social Archaeology* (London), pp. 309-32

Adkins, R.A., Perry, J.G., with Evans, J. 1989, '... of sherds and soil and sealing layers, of cobbling and coins ...', *Oxford Journal of Archaeology* 8, 119-29

Aitchison, N. B. 1988, 'Roman wealth, native ritual: coin hoards within and beyond Roman Britain', *World Archaeology* 20, 270-84

Aitken, M.J. 1990, *Science-Based Dating in Archaeology* (London)

Alcock, L. 1963, *Dinas Powys – an Iron Age, Dark Age, and Early Medieval Settlement in Glamorgan* (Cardiff)

————— 1971, *Arthur's Britain* (Harmondsworth)

————— 1987, *Economy, Society and Warfare among the Britons and the Saxons* (Cardiff)

Allen, P.M. 1982, 'The genesis of structure in social systems: the paradigm of self-organisation', in C. Renfrew, M.J. Rowlands and B.A. Segraves (eds), *Theory and Explanation in Archaeology: The Southampton Conference* (New York), 347-76

Althusser, L. 1977, *For Marx* (London)

Ammerman, A.J. and Cavalli-Sforza, L.L. 1979, 'A population model for the diffusion of early farming in Europe', in C. Renfrew and K.L. Cooke (eds), *Transformations: Mathematical Approaches to Culture Change* (New York), 275-94

Andah, B.W. 1983, 'No past! no present! no future! Anthropological education and African revolution', Inaugural Lecture, Department of Archaeology and Anthropology, University of Ibadan

Arnold, B. 1990, 'The past as propaganda: totalitarian archaeology in Nazi Germany', *Antiquity* 64, 464-78

Arnold, C.J. 1984, *Roman Britain to Saxon England* (London)

————— 1988, *An Archaeology of the Early Anglo-Saxon Kingdoms* (London)

Ascher, R. 1961, 'Analogy in archaeological interpretation', *Southwestern Journal of Anthropology* 17:4, 317-25

Ashbee, P. 1986, 'Ancient Scilly: retrospect, aspect and prospect', *Cornish Archaeology* 25, 186-219

Atkinson, R.J.C. 1953, *Field Archaeology*, 2nd edn. (London)

———— 1957, 'Worms and weathering', *Antiquity* 31, 219-33

Austin, D. and Alcock L. (eds) 1990, *From the Baltic to the Black Sea* (London)

Avent, R.1975, *Anglo-Saxon Garnet Inlaid and Composite Brooches* (Oxford)

Bacus, E.A. *et al.* (eds) 1993, *Gendered Past. A Critical Bibliography of Gender in Archaeology* (Ann Arbor)

Bailey, D.W. 1994, 'Reading prehistoric figurines as individuals', *World Archaeology* 25.3, 321-31

Bailey, G.N. 1981, 'Concepts, time scales and explanations in economic prehistory', in A. Sheridan and G. Bailey (eds), *Economic Archaeology* (Oxford), 97-117

———— 1983, 'Concepts in time in Quaternary prehistory', *Annual Review of Anthropology* 12, 165-92

———— 1987, 'Breaking the time barrier', *Archaeological Review from Cambridge* 6, 5-20

———— (ed.) 1983, *Hunter-Gatherer Economy in Prehistory: A European Perspective* (Cambridge)

Baillie, M.G.L. 1989, 'Do Irish Bog Oaks date the Shang Dynasty?', *Current Archaeology* 117, 310-13

———— 1991a, 'Marking in marker dates: towards an archaeology with historical precision', *World Archaeology* 23, 233-43

———— 1991b, 'Suck-in and smear: two related chronological problems for the 1990s', *Journal of Theoretical Archaeology* 2, 12-16

———— 1992, 'Dendrochronology and past environments', in A.M. Pollard (ed.), *New Developments in Archaeological Science* (Oxford), 5-23

———— 1994, 'Dendrochronology raises questions about the nature of the AD 536 dust-veil event', *Holocene* 4, 212-17

———— and Munro, M.A.R. 1988, 'Irish tree-rings, Santorini and volcanic dust veils', *Nature* 332, 344-6

Baker, F. and Thomas, J. (eds) 1990, *Writing the Past in the Present* (Lampeter)

Bapty, I. and Yates, T. (eds) 1991, *Archaeology after Structuralism* (London)

Barfoot, J. and Price Williams, D. 1976, 'The Saxon Barrow at Gally Hills, Banstead Downs, Surrey', *Surrey Archaeological Society Research Volume 3*, 59-76

Barich, B.E. 1977-1982, 'Archeologia teoretica: il problema della teoria in archeologia preistorica e nelle scienze umane', *Origini* 2, 7-44

Barker, G. 1981, *Landscape and Society: Prehistoric Central Italy* (London)

———— and Gamble, C. (eds) 1985, *Beyond Domestication in Prehistoric Europe: Investigations in Subsistence Archaeology and Social Complexity* (London)

Barker, P. 1977, *Techniques of Archaeological Excavation* (London)

———— 1986, *Understanding Archaeological Excavation* (London)

Barrett, J.C. 1987, 'Contextual archaeology', *Antiquity* 61, 468-73

———— 1988, 'Fields of discourse: reconstituting a social archaeology', *Critiques of Anthropology* 7(3), 5-16

———— 1990, 'Archaeology in the age of uncertainty', *Scottish Archaeological Review* 7, 31-7

———— 1994, *Fragments from Antiquity* (Oxford)

Bartel, B. 1982, 'A historical review of ethnological and archaeological analyses of mortuary practice', *Journal of Anthropological Archaeology* 1, 32-58

Barthes, R. 1977, *Image-Music-Text*, transl. S. Heath (London)

Bayard, D.T. 1969, 'Science, theory, and reality in the "new archaeology"', *American Antiquity* 34, 376-84

———— 1978, '15 Jahre "New Archaeology"', *Saeculum* 29, 69-109

Beaudry, M.C. (ed.) 1993, *Documentary Archaeology in the New World* (Cambridge)

Bell, J.A. 1981, 'Scientific method and the formulation of testable computer simulation models', in J. Sabloff (ed.), *Simulations in Archaeology* (Albuquerque), 51-64

———— 1982, 'Archaeological explanation: progress through criticism', in C. Renfrew *et al.* (eds), *Theory and Explanation in Archaeology* (New York), 65-72

———— 1988, 'Rationality versus relativism: a review of *Reading the Past* by Ian Hodder', *Archaeological Review from Cambridge* 7, 2

———— 1990, 'Method in spite of rhetoric', *Journal of Theoretical Archaeology* 1, 3-12

———— 1991, 'Anarchy and archaeology', in R.W. Preucel (ed.), *Processual and Postprocessual Archaeologies* (Carbondale), 71-80

———— 1992, 'Universalization in archaeological explanation', in L. Embree (ed.), *Metaarchaeology* (Dordrecht), 143-64

Bellman, R. 1979, 'Mathematics in the field of history', in C. Renfrew and K.L. Cooke (eds), *Transformations: Mathematical Approaches to Culture Change* (New York), 83-90

Bender, B. 1978, 'Gatherer-hunter to farmer: a social perspective', *World Archaeology* 19, 204-22

Bettess, F. 1991, 'The Anglo-Saxon foot: a computerized assessment', *Medieval Archaeology* 35, 44-50

Biddle, M. 1975, 'The evolution of towns: planned towns before 1066', in M.W. Barley (ed.), *The Plans and Topography of Medieval Towns in England and Wales* (London), 19-32

———— and Hill, D.H. 1971, 'Late Saxon planned towns', *Antiquaries Journal* 51, 70-85

Binchy, D.A. 1962, 'The passing of the Old Order', *Proceedings of the International Congress of Celtic Studies, Dublin, 1959*, 119-32

Binford L.R. 1962, 'Archaeology as anthropology', *American Antiquity* 28, 217-25

———— 1967, 'Smudge pits and hide smoking: the use of analogy in archaeological reasoning', *American Antiquity* 32, 1-12

———— 1971, 'Mortuary practices: their study and their potential', in J.A. Brown (ed.), *Approaches to the Social Dimensions of Mortuary Practices* (Washington), 58-67

———— 1972, *An Archaeological Perspective* (London)

———— 1978, *Nunamiut Ethnoarchaeology* (New York)

———— 1981 *Bones: Ancient Men and Modern Myths* (New York)

———— 1982, 'Meaning, inference and the material record', in A.C. Renfrew and S. Shennan (eds), *Ranking, Resource and Exchange* (Cambridge), 160-3

———— 1983a, *In Pursuit of the Past* (London)

———— 1983b, 'Historical archaeology: is it historical or archaeological', in L.R. Binford (ed.), *Working at Archaeology* (New York), 169-78

———— 1989, *Debating Archaeology* (New York)

Binford, S.R. and Binford, L.R. 1968, *New Perspectives in Archaeology* (Chicago)

Bintliff, J. 1991a, *The Annales School and Archaeology* (London)

214　　　　　　　　　　　　　　*Bibliography*

──── (ed.) 1988, *Extracting Meaning from the Past* (Oxford)
──── (ed.) 1991b, 'Post-modernism, rhetoric and scholasticism at TAG: the
current state of British archaeological theory', *Antiquity* 65, 274-8
────, Davidson, D.A. and Grant, E.G. (eds) 1988, *Conceptual Issues in
Environmental Archaeology* (Edinburgh)
Birch, E.S. and Ellaanna, L.J. (eds) forthcoming, *Key Issues in Hunter Gatherer
Research* (Oxford).
Bloch, M. 1971, *Placing the Dead* (London)
Boado, F.C. and Damm, C. 1988, 'Archaeology: science or politics? An interview
with Colin Renfrew', *Journal of Danish Archaeology* 7, 231-4
Boardman, J. and Bell, M. (eds) 1992, *Past and Present Soil Erosion* (Oxford)
Boddington, A., Garland, A.N., and Janaway, R.C. 1987, *Death, Decay and
Reconstruction: Approaches to Archaeology and Forensic Science* (Manchester)
Bogucki, P. 1989, *Forest Farmers and Stockherders* (Cambridge)
Bonney, D.J. 1972, 'Early boundaries in Wessex', in P.J. Fowler (ed.), *Archaeology
and the Landscape* (London), 168-86
──── 1976, 'Early boundaries and estates in Southern England', in P.H. Sawyer
(ed.), *Medieval Settlement: Continuity and Change* (London), 72-82
Bonnischen, R. 1973, 'Millie's Camp: an experiment in archaeology', *World
Archaeology* 4, 277-91
──── and Sorg, N. 1989, *Bone Modification* (Orono, Maine)
Boon, G.C. 1991, 'Byzantine and other exotic ancient bronze coins from Exeter', in
N. Holbrook and P.T. Bidwell (eds), *Roman Finds from Exeter*, 38-45
Bordes, F. 1971, 'Physical evolution and technological evolution in man. A
parallelism', *World Archaeology* 3, 1-5
Borillo, M. (ed.) 1975, *Les Méthodes mathématiques de l'archéologie* (Marseilles)
Bourdieu, P. 1977, *Outline of a Theory of Practice* (Cambridge)
Bowden, M. and McOrmish, D. 1983, 'The required barrier', *Scottish
Archaeological Review* 2, 76-84
Boyle, K.V. 1990, *Upper Palaeolithic Faunas from South-west France* (Oxford)
Bradley, R. 1970, 'The excavation of a Beaker settlement at Belle Tout, East
Sussex, England', *Proceedings of the Prehistoric Society* 36, 312-79
──── 1978, *The Prehistoric Settlement of Britain* (London)
──── 1984, *The Social Foundations of Prehistoric Britain: Themes and
Variations in the Archaeology of Power* (Harlow)
──── 1986, *Consumption, Change and the Archaeological Record* (Edinburgh)
──── 1989, 'Darkness and light in the design of Megalithic tombs', *Oxford
Journal of Archaeology* 8, 251-9
──── 1990, *The Passage of Arms* (Cambridge)
──── 1991, 'Ritual time and history', *World Archaeology* 23, 209-19
──── 1993, *Altering the Earth* (Edinburgh)
Braithwaite, M. 1982, 'Decoration as ritual symbol: a theoretical proposal and an
ethnographic study in Southern Sudan', in I. Hodder (ed.), *Symbolic and
Structural Archaeology* (Cambridge), 80-8
Brandt, R. and Slofstra, J. (eds) 1983, *Roman and Native in the Low Countries:
Spheres of Interaction* (Oxford)
Breeding, K.J. and Amoss, J.O. 1972, 'A pattern description language – PADEL',
Pattern Recognition 4, 19-36
Brothwell, D.R. 1963, *Digging up Bones* (London)
──── and Sandison, A.T. 1967, *Diseases in Antiquity* (Springfield)
Brown, J.A. 1981, 'The search for rank in prehistoric burials', in R. Chapman *et

al. (eds), *The Archaeology of Death* (Cambridge), 25-37

———— (ed.) 1971, *Approaches to the Social Dimensions of Mortuary Practices* (Washington)

Brumfiel, E.M. and Earle, T. 1987, 'Specialization, exchange, and complex societies: an introduction', in E. Brumfiel and T. Earle (eds), *Specialization, Exchange, and Complex Societies* (Cambridge), 1-9

———— and Fox, J.W. (eds) forthcoming, *Factional Competition and Political Development in the New World* (Cambridge)

Bryson, R.A., Lamb, A.H. and Donley, D.L. 1974, 'Drought and the decline of Mycenae', *Antiquity* 48, 46-50

Buck, C.E., Kenworthy, J.B., Litton, C.D. and Smith, A.F.M. 1991, 'Combining archaeological and radiocarbon information: a Bayesian approach to calibration', *Antiquity* 65, 808-21

Burgess, C. 1980, 'The Bronze Age in Wales', in J.A. Taylor (ed.), *Culture and Environment in Prehistoric Wales*, 243-86

———— 1985, 'Population, climate and upland settlement', in D. Spratt and C. Burgess (eds), *Upland Settlement in Britain* (Oxford), 195-230

———— 1989, 'Volcanoes, catastrophe and the global crisis of the late second millennium BC', *Current Archaeology* 117, 325-9

Butler, L. 1987, 'Symbols on medieval memorials', *Archaeological Journal* 144, 246-55

Butzer, K.W. 1971, *Environment and Archaeology*, 2nd edn. (Chicago)

———— 1982, *Archaeology as Human Ecology* (Cambridge)

Caldwell, J.R. 1959, 'The New American Archaeology', *Science* 129/3345, 303-7

———— 1964, 'Interaction spheres in prehistory', in J.R. Caldwell and R.L. Hall (eds), *Hopewellian Studies* (Illinois), 133-43

Cameron, C.M. and Tomka, S.A. (eds) 1993, *The Abandonment of Settlements and Regions* (Cambridge)

Cannon, A. 1989, 'The historical dimension in mortuary expressions of status and sentiment', *Current Anthropology* 30, 437-58

Carman, J. and Meredith, J. (eds) 1992, *Affective Archaeology* (= *Archaeological Review from Cambridge*) 9:2

Carver, M.O.H. 1986, 'Contemporary artefacts illustrated in Late Saxon manuscripts', *Archaeologia* 108, 117-43

———— 1987, *Underneath English Towns: Interpreting Urban Archaeology* (London)

———— 1988, 'In the steps of a master: Philip Barker and the future of archaeological excavation', in A. Burl (ed.), *From Roman Town to Norman Castle* (Birmingham), 11-29

———— 1989, 'Kingship and material culture in early Anglo-Saxon East Anglia', in S. Bassett (ed.), *The Origins of Anglo-Saxon Kingdoms* (London), 141-58

———— 1990, 'Pre-Viking traffic in the North Sea', in S. McGrail (ed.), *Maritime Celts, Frisians and Saxons* (London), 117-25

———— 1992a, 'The Anglo-Saxon cemetery at Sutton Hoo: an interim report', in M.O.H. Carver (ed.), *The Age of Sutton Hoo* (Woodbridge), 343-71

———— (ed.) 1992b, *The Age of Sutton Hoo* (Woodbridge)

Casey, J. 1986, *Understanding Ancient Coins* (London)

Chadwick, H.M. 1907, *Origin of the English Nation* (Cambridge)

Champion, T.C. 1985, 'Written sources and the study of the European Iron Age', in T.C. Champion and J.V.S. Megaw (eds), *Settlement and Society: Aspects of West European Prehistory in the First Millennium BC* (Leicester), 9-22

———— 1990, 'Migration revived', *Journal of Danish Archaeology* 9, 214-18

———— (ed.) 1989, *Centre and Periphery: Comparative Studies in Archaeology* (London)

Chang, K-C. (ed.) 1968, *Settlement Archaeology* (Palo Alto)

Chapman, R. 1990, *Emerging Complexity* (Cambridge)

Chapman, R., Kinnes, I. and Randsborg, K. (eds) 1981, *The Archaeology of Death* (Cambridge)

Charles-Edwards, T.M. 1976, 'Boundaries in Irish Law', in P.H. Sawyer (ed.), *Medieval Settlement: Continuity and Change*, 83-7

Cherry, J.F. 1978, 'Generalisation and the archaeology of the State', in D. Green, C. Haselgrove and M. Spriggs (eds), *Social Organisation and Settlement* (Oxford), 411-37

Childe, V.G. 1929, *The Danube in Prehistory* (Oxford)

———— 1936, *Man Makes Himself* (London)

———— 1949, *Social Worlds of Knowledge* (Oxford)

———— 1950, *Prehistoric Migration in Europe* (Oslo)

———— 1951, *Social Evolution* (New York)

———— 1979, 'Prehistory and Marxism', *Antiquity* 53, 93-5

Claassen, C. (ed.) 1992, *Exploring Gender Through Archaeology* (Madison, Wi.)

Claessen, H.J.M. 1983, 'Kinship, chiefdom and reciprocity – on the use of anthropological concepts in archaeology', in R. Brandt and J. Slofstra (eds), *Roman and Native in the Low Countries: Spheres of Interaction* (Oxford), 211-22

———— and Skalnik, P. (eds) 1984, *The Early State* (The Hague)

Clare, T. 1987, 'Towards a reappraisal of henge monuments: origins, evolution and hierarchies', *Proceedings of the Prehistoric Society* 33, 457-77

Clark, G. and Piggott, S. 1965, *Prehistoric Societies* (Harmondsworth)

Clark, J.G.D. 1939, *Archaeology and Society* (London)

———— 1952, *Prehistoric Europe: The Economic Basis* (London)

———— 1954, *Excavations at Star Carr* (Cambridge)

———— 1961, *World Prehistory* (Cambridge)

———— 1972, *Star Carr: A Case Study in Bioarchaeology* (Reading, Massachusetts)

———— 1989, *Economic Prehistory* (Cambridge)

Clarke, D.L. 1965, 'Matrix analysis and archaeology, with particular reference to British Beaker pottery, *Atti del VI Congresso Internazionale delle Scienze Preistoriche e Protoistoriche*, vol. 2, 37-42

———— 1968, *Analytical Archaeology* (London)

———— 1970, *Beaker Pottery of Great Britain and Ireland* (Cambridge)

———— 1972b, 'A provisional model of an Iron Age society and its settlement system', in D.L. Clarke (ed.). *Models in Archaeology* (London), 801-69

———— 1973, 'Archaeology: the loss of innocence', *Antiquity* 47, 6-18

———— 1978, *Analytical Archaeology*, rev. by R. Chapman (London, 2nd edn.)

———— (ed.) 1972a, *Models in Archaeology* (London)

Cleary, A.S.E. 1989, *The Ending of Roman Britain* (London)

Clifford, J. and Marcus, G. (eds) 1986, *Writing Culture: The Politics and Poetics of Ethnography* (Berkeley)

Coe, M.D. 1978, 'The churches on the Green: a cautionary tale', in R.C. Dunnell and E.S. Hall (eds), *Archaeological Essays in Honour of Irving B. Rouse* (The Hague), 75-85

Coles, B. (ed.) 1991, *Wetland Revolution in Prehistory* (London)

Coles, J.M. 1962, 'European bronze shields', *Proceedings of the Prehistoric Society* 28, 156-90

———— 1973, *Archaeology by Experiment* (London)

———— 1979, *Experimental Archaeology* (New York)

Collingwood, R.G. 1924, *Roman Britain* (Oxford)

———— 1946, *The Idea of History* (Oxford)

Combes, J.D. 1974, 'Ethnography, archaeology and burial practice among South Carolina blacks', *Conference on Historic Site Archaeology Papers* 7, 52-61

Conkey, M.W. 1982, 'Boundedness in art and society', in I. Hodder (ed.), *Symbolic and Structural Archaeology* (Cambridge), 115-28

———— and Spector, J. 1984, 'Archaeology and the study of gender' in M.B. Schiffer (ed.), *Advances in Archaeological Method and Theory* (New York), 1-38

Corillo, R.F. 1975, 'Archaeological variability – sociocultural variability', in R.A. Gould (ed.), *Explorations in Ethnoarchaeology* (Albuquerque), 73-90

Coupland, S. 1990, 'Carolingian arms and armour', *Viator* 21, 29-50

Crawford, O.G.S. 1953, *Archaeology in the Field* (London)

Crawford, S. 1991, 'When do Anglo-Saxon children count?', *Journal of Theoretical Archaeology* 2, 17-24

Cribb, R. 1991, *Nomads in Archaeology* (Cambridge)

Cullberg, C. 1968, 'On artifact analysis: a study in the systematics and classification of Scandinavian early Bronze Age material with metal analysis and chronology as contributing factors', *Acta Archaeologica Ludensia* 4, 7

D'Altoy, T. and Earle, T.K. 1985, 'State finance, wealth finance, and storage in the Inka political economy', *Current Anthropology* 26, 187-206

Dalton, G. 1977, 'Aboriginal economies in stateless societies', in T.K. Earle and J. Ericson (eds), *Exchange Systems in Prehistory* (London), 191-212

Daly, R.H. 1978, 'Dynamics, systems and epochal change', in J. Sabloff (ed.), *Simulations in Archaeology* (Albuquerque), 189-227

Damm, C. 1991, 'The Danish Single Grave culture – ethnic migration or social construction', *Journal of Danish Archaeology* 10, 199-204

Dangen, V. 1990, 'Dwarfs in Athens', *Oxford Journal of Archaeology* 9, 191-207

Daniel, G.E. 1975, *A Hundred and Fifty Years of Archaeology*, 2nd edn. (London)

———— and Renfrew, C. 1988, *The Idea of Prehistory* (Edinburgh)

Dark, K.R. 1985, 'Studying the past and improving the present', in J. Isitt (ed.), *Hemispheres* (Cambridge), 63-7

———— 1987, 'Towards a post-numerate taxonomy', *Nicolay* 47, 41-9

———— 1993, 'Roman-period activity at prehistoric ritual monuments in Britain and the Armorican peninsula', in E. Scott (ed.), *Theoretical Roman Archaeology* (Aldershot), 133-46

———— 1994a, *Civitas to Kingdom* (London)

———— 1994b, *Discovery by Design* (Oxford)

———— forthcoming (a), *The Waves of Time*

———— forthcoming (b), 'Proto-industrialisation and the end of Roman economy', in K.R. Dark (ed.), *External Contacts and the Economy of Late Roman and Post-Roman Britain*

Darwin, C. 1859, *The Origin of Species* (London)

———— 1881, *The Formation of Vegetable Mould Through the Action of Worms with Observations on their Habits* (London)

David, N. 1971, 'The Fulani compound and the archaeologist', *World Archaeology* 3, 111-31

David, N., Sterner, J. and Gavua, K. 1988, 'Why pots are decorated', *Current*

Anthropology 29, 365-89

Davidson, H.E. 1992, 'Human sacrifice in the Late Pagan Period in north-western Europe', in M.O.H. Carver (ed.), *The Age of Sutton Hoo* (Woodbridge), 331-40

Davies, W. and Vierck, H. 1974, 'The contexts of tribal hidage: social aggregates and settlement patterns', *Frühmittelalterliche Studien* 8, 223-93

Davis, L.B. and Reeves, B.O.K. (eds) 1989, *Hunters of the Recent Past* (London)

Day, S.P. 1993, 'Preliminary results of high-resolution palaeoecological analyses at Star Carr, Yorkshire', *Cambridge Archaeological Journal* 3:1, 129-40

Deagan, K. 1982, 'Avenues and inquiry in historical archaeology', *Advances in Archaeological Method and Theory* 5, 151-77

Deetz, J. 1977, *In Small Things Forgotten* (New York)

———— 1983, 'Scientific humanism and humanistic science: a plea for paradigmatic pluralism in historical archaeology', *Geoscience and Man* 23, 27-34

———— 1988, 'History and archaeological theory: Walter Taylor revisited', *American Antiquity* 53, 13-22

Deetz, J. and Dethlefsen, E. 1965, 'The Doppler effect and archaeology: a consideration of the spatial aspects of seriation', *Southwestern Journal of Anthropology* 21, 196-206

———— 1971, 'Some social aspects of New England Colonial mortuary art', in J.A. Brown (ed.), *Approaches to the Social Dimensions of Mortuary Practices* (Washington D.C.), 30-8

De Montmollin, O. 1989, *The Archaeology of Political Structure* (Cambridge)

Dendrinos, D.S. and Sonis, M. 1990, *Chaos and Socio-Spatial Dynamics* (New York)

Dennell, R. 1983, *European Economic Prehistory: A New Approach* (London)

Dent, J.S. 1983, 'Weapons, wounds and war in the Iron Age', *Archaeological Journal* 140, 120-8

Derrida, J. 1976, *Of Grammatology*, transl. G.C. Spivak (Baltimore)

———— 1978, *Writing and Difference* (London)

———— 1981a, *Positions*, transl. A. Bass (London)

———— 1981b, *Disseminations*, transl. B. Johnson (London)

———— 1987, *The Truth in Painting*, transl. G. Bennington and I. Macleod (Chicago)

Dethlefsen, E. and Deetz, J. 1966, 'Death's heads, cherubs, and willow trees: experimental archaeology in Colonial cemeteries', *American Antiquity* 31.4, 502-11

Dixon, P. 1981, 'Crickley Hill', *Current Archaeology* 76, 145-7

Dobres, M. 1988, 'Feminist archaeology and enquiries into gender relations: some thoughts on universals, origin stories and alternating paradigms', *Archaeological Review from Cambridge* 7, 30-44

Dolukhanov, P.M. 1979, *Ecology and Economy in Neolithic Eastern Europe* (London)

Dommasnes, L.H. 1992, 'Two decades of women in prehistory and in archaeology in Norway: a review', *Norwegian Archaeological Review* 25, 1-14

Donan, C.B. and Clewlow, C.W. (eds) 1974, *Ethnoarchaeology* (Los Angeles)

Doran, J. 1982, 'A computational model of sociocultural systems and their dynamics', in C. Renfrew, M.J. Rowlands and B.A. Segraves (eds), *Theory and Explanation in Archaeology* (New York), 375-88

Doran, J.E. and Hodson, F.R. 1975, *Mathematics and Computers in Archaeology* (Edinburgh)

Drennan, R.D. 1992, 'What is the archaeology of chiefdoms about?', in L. Embree (ed.), *Metaarchaeology* (Dordrecht), 53-74

Drewett, P. 1982, 'Later Bronze Age downland economy and excavations at Black Patch, East Sussex', *Proceedings of the Prehistoric Society* 48, 321-409

Dunnell, R.C. 1971, *Systematics in Prehistory* (New York)

——— 1980, 'Evolutionary theory and archaeology', in M.B. Schiffer (ed.), *Advances in Archaeological Method and Theory* (New York), 35-99

Earle, T. (ed.) 1991, *Chiefdoms: Power, Economy and Ideology* (Cambridge)

Earle, T.K. and Christensen, A.L. 1980, *Modelling Change in Prehistoric Subsistence Economies* (New York)

——— and Ericson, J.E. (eds) 1977, *Exchange Systems in Prehistory* (New York)

Edmonds, M. 1990, 'Science, technology and society', *Scottish Archaeological Review* 7, 23-30

——— and Thomas, J. 1990, 'Science fiction: scientism and technism in archaeology', *Scottish Archaeological Review* 7, 1-2

Eggers, H.J. 1950, 'Das Problem der ethnischen Deutung in der Frühgeschichte', in H. Kirchner (ed.), *Ur- und Frühgeschichte als historische Wissenschaft: Wahle Festschrift* (Heidelberg), 49-59

——— 1959, *Einführung in die Vorgeschichte* (Munich)

Eggert, M.K.H. 1976, 'On the interrelationship of prehistoric archaeology and cultural anthropology', *Prähistorische Zeitschrift* 51, 56-60

——— 1978, 'Prähistorische Archäologie und Ethnologie: Studien zur amerikanischen New Archaeology', *Berliner Jahrbuch für Vor- und Frühgeschichte* 4, 102-45

Ehrenberg, M. 1980, 'The occurrence of Bronze Age metalwork in the Thames: an investigation', *Transactions of the London and Middlesex Archaeological Society* 31, 1-15

——— 1989, *Women in Prehistory* (London)

Embree, L. (ed.) 1992, *Metaarchaeology* (Dordrecht)

Engelstead, E. 1991, 'Images of power and contradiction', *Antiquity* 65, 502-14

Evans, E.E. 1957, *Irish Folk Ways* (London)

Evans, J.D. 1973, 'Islands as laboratories of culture change', in C. Renfrew (ed.), *The Explanation of Culture Change* (London), 517-20

Evans, J.G. 1975, *The Environment of Early Man in the British Isles* (London)

Fernie, E.C. 1991, Anglo-Saxon lengths and the evidence of the buildings', *Medieval Archaeology* 35, 1-5

Fischer, J.L. 1961, 'Art styles as cultural cognitive maps', *American Anthropologist* 63, 79-93

Fisher, A.R. 1985, 'The early state module: a critical assessment', *Oxford Journal of Archaeology* 4, 1-8

Flannery, K.V. 1967, 'Culture history vs cultural process: a debate in American archaeology', *Scientific American* 217, 119-22

——— 1968, 'Archaeological systems theory and early Mesoamerica', in B. Meggers (ed.), *Anthropological Archaeology in the Americas* (Washington), 67-87

——— 1972, 'The cultural evolution of civilizations', *Annual Review of Ecology and Systematics* 3: 399-425

——— 1973, 'Archaeology with a capital S', in C.L. Redman (ed.), *Research and Theory in Current Archaeology* (New York), 47-53

——— (ed.) 1976, *The Early Mesoamerican Village* (New York)

——— and Marcus, J. (eds) 1983, *The Cloud People: Divergent Evolution of the*

Zapotec and Mixtec Civilizations (New York)

Fleming, A. 1973, 'Models for the development of the Wessex Culture', in C. Renfrew (ed.), *The Explanation of Culture Change* (London), 571-85

———— 1982, 'Social boundaries and land boundaries', in C. Renfrew and S. Shennan (eds), *Ranking, Resource and Exchange* (Cambridge), 52-5

Fletcher, J.M. and Tapper, M.C. 1984, 'Medieval artefacts and structures dated by dendrochronology', *Medieval Archaeology* 28, 112-32

Fletcher, R. 1992, 'Time perspectivism, *Annales*, and the potential of archaeology', in A.B. Knapp (ed.), *Archaeology, Annales, and Ethnohistory* (Cambridge), 35-49

Ford, R.I. 1973, 'Archaeology serving humanity', in C.L. Redman (ed.), *Research and Theory in Current Archaeology* (New York), 83-93

Foster, S.M. 1989, 'Analysis of spatial patterns in buildings (Access analysis) as an insight into social structure: examples from Scottish Atlantic Iron Age', *Antiquity* 63, 40-50

Foucault, M. 1972, *The Archaeology of Knowledge*, transl. A.M. Sheridan (London)

———— 1977, *Discipline and Punish* (New York)

———— 1986, *The History of Sexuality*, Vol, 2: *The Use of Pleasure*, transl. R. Hurley (London)

———— 1988, 'Technologies of the Self', in L. Martin, H. Gutman and P. Hutton (eds), *Technologies of the Self* (London), 16-49

Fowler, P.J. 1988/9, 'The experimental earthworks 1958-88', *Annual Report of the Council for British Archaeology* 39, 83-98

Fox, A. 1976, *Prehistoric Maori Fortifications in the North Island of New Zealand* (Auckland)

Fox, C. 1923, *The Archaeology of the Cambridge Region* (Cambridge)

———— 1932, *The Personality of Britain* (Cardiff)

Frankenstein, S. and Rowlands, M. 1978, 'The internal structure and regional context of early Iron Age society in south-western Germany', *Bulletin of the Institute of Archaeology* 15, 73-112

Frantzen, A.J. and Moffat, D. (eds) 1994, *The Work of Work: Servitude, Slavery, and Labour in Medieval England* (Glasgow)

Freid, M. 1967, *The Evolution of Political Society* (New York)

Frere, S.S. 1987, *Britannia: A History of Roman Britain*, 3rd edn. (London)

Friedman, J. 1974, 'Marxism, structuralism and vulgar materialism', *Man* 9, 444-69

———— and Rowlands, M.J. 1978, 'Notes towards an epigenetic model of the evolution of "civilisation" ', in J. Friedman and M.J. Rowlands (eds), *The Evolution of Social Systems* (London), 201-78

Fritz, J.M. 1978, 'Palaeopsychology today: ideational systems and human adaptation in prehistory', in C.L. Redman *et al.* (eds), *Social Archaeology: Beyond Subsistence and Dating*, (New York) 37-59

Fulford, M.G. 1979, 'Pottery production and trade at the end of Roman Britain: the case against continuity', in P.J. Casey (ed.), *The End of Roman Britain* (Oxford), 120-32

Gall, P.L. and Saxe, A.A. 1977, 'The ecological evolution of culture: the state as predator in succession theory', in T.K. Earle and J. Ericson (eds), *Exchange Systems in Prehistory* (New York), 255-68

Gallay, A. 1986, *L'Archéologie demain* (Paris)

———— 1989, 'Logicism: a French view of archaeological theory founded in a computational perspective', *Antiquity* 63, 27-39

Gamble, C. 1987, 'Archaeology, geography and time', *Progress in Human Geography* 11, 227-46

Gardin, J.-C. 1955, 'Problèmes de la documentation', *Diogène* 11, 107-24

———— 1978, *Code pour l'analyse des ornements* (Paris)

———— 1980, *Archaeological Constructs: An Aspect of Theoretical Archaeology* (Cambridge)

———— 1987, 'Questions d'epistémologie pratique dans les perspectives de l'intelligence artificielle', *Bulletin de la Société Française de Philosophie* 81, 69-112

———— and Peebles, C.S. (eds) 1992, *Representations in Archaeology* (Bloomington)

Garlake, P.S. 1973, *Great Zimbabwe* (London)

Garland, A.N., Janaway, R.C., and Roberts, C. 1988, 'A study of the decay processes of human skeletal remains from the parish church of the Holy Trinity, Rothwell, Northamptonshire', *Oxford Journal of Archaeology* 7, 235-52

Gathercole, P. 1984, 'A consideration of ideology', in M. Spriggs (ed.), *Marxist Perspectives in Archaeology* (Cambridge), 149-54

———— and Lowenthal, D. (eds) 1989, *The Politics of the Past* (London)

Gebauer, A.B. and Price, T.D. (eds), *Transitions to Agriculture in Prehistory* (Wisconsin)

Gellner, E. 1982, 'What is Structuralisme?', in C. Renfrew, M. Rowlands and B. Segraves (eds), *Theory and Explanation in Archaeology* (London), 97-124

Gero, J. 1985, 'Socio-politics and the woman-at-home ideology', *American Antiquity* 50, 342-50

———— and Conkey, M. (eds) 1990, *Engendering Archaeology: Women and Prehistory* (Oxford)

———— and Mazzullo, J. 1984, 'Analysis of artefact shape using Fourier series in closed form', *Journal of Field Archaeology* 11, 315-22

Gibbon, G. 1989, *Explanation in Archaeology* (Oxford)

Gibbs, L. 1987, 'Identifying gender representation in the archaeological record: a contextual study', in I. Hodder (ed.), *The Archaeology of Contextual Meaning* (Cambridge), 79-89

Giddens, A. 1981, *A Contemporary Critique of Historical Materialism* (London)

———— 1984, *The Constitution of Society: Outline of the Theory of Structuration* (Cambridge)

———— 1989, *Sociology: A Brief but Critical Introduction*, 2nd edn. (London)

———— 1992, *Human Societies: An Introductory Reader in Sociology*, 2nd edn. (Cambridge)

———— and Turner, J. (eds) 1987, *Social Theory Today* (Cambridge)

Gifford-Gonzalez, D. 1991, 'Bones are not trash: analogues, knowledge and interpretative strategies in zooarchaeology', *Journal of Anthropological Archaeology* 10, 215-54

Gilchrist, R. 1991, 'Women's archaeology? Political feminism, gender theory and historical revision', *Antiquity* 65, 248

Gjessing, G. 1975, 'Socioarchaeology', *Current Anthropology* 16, 323-42

Gladfelter, B.G. 1977, 'Geoarchaeology: the geomorphologist and archaeology', *American Antiquity* 42, 519-38

Glassie, J. 1975, *Folk Housing of Middle Virginia* (Knoxville)

Gledhill, J. 1984, 'The transformation of Asiatic formations: the case of late prehispanic Mesoamerica', in M. Spriggs (ed.), *Marxist Perspectives in Archaeology* (Cambridge), 135-48

Glob, P.V. 1969, *The Bog People: Iron Age Man Preserved* (London)

Godelier, M. 1977, *Perspectives in Marxist Anthropology* (Cambridge)

Going, C.J. 1992, 'Economic "long waves" in the Roman period? A reconnaissance of the Romano-British ceramic evidence', *Oxford Journal of Archaeology* 11, 93-117

Golvin, J.C. 1988, *L'amphithéâtre Romain: essai sur la théorisation de sa forme et ses fonctions* (Paris)

Goode, T.M. 1977, 'Explanation and the aims of historians: toward an alternative account of historical explanation', *Philosophy of the Social Sciences* 7, 367-84

Goodier, A. 1984, 'The formation of boundaries in Anglo-Saxon England: a statistical study', *Medieval Archaeology* 28, 1-21

Gosden, C. 1994 *Social Being and Time* (Oxford)

Gould, R.A. 1980, *Living Archaeology* (Cambridge)

———— (ed.) 1978, *Explorations in Ethnoarchaeology* (Albuquerque)

———— and Schiffer, M.B. (eds) 1981, *Modern Material Culture: The Archaeology of Us* (New York)

Grant, E. (ed.) 1986, *The Concept of Central Places* (Sheffield)

Graves, P. 1991, 'Relative values? Criticisms of critical theory', *Archaeological Review from Cambridge* 10, 86-93

Grebingen, P. 1978, *Discovering Past Behaviour* (New York)

Greeves, T. 1989, 'Archaeology and the Green Movement: a case for *Perestroika*', *Antiquity* 63, 659-66

Gregg, S. 1988, *Foragers and Farmers* (Chicago)

Grierson, P. 1978, 'The origins of money', *Research in Economic Anthropology* 1, 1-35

Grigson, C. and Brock, J.C. (eds) 1984, *Early Herders and their Flocks* (Oxford)

Guilbert, G.C. 1975, 'Planned hillfort interiors', *Proceedings of the Prehistoric Society* 41, 203-21

Haas, J. 1990, *The Anthropology of War* (Cambridge)

Hachmann, R., Kossak, G. and Kuhn, H. 1962, *Völker zwischen Germanen und Kelten: Schriftquellen, Bodenfunde und Namengut zur Geschichte des nördlichen Westdeutschlands um Christi Geburt* (Neumünster)

Halsall, G. 1989, 'Anthropology and the study of pre-Conquest warfare and society: the ritual war in Anglo-Saxon England', in S.C. Hawkes (ed.), *Weapons and Warfare in Anglo-Saxon England* (Oxford), 155-77

Halstead, P. and O'Shea, J. 1982, 'A friend in need is a friend indeed: social storage and the origins of social ranking', in C. Renfrew and S. Shennan (eds), *Ranking, Resource and Exchange* (Cambridge), 92-9

———— and ———— (eds) 1989, *Bad Year Economics* (Cambridge)

Härke, H. 1989, 'Early Saxon weapon burials, frequencies, distributions and weapon combinations', in S.C. Hawkes (ed.), *Weapons and Warfare in Anglo-Saxon England* (Oxford), 49-62

———— 1990, ' "Warrior graves"? The background of the Anglo-Saxon burial rite', *Past and Present* 126, 22-43

Harris, D.R. 1977, 'Alternative pathways toward agriculture', in C.A. Reed (ed.), *Origins of Agriculture* (Hague), 179-243

———— and Hillman, G.C. (eds) 1989, *Foraging and Farming: The Evolution of Plant Exploitation* (London)

Harris, E.C. 1979, *Principles of Archaeological Stratigraphy* (London)

Hart, K. 1983, 'On commoditisation', in E.N. Goody (ed.), *From Craft to Industry* (Cambridge), 38-49

Hastorf, C. 1990, 'Gender, space and food in prehistory', in J. Gero and M. Conkey (eds), *Engendering Archaeology: Women and Prehistory* (Oxford), 132-59

Haverfield, F. 1912, *The Romanisation of Britain* (Oxford)

Hawkes, C. 1973, 'Innocence retrieval in archaeology', *Antiquity* 47, 176-8

Hawkes, J. 1968, 'The proper study of mankind', *Antiquity* 42, 255-62

———— 1982, *Mortimer Wheeler, Adventurer in Archaeology* (London)

Hawkes, S.C. 1986, 'The Early Saxon period', in G. Briggs *et al.* (eds), *The Archaeology of the Oxford Region* (Oxford), 64-108

———— 1989, 'The south-east after the Romans: the Saxon settlement', in V.A. Maxfield (ed.), *The Saxon Shore* (Exeter), 78-95

Heather, P. and Matthews, J. 1991, *The Goths in the Fourth Century* (Liverpool)

Hedeager, L. 1992, 'Kingdoms, ethnicity and material culture: Denmark in a European perspective', in M.O.H. Carver (ed.), *The Age of Sutton Hoo* (Woodbridge), 279-300

———— 1992, *Iron Age Societies: From Tribe to State in Northern Europe, 500 BC to 700 AD* (Oxford)

Heider, K.G. 1967, 'Archaeological assumptions and ethnographical facts: a cautionary tale from New Guinea', *Southwestern Journal of Anthropology* 23.1, 52-64

Hempel, C.G. 1942, 'The function of general laws in history', *Journal of Philosophy* 39, 35-48

———— 1966, *Philosophy of Natural Science* (Englewood Cliffs, N.J.)

Hencken, H. 1950, 'Lagore Crannog: an Irish royal residence of the seventh to tenth century AD', *Proceedings of the Royal Irish Academy* 53c, 1-248

Henig, W. 1966, *Phylogenetic Systematics* (Urbana)

Hietala, H.J. (ed.) 1984, *Intrasite Spatial Analysis* (Cambridge)

Higgs, E.S. (ed.) 1972, *Papers in Economic Prehistory* (Cambridge)

———— (ed.) 1975, *Palaeoeconomy* (Cambridge)

Higham, N.J. 1992, *Rome, Britain, and the Anglo-Saxons* (London)

Hill, J.N. 1968, 'Broken K Pueblo: patterns of form and function', in S.R. and L.R. Binford (eds), *New Perspectives in Archaeology* (Chicago), 103-43

———— 1970, *Broken K Pueblo: Prehistoric Social Organisation in the American Southwest* (Tucson)

———— 1991, 'Archaeology and the accumulation of knowledge', in R.W. Preucel (ed.), *Processual and Postprocessual Archaeologies* (Carbondale), 42-53

———— and Evans, R.K. 1972, 'A model for classification and typology', in D.L. Clarke (ed.), *Models in Archaeology* (London), 231-73

———— and Gunn, J. (eds) 1977, *The Individual in Prehistory: Studies of Variability in Style in Prehistoric Technologies* (New York)

Hillman, G.C., Colledge, S.M. and Harris, D.R. 1990, 'Plant-food economy during the Epi-Palaeolithic period at Tell Abu Hureyra, Syria: dietary diversity, seasonality and modes of exploitation', in D.R. Harris and G.C. Hillman (eds), *Foraging and Farming: The Evolution of Plant Exploitation* (London), 240-68

Hills, C. 1978, 'The archaeology of Anglo-Saxon England in the pagan period: a review', *Anglo-Saxon England* 8, 297-329

Hines, J. 1989, 'Ritual hoarding in Migration-period Scandinavia: a review of recent interpretations', *Proceedings of the Prehistoric Society* 55, 193-205

Hingley, R. 1984, 'The archaeology of settlement and the social significance of space', *Scottish Archaeological Review* 3, 22-7

Hirst, S. 1976, *Recording on Excavations I, the Written Record* (Hertford)

Hodder, I. 1979, 'Social and economic stress and material culture patterning', *American Antiquity* 44, 446-54

————— 1982a, 'Theoretical archaeology: a reactionary view', in I. Hodder (ed.), *Symbolic and Structural Archaeology* (Cambridge), 1-16

————— 1982b, *Symbols in Action* (Cambridge)

————— 1982c, *The Present Past* (London)

————— 1984, 'Burials, houses, women and men in the European Neolithic', in D. Miller and C. Tilley (eds) *Ideology, Power and Prehistory* (Cambridge), 51-68

————— 1986, *Reading the Past: Current Approaches to Interpretation in Archaeology* (Cambridge)

————— 1987a, *The Archaeology of Contextual Meanings* (Cambridge)

————— 1987b, *Archaeology as Long-Term History* (Cambridge)

————— 1988, 'Material culture texts and social change: a theoretical discussion and some examples', *Proceedings of the Prehistoric Society* 54, 67-75

————— 1989, 'This is not an article about material culture as text', *Journal of Anthropological Archaeology* 8, 250-69

————— 1990, *The Domestication of Europe* (Oxford)

————— 1992, *Theory and Practice in Archaeology* (London)

————— (ed.) 1982d, *Symbolic and Structural Archaeology* (Cambridge)

————— 1991a, *The Meaning of Things* (London)

————— 1991b, *Archaeological Theory in Europe* (London)

————— Isaac, G. and Hammond, N. (eds) 1981, *Pattern of the Past: Studies in Honour of David Clarke* (Cambridge)

Hodges, R. 1978, 'State formation and the role of trade in Middle Saxon England', in D. Green, C. Haselgrove and M. Spriggs (eds), *Social Organisation and Settlement* (Oxford), 439-53

————— 1979, 'Trade and urban origins in Dark Age England – an archaeological critique of the evidence', *ROB* 27, 191-215

————— 1982, *Dark Age Economics* (London)

————— 1983, 'New approaches to medieval archaeology, Part 2', in D.A. Hinton (ed.), *25 Years of Medieval Archaeology* (Sheffield), 24-32

————— 1989, *The Anglo-Saxon Achievement* (London)

————— *et al.* 1978, 'Ports of trade in early medieval Europe', *Norwegian Archaeological Review* 11, 97-117

Hope-Taylor, B. 1979, *Yeavering: An Anglo-British Centre of Early Northumbria* (London)

Huggins, P.J. 1991, 'Anglo-Saxon timber building measurements: recent results', *Medieval Archaeology* 35, 6-28

Humphrey, J.H. 1986, *Roman Circuses* (London)

Hunter, M.C.W. 1971, 'The Royal Society and the origins of British archaeology: I', *Antiquity* 45, 187-91

————— 1973, 'Germanic and Roman antiquity and the sense of the past in Anglo-Saxon England', *Anglo-Saxon England* 3, 29-50

Huntingdon, R. and Metcalf, P. 1979, *Celebrations of Death* (Cambridge)

Hyenstrand, Å. 1982, *Forntida samhällsformer och arkeologiska forskningsprogram* (Riksantikvarieämbetet Sth.)

Impey, O.R. and Pollard, M. 1985, 'A multivariate metrical study of ceramics made by three potters', *Oxford Journal of Archaeology* 4 (2), 157-64

Ingersoll, D., Yellen, J.E. and MacDonald, W. (eds) 1977, *Experimental*

Archaeology (New York)

Ingold, T. 1983, 'The significance of storage in hunting societies', *Man* 18, 553-71

————, Riches, D. and Woodburn, J. (eds) 1991, *Hunters and Gatherers* (Oxford, 2 vols)

Irwin, G. 1992, *The Prehistoric Exploration and Colonisation of the Pacific* (Cambridge)

————, Bickler, S. and Quicke, P. 1990, 'Voyaging by canoe and computer: experiments in the settlement of the Indian Ocean', *Antiquity* 64, 34-50

Jochim, M. 1976, *Hunter-Gatherer Subsistence and Settlement: A Predictive Model* (New York)

Johansen, A.B. 1969, 'Hofjellsfunn ved Laerdalsvassdraget. Den teoretiske bakgrunn og de forste analyseforsok', *Årbok for Universitet i Bergen 1968* 4, 1-159

Johnson, M.H. 1986, 'Assumptions and interpretations in the study of the Great Rebuilding', *Archaeological Review from Cambridge* 5, 141-53

———— 1990, 'Late medieval houses in western Suffolk: new directions in the study of vernacular architecture', *Scottish Archaeological Review* 7, 114-20

———— 1993, *Housing Culture* (London)

Jones, G.R. 1971, 'The multiple estate as a model framework for tracing early stages in the evolution of rural settlement', in F. Dussart (ed.), *L'habitat et les paysages ruraux d'Europe* (Liege), 251-67

Jones, M.E. 1979, 'Climate, nutrition and disease: an hypothesis of Romano-British population', in P.J. Casey (ed.), *The End of Roman Britain* (Oxford), 231-51

Jones, M.K. 1992, 'Food remains, food webs and ecosystems', in A.M. Pollard (ed.), *New Developments in Archaeological Science* (Oxford), 209-19

Kamenetsky, I.S., Marshak, B.I. and Sher, Ya.A. 1975, *Analiz Arkheologicheskikh Istochnikov* (Leningrad)

Keeley, H.C.M. and Macphail, R.I. 1981, *A Soil Handbook for Archaeologists* (London)

Kelly, J.H. and Hanen, M.P. 1988, *Archaeology and the Methodology of Science* (Albuquerque)

Kent, S. 1984, *Analysing Activity Areas* (Albuquerque)

———— 1990, *Domestic Architecture and the Use of Space* (Cambridge)

———— (ed.) 1989, *Farmers as Hunters* (Cambridge)

Keur, D.L. 1941, *Big Bead Mesa* (Menasha)

Klejn, L.S. 1970, 'Archaeology in Britain: a Marxist view', *Antiquity* 44, 296-303

———— 1971, 'Was ist eine archäologische Kultur', *Ethnographisch-Archäologische Zeitschrift* 12, 321-45

———— 1973, 'Marxism, the systematic approach, and archaeology', in A.C. Renfrew (ed.), *The Explanation of Culture Change: Models in Prehistory* (London), 691-710

———— 1977, 'A panorama of theoretical archaeology', *Current Anthropology* 18, 1-42

———— 1982, *Archaeological Typology* (Oxford)

———— forthcoming (a), 'Metaarchaeology in the West', *Journal of Theoretical Archaeology* 3-4

———— forthcoming (b), 'The functions of archaeological theory', *Journal of Theoretical Archaeology* 3-4

———— (ed.) 1979, *Tipy v Kulture* (Leningrad)

————, Lebedev, G.S. and Stoljar, A.D. (eds) 1973, *Problemy Arheologii II*

(Leningrad)

Kluckhohn, C. 1940, 'The conceptual structure in Middle American Studies', in C.L. Hay (ed.), *The Maya and their Neighbours* (New York), 41-51

Knapp, A.B. (ed.) 1992, *Archaeology, Annales and Ethnohistory* (Cambridge)

Koch, J.T. 1987, 'A Welsh window on the Iron Age: Manawydan Mandubracios', *Cambridge Medieval Celtic Studies* 14, 17-52

Kosse, K. 1994, 'The evolution of large, complex groups: a hypothesis', *Journal of Anthropological Archaeology* 13, 35-50

Kottak, C.P. 1972, 'Ecological variables in the origin and evolution of African states: the Buganda example', *Comparative Studies in Society and History* 14, 351-80

Kramer, C. (ed.) 1979, *Ethnoarchaeology* (New York)

Krause, R.A. 1990, 'Ceramic practice and semantic space', *Antiquity* 64, 245

Kristiansen, K. 1989, 'Prehistoric migrations – the case of Single Grave and Corded Ware cultures', *Journal of Danish Archaeology* 8, 211-25

———— 1991, 'Chiefdoms, states and systems of social evolution', in T. Earle (ed.), *Chiefdoms: Power, Economy and Ideology* (Cambridge), 16-43

———— (ed.) 1985, *Archaeological Formation Processes: The Representivity of Archaeological Remains from Danish Prehistory* (Copenhagen)

Kroll, E. and Price, T.D. (eds) 1991, *The Interpretation of Archaeological Spatial Patterning* (London)

Kuhn, T.S. 1962, *The Structure of Scientific Revolutions* (Chicago)

Kushner, G. 1970, 'A consideration of some processual designs for archaeology as anthropology', *American Antiquity* 35, 125-32

Lagrange, M.-S. and Bonnet, C. 1978, *Les Chemins de la 'Memoria'. Nouvel essai du discours archéologique* (Paris)

———— and Renaud, M. 1984, 'Deux expériences de simulation du raisonnement en archéologie au moyen d'un système expert: le système SNARK', *Informatique et Sciences Sociales* 14, 161-88

Lane, P. 1987, 'Reordering residues of the past', in I. Hodder (ed.), *Archaeology as Long-term History* (Cambridge), 54-62

Lancaster, Sir Osbert 1947, *Classical Landscape with Figures* (London)

Laplace, G.L.L.P. 1957, 'Typologie analytique: application d'une nouvelle méthode d'étude des formes et des structures aux industries à lames et lamelles', *Quaternaria* 4, 133-64

Latham, R.G. and Franks, A.W. (eds) 1856, *Horae Ferales* (London)

Layton, R. (ed.) 1989a, *Who Needs the Past? Indigenous Values and Archaeology* (London)

———— 1989b, *Conflict in the Archaeology of Living Traditions* (London)

Lee, R.B. and De Vore, I. (eds) 1968, *Man the Hunter* (Chicago)

Leeds, E.T. 1913, *The Archaeology of the Anglo-Saxon Settlements* (Oxford)

Leigh, D. 1980, 'Ambiguity in Anglo-Saxon Style I art', *Antiquaries Journal* 63, 34-42

Lemmonnier, P. 1993, *Technological Choices* (London)

Leone, M.P. 1982, 'Some opinions about recovering Mind', *American Antiquity* 47, 742-60

———— 1986, 'Symbolic, structural, and critical archaeology', in D.J. Meltzer, D.D. Fowler and J.A. Sabloff (eds), *American Archaeology Past and Future: A Celebration of the Society for American Archaeology 1935-1985* (Washington), 415-38

———— Parker, B. and Shakel, P. 1987, 'Toward a critical archaeology',

Current Anthropology 28, 283-302

Leroi-Gourhan, A. 1943, *L'Homme la matière* (Paris)

———— 1945, *Milieu et techniques* (Paris)

Lewis, T.M. and Kneberg, M. 1941, *The Prehistory of Chickamduga Basin in Tennessee* (Knoxville)

Lewthwaite, J. 1987, 'The Braudelian Beaker: a Chalcolithic *conjoncture* in the Western Mediterranean?', in R.H. Waldren and R.C. Kennard (eds), *Bell Beakers of the Western Mediterranean* (Oxford), 31-60

———— 1988, 'Trial by durée: the application of historical-geographical concepts to the archaeology of settlement on Corsica and Sardinia', in J.L. Bintliff, D. Davidson and A. Grant (eds), *Conceptual Issues in Environmental Archaeology* (Edinburgh), 161-86

Limbrey, S. 1975, *Soil Science and Archaeology* (London)

Little, B.J. (ed.) 1992, *Text-aided Archaeology* (Boca Raton, Florida)

Longacre, W. 1964, 'Archaeology as anthropology: a case study', *Science* 144, 1454-5

———— 1970, *Archaeology as Anthropology*, Tucson: Anthropological Papers of the University of Arizona, 17

Lubar, S. and Kingery, W.D. (eds) 1993, *History From Things* (Smithsonian Institution)

Lubbock, Sir J. 1865, *Prehistoric Times* (London)

Lyman, R.L. forthcoming, *Vertebrate Taphonomy* (Cambridge)

McGhee, R. 1977, 'Ivory for the Sea Woman: the symbolic attributes of a prehistoric technology', *Canadian Journal of Archaeology* 1, 141-59

McGuire, R.H. 1992, *A Marxist Archaeology* (New York)

———— and Paynter, R. (eds) 1991, *The Archaeology of Inequality* (Oxford)

Macinnes, L. and Wickham-Jones C.R. (eds) 1992, *All Natural Things: Archaeology and the Green Debate* (Oxford)

Mackenzie, I.M. 1994, *Archaeological Theory: Progress or Posture?* (Aldershot)

Malina, J. and Vasicek, Z. 1990, *Archaeology Yesterday and Today* (Cambridge)

Malmer, M.P. 1962, 'Jungneolithische Studien', *Acta Archaeologia Lundensia* Series in 8°, 2

Mango, C. 1963, 'Antique statuary and the Byzantine beholder', *Dumbarton Oaks Papers*

———— 1986, *The Art of the Byzantine Empire 312-1452* (Toronto)

Manley, J. 1987, 'Feasting and fighting: the "connection" between Celt and Maori', *Archaeology in Clwyd* 9, 20-1

Marshak, A. 1972a, *The Roots of Civilization: The Cognitive Beginnings of Man's First Art, Symbol and Notation* (New York)

———— 1972b, 'Cognitive aspects of Upper Palaeolithic engraving', *Current Anthropology* 13, 445-77

———— 1975, 'Exploring the mind of Ice Age man', *National Geographic* 147 (1), 64-89

———— 1991, 'The Taï plaque and calendrical notation in the Upper Palaeolithic', *Cambridge Archaeological Journal* 1, 25-61

Marshall, A. and Marshall, G. 1991, 'A survey and analysis of the buildings of Early and Middle Anglo-Saxon England', *Medieval Archaeology*, 35, 29-43

Martin, P.S. and Plog, F. 1973, *The Archaeology of Arizona* (Garden City)

Meggers, B.J. 1954, 'Environmental limitation on the development of culture', *American Anthropologist* 56, 801-24

———— 1955, 'The coming of age of American archaeology', in *New Interpretations*

of Aboriginal American Culture History (Washington D.C.), 116-29
———— 1956, 'Functional and evolutionary implications of community patterning', in R. Wauchope (ed.), *Seminars in Archaeology* (Salt Lake City), 129-57
———— 1957, 'Environment and culture in the Amazon Basin: an appraisal of the theory of environmental determinism', in A. Palerm *et al.* (eds), *Studies in Human Ecology* (Washington D.C.), 71-90
———— 1961, 'Field testing of cultural law: a reply to Morris Opler', *Southwestern Journal of Anthropology* 17, 352-4
Meinander, C.F. 1981, 'The concept of culture in European archaeological literature', in G. Daniel (ed.), *Towards a History of Archaeology* (London), 100-11
Mellars, P. 1976, 'Fire ecology, animal populations and man: a study in some ecological relationships in prehistory', *Proceedings of the Prehistoric Society* 42, 15-45
———— 1985, 'The ecological basis of social complexity in the Upper Palaeolithic of south-west France', in T.D. Price and J. Brown (eds), *Prehistoric Hunter-Gatherers: The Emergence of Social Complexity* (New York), 271-97
Meltzer, D.J. *et al.* (eds) 1986, *American Archaeology Past and Future: A Celebration of the Society for American Archaeology* (Washington)
Miles, A., Williams, D. and Gardner, N. (eds) 1989, *The Beginnings of Agriculture* (Oxford)
Miller, D. 1980, 'Archaeology and development', *Current Anthropology* 21, 709-26
———— 1982, 'Explanation and social theory in archaeological practice', in C. Renfrew *et al.* (eds), *Theory and Explanation in Archaeology* (New York)
———— 1984, 'Modernism and suburbia as material ideology', in D. Miller and C. Tilley (eds), *Ideology, Power and Prehistory* (Cambridge), 37-49
———— 1985a, *Artefacts as Categories: A Study of Ceramic Variability in Central India* (Cambridge)
———— 1985b, 'Ideology and the Harappan Civilization', *Journal of Anthropological Archaeology* 4, 34-71
———— 1987, *Material Culture and Mass Consumption* (Oxford)
————, Rowlands, M. and Tilley, C. (eds) 1989, *Domination and Resistance* (London)
———— and Tilley, C. (eds) 1984, *Ideology, Power and Prehistory* (Cambridge)
Millett, M. and James, S. 1983, 'Excavations at Cowdrey's Down, Basingstoke, Hampshire, 1978-81', *Archaeological Journal* 140, 151-279
Mithen, S.J. 1989, 'Evolutionary theory and post-processual archaeology', *Antiquity* 63, 483-94
———— 1990, *Thoughtful Foragers: A Study of Prehistoric Decision Making* (Cambridge)
———— 1991a, 'A cybernetic wasteland? Rationality, emotion and Mesolithic foraging', *Proceedings of the Prehistoric Society* 57, 9-14
———— 1991b, 'Ecological interpretations of Palaeolithic art', *Proceedings of the Prehistoric Society* 57, 103-14
Mizoguchi, K. 1993, 'Time in the reproduction of mortuary practices', *World Archaeology* 25.2, 223-35
Monaghan, J. 1982, 'Modelling variations in ceramic fabric descriptions. Some theoretical observations based on a Roman example', *Bulletin of the Institute of Archaeology* 19, 119-23
Monks, G.G. 1981, 'Seasonality studies', *Advances in Archaeological Method and Theory* 4, 177-240

Moore, H.L. 1982, 'The interpretation of spatial patterning in settlement residues' in I. Hodder (ed.), *Symbolic and Structural Archaeology* (Cambridge), 74-9

———— 1986, *Space, Text and Gender* (Cambridge)

———— 1988, *Feminism and Anthropology* (Oxford)

Moore, J.A. and Keen, A.S. 1983, 'Archaeology and the law of the hammer', in J.A. Moore and A.S. Keen (eds), *Archaeological Hammers and Theories* (New York), 3-17

Moreland, J.F. 1992, 'Restoring the dialectic: settlement patterns and documents in medieval central Italy', in A.B. Knapp (ed.), *Archaeology, Annales, and Ethnohistory* (Cambridge), 112-29

Morris, C. 1993, 'Hands up for the individual! The role of attribution studies in Aegean prehistory', *Cambridge Archaeological Journal* 3, 41-66

Morris, I. 1991, 'The archaeology of ancestors: the Saxe/Goldstein hypothesis revisited', *Cambridge Archaeological Journal* 1, 147-69

———— 1991, *Burial and Ancient Society* (Cambridge)

———— 1992, *Death-ritual and Social Structure in Classical Antiquity* (Cambridge)

Myhre, B. 1987, 'Chieftains' graves and chieftains' territories in south-west Norway in the Migration Period', *Studien zur Sachsenforschung* 6, 169-88

Mytum, H. 1982, 'The location of early churches in northern County Clare', in S. Pearce (ed.), *The Early Church in Western Britain and Ireland* (Oxford), 351-60

———— 1992, *The Origins of Early Christian Ireland* (London)

Nash, D.T. and Petraglia, M.D. (eds) 1987, *Natural Formation Processes and the Archaeological Record* (Oxford)

O'Connor, T.P. 1991, 'Science, evidential archaeology and the New Scholasticism', *Scottish Archaeological Review* 8, 1-7

O'Kelly, M.J. 1982, *Newgrange, Archaeology, Art and Legend* (London)

O'Shea, J. 1981a, 'Social configurations and the archaeological study of mortuary practices: a case study', in R. Chapman *et al.* (eds), *The Archaeology of Death* (Cambridge), 39-52

———— 1981b, 'Coping with scarcity: exchange and social storage', in A. Sheridan and G. Bailey (eds), *Economic Archaeology* (Oxford), 167-83

———— 1984, *Mortuary Variability: An Archaeological Investigation* (New York)

Odner, K. 1972, 'Ethno-historic and ecological settings for economic and social models of an Iron Age society', in D.L. Clarke (ed.), *Models in Archaeology* (London), 623-51

Orme, B. 1981, *Anthropology for Archaeologists* (London)

Orton, C. 1980, *Mathematics in Archaeology* (London)

Ovrevik, S.E. 1991, 'Engendering archaeology', *Antiquity* 65, 738-41

Pader, E.-J. 1982, *Symbolism, Social Relations and the Interpretation of Mortuary Remains* (Oxford)

Parker-Pearson, M. 1982, 'Mortuary practices society and ideology: an ethnoarchaeological study', in I. Hodder (ed.), *Symbolic and Structural Archaeology* (Cambridge), 99-113

———— 1984, 'Economic and ideological change: cyclical growth in the pre-state societies of Jutland', in D. Miller and C. Tilley (eds), *Ideology, Power and Prehistory* (Cambridge), 69-92

———— and Richards, C. (eds) 1994, *Architecture and Order* (London)

Parrington, M. and Widerman, J. 1986, 'Acculturation in an urban setting', *Expedition* 28, 55-62

Patrick, J. 1974, 'Midwinter sunrise at Newgrange, Co. Meath', *Nature* 249, 517-19

Patrik, L. 1985, 'Is there an archaeological record?', in M.B. Schiffer (ed.), *Advances in Archaeological Method and Theory* (London), 27-62

Paynter, R. 1992, 'The archaeology of equality and inequality', *Annual Review of Anthropology* 21, 517-36

Peacock, D.P.S. 1982, *Pottery in the Roman World: An Ethnoarchaeological Approach* (London)

Peebles, C.S. and Kus, S.M. 1977, 'Some archaeological correlates of ranked societies', *American Antiquity* 42, 421-48

Phillips, E.D. 1974, 'The Greek vision of prehistory', *Antiquity* 60, 171-8

Piggot, S. 1965, *Ancient Europe* (Edinburgh)

Pimental, D. and M. 1979, *Food, Energy and Society* (London)

Pitt-Rivers, A.H.L.-F. 1887-98, *Excavations in Cranbourne Chase*, 4 vols (London)

———— 1906, *The Evolution of Culture and Other Essays* (Oxford)

Platt, C, 1978, *Medieval England* (London)

Plog, F.T. 1974, *The Study of Prehistoric Change* (New York)

———— 1975, 'Systems theory in archaeological research', *Annual Review of Anthropology* 4, 207-24

Polanyi, K. 1963, 'Ports of trade in early societies', *Journal of Economic History*, 30-45

————, Arensberg, C.M. and Pearson, H.W. 1957, *Trade and Market in the Early Empires* (Glencoe)

Popper, K. 1985, *Conjectures and Refutations: The Growth of Scientific Knowledge*, 4th edn. (London)

Prag, J. 1984, 'Philip of Macedon – the flesh on the bones', *Popular Archaeology* 5 (9), 8-11

————, Musgrave, J.H. and Neave, R.A.H. 1984, 'The skull from Tomb II at Vergina: King Philip of Macedon', *Journal of Hellenic Studies* 104, 65-8

Preucel, R.W. (ed.) 1991, *Processual and Post-processual Archaeologies* (Carbondale, Illinois)

Pryor, F. 1990, 'The reluctant greening of archaeology', *Antiquity* 64, 147-50

Pulsipher, L.M. 1990, 'They have Saturdays and Sundays to feed themselves', *Expedition* 32, 24-33

Raab, L.C. and Goodyear, A.C. 1984, 'Middle range theory in archaeology: a critical review of origins and applications', *American Antiquity* 49, 255-68

Rahtz, P. 1974, 'Monasteries as settlements', *Scottish Archaeological Forum* 5, 125-35

———— 1978, 'Grave orientation', *Archaeological Journal* 135, 1-14

———— 1983, 'New approaches to medieval archaeology Part 1', in D.A. Hinton (ed.), *25 Years of Medieval Archaeology* (Sheffield), 12-21

———— 1985, *Invitation to Archaeology* (Oxford)

———— 1988, 'Decision-making in the past', *Archaeological Review from Cambridge* 7.2, 210-18

————, Dickinson, T. and Watts, L. (eds) 1980, *Anglo-Saxon Cemeteries 1979* (Oxford)

———— and Watts, L. 1986, 'The archaeologist on the road to Lourdes and Santiago de Compostela', in L.A.S. Butler and R.K. Morris (eds), *The Anglo-Saxon Church* (London), 51-73

Raikes, R. 1967, *Water, Weather and Prehistory* (London)

Randsborg, K. 1992, *Archaeology and the Man-Made Material and Reality* (Aarhus)

Rathje, W.L. 1974, 'The Garbage Project: a new way of looking at the problems of archaeology', *Archaeology* 27, 236-41

———— 1975, 'The last tango in Mayapán: a tentative trajectory of production-distribution systems', in J.A. Sabloff and C.C. Lamberg-Karlovsky (eds), *Ancient Civilization and Trade* (Albuquerque), 409-48

———— 1979, 'Modern material culture studies', *Advances in Archaeological Method and Theory* 2, 1-37

Rault, S. forthcoming, 'Neolithic passage graves', *Journal of Theoretical Archaeology* 3-4

Read, D.W. and LeBlanc, S.A. 1978, 'Descriptive statements, covering laws, and theories in archaeology', *Current Anthropology* 19, 307-35

Redding, R.W. 1988, 'A general explanation of subsistence change: from hunting to food production', *Journal of Anthropological Archaeology* 7, 56-97

Redman, C.L. (ed.) 1973, *Research and Theory in Current Archaeology* (New York)

————, Berman, M.J., Curtin, E.V., Langhorne Jnr, W.T., Versaggi, N.M. and Wanser, J.C. (eds) 1978, *Social Archaeology: Beyond Subsistence and Dating* (New York)

Reece, R. 1981, 'Town and country and the end of Roman Britain', *World Archaeology* 12, 77-92

———— 1982, 'Thinking about archaeology', *Bulletin of the Institute of Archaeology* 25, 191-204

———— 1983, 'Sequence is all: or archaeology in an historical period', *Scottish Archaeological Review* 2, 113-15

———— 1984, 'The uses of Roman coinage', *Oxford Journal of Archaeology* 3, 197-210

———— 1987, *My Roman Britain* (Cirencester)

Reid, M.L. 1989, 'A room with a view: an examination of round-houses, with particular reference to Northern Britain', *Oxford Journal of Archaeology* 8, 1-39

Reilly, P. 1988, *Computer Analysis of an Archaeological Landscape* (Oxford)

Renfrew, A.C. 1972, *The Emergence of Civilisation* (London)

———— 1973b, *Before Civilisation* (London)

———— 1973c, 'Monuments, mobilization and social organization in Neolithic Wessex', in C. Renfrew (ed.), *The Explanation of Culture Change: Models in Prehistory* (London), 539-58

———— 1975, 'Trade as action at a distance: questions of integration and communication', in J. Sabloff and C.C. Lamberg-Karlovsky (eds), *Ancient Civilisation and Trade* (Albuquerque), 3-59

———— 1976, 'Megaliths, territories and populations', in S.J. de Lact (ed.), *Acculturation and Continuity in Atlantic Europe* (Bruges), 298-320

———— 1977, 'Alternative models for exchange and spatial distribution', in T. Earle and J. Ericson (eds), *Exchange Systems in Prehistory* (London), 71-90

———— 1979a, 'Systems collapse as social transformation', in C. Renfrew and K.L. Cooke (eds), *Transformations: Mathematical Approaches to Culture Change* (New York), 275-94

———— 1979b, *Problems in European Prehistory* (Edinburgh)

———— 1982, 'Explanation revisited', in C. Renfrew, M.J. Rowlands and B.A. Segraves (eds), *Theory and Explanation in Archaeology* (New York), 1-24

———— 1984, *Approaches to Social Archaeology* (Edinburgh)

———— 1985a, *Towards an Archaeology of Mind* (Cambridge)

———— 1985b, *The Archaeology of Cult* (London)

———— 1987, *Archaeology and Language* (London)

———— (ed.) 1973a, *The Explanation of Culture Change: Models in Prehistory* (London)

———— and Bahn, P. 1991, *Archaeology: Theories, Methods and Practice* (London)

———— and Cherry, J.F. (eds) 1986, *Peer-Polity Interaction and Sociopolitical Change* (Cambridge)

———— and Cooke, K. L. (eds) 1979, *Transformations: Mathematical Approaches to Culture Change* (New York)

———— and Shennan, S. (eds) 1982, *Ranking Resource and Exchange* (Cambridge)

———— and Zubrow, E.B.W. (eds) 1994, *The Ancient Mind* (Cambridge)

Reynolds, N. 1983, 'To the last syllable of recorded time', *Scottish Archaeological Review* 2, 153-5

Reynolds, P.J. 1982, 'Substructure to superstructure', in P.J. Drury (ed.) *Structural Reconstruction* (Oxford), 173-98

Richards, C. and Thomas, J. 1984, 'Ritual activity and structured deposition in Later Neolithic Wessex', in R.J. Bradley and J. Gardiner (eds), *Neolithic Studies: A Review of Some Current Research* (Oxford), 189-218

Richards, J.D. 1987, *The Significance of Form and Decoration of Anglo-Saxon Cremation Urns* (Oxford)

———— 1988, 'Style and symbol: explaining variability in Anglo-Saxon cremation burials', in S.T. Driscoll and M.R. Nieke (eds), *Power and Politics in Early Medieval Britain and Ireland* (Edinburgh), 145-61

———— 1992, 'Anglo-Saxon symbolism', in M. Carver (ed.), *The Age of Sutton Hoo* (Woodbridge), 131-47

Ricoeur, P. 1971, 'The model of the text: meaningful action considered as text', *Social Research*, 529-62

Rindos, D. 1984, *The Origins of Agriculture: An Evolutionary Perspective* (New York)

Robbins, M.C. 1966, 'House types and settlement patterns: an application of ethnology to archaeological interpretation', *Minnesota Archaeologist* 28, 3-26

Roberts, C.A., Lee, F. and Bintliff J. (eds) 1989, *Burial Archaeology: Current Research, Methods and Developments* (Oxford)

Rostow, W.W. 1978, *The World Economy* (London)

Rouse, I.B. 1970, 'Comments on *Analytical Archaeology*', *Norwegian Archaeological Review* 34, 4-12

———— 1972, *Introduction to Prehistory* (New York)

Rowlands, M.J. 1982, 'Processual archaeology as historical social science', in C. Renfrew, M.J. Rowlands and B.A. Segraves (eds), *Theory and Explanation in Archaeology* (New York), 155-74

———— 1984, 'Conceptualising the European Bronze Age and Early Iron Ages', in J. Bintliff (ed.), *European Social Evolution* (Bradford), 147-56

———— 1986, 'Modernist fantasies in prehistory', *Man* 21, 745-6

———— 1987, 'The concept of Europe in prehistory', *Man* 22, 558-9

————, Larsen, L. and Kristiansen, K. (eds) 1987, *Centre and Periphery in the Ancient World* (Cambridge)

Rowley Conwy, P. 1983, 'Sedentary hunters: the Ertebolle case', in G. Bailey (ed.), *Hunter-Gatherer Economy in Prehistory* (Cambridge), 11-126

Sabloff, J.A. (ed.) 1978, *Explorations in Ethnoarchaeology* (Albuquerque)

Saitta, D.J. 1983, 'The poverty of philosophy in archaeology', in J.A. Moore and A.S. Keene (eds), *Archaeological Hammers and Theories* (New York), 299-304

———— 1991, 'Radical theory and the processual critique', in R.W. Preucel (ed.), *Processual and Post-processual Archaeologies* (Carbondale, Illinois), 54-9

Salmon, M.H. and Salmon, W. 1982, *Philosophy and Archaeology* (New York)

Samson, R. 1989, 'Rural slavery, inscriptions, archaeology and Marx. A response to Ramsay Macmullen's "Late Roman Slavery" ', *Historia* 38, 99-110

———— 1990, *The Social Archaeology of Houses* (Glasgow)

———— 1992, 'Slavery, the Roman legacy', in J. Drinkwater and H. Elton (eds), *Fifth-century Gaul: A Crisis of Identity?* (Cambridge), 218-27

———— 1994, 'The end of early medieval slavery', in A.J. Frantzen and D. Moffat (eds), *The Work of Work: Servitude, Slavery, and Labour in Medieval England* (Glasgow), pp. 95-124

Saunders, T. (ed.) forthcoming, *Revenge of the Grand Narrative. Marxist Perspectives in Archaeology* (Aldershot)

Saussure, F. de 1959, *A Course in General Linguistics* (New York)

Sawyer, P.H. (ed.) 1976, *Medieval Settlement, Continuity and Change* (London)

Saxe, A. 1970, *Social Dimensions of Mortuary Practices*, unpublished Ph.D. thesis, University of Michigan

Schaller, G.B. and Lowther, G.R. 1969, 'The relevance of carnivore behaviour to the study of early hominids', *South-Western Journal of Anthropology* 25, 307-41

Schiffer, M.B. 1976, *Behavioural Archaeology* (New York)

———— 1987, *Formation Processes of the Archaeological Record* (New Mexico)

Schmitz, B. and Steffgen, U. (eds) 1989, *Warren sie nur schön?* (Zabern)

Schnapp, A. 1981, 'Les *Annales* et l'archéologie: une rencontre difficile', *Mélanges de l'Ecole Française de Rome, Antiquité* 93, 469-78

Schulyer, R.S. (ed.) 1980, *Archaeological Perspectives on Ethnicity in America: Afro-American and Asian American Cultural History* (New York)

Scott, B.G. 1978, 'Irish "slave-collars" from Lagore Crannog, Co. Meath', *Proceedings of the Royal Irish Academy* 78c, 213-30

Scott, E. 1990, 'A critical review of the interpretation of infant burials in Roman Britain, with particular reference to villas', *Journal of Theoretical Archaeology* 1, 30-46

———— 1991, 'Animal and infant burials in Romano-British villas: a revitalisation movement', in P. Garwood, D. Jennings, R. Skeates and J. Toms (eds), *Sacred and Profane*, 115-21

Segobye, A.K., Reid, A. and Murambiwa, I. 1990, 'Communication in archaeology: the production, consumption and status of archaeology in eastern and southern Africa', *Archaeological Review from Cambridge* 9:2, 263-74

Segraves, B.A. 1982, 'Central elements in the construction of a general theory of the evolution of societal complexity', in C. Renfrew, M.J. Rowlands and B.A. Segraves (eds), *Theory and Explanation in Archaeology* (New York), 287-300

Sellwood, L. 1980, 'Tribal boundaries from numismatic evidence', in B. Cunliffe and D. Miles (eds), *Aspects of the Iron Age in Central Southern Britain*, 191-204

Service, E. 1971, *Primitive and Social Organisation: An Evolutionary Perspective*, 2nd edition Random House (New York)

———— 1975, *Origins of the State and Civilization* (New York)

Shanks, M. 1991, *Experiencing the Past* (London)

———— and Tilley, C. 1982, 'Ideology, symbolic power and ritual communication: a reinterpretation of Neolithic mortuary practices', in I. Hodder (ed.), *Symbolic and Structural Archaeology* (Cambridge), 129-54

———— and ———— 1987a, *Social Theory and Archaeology* (Cambridge)

———— and ———— 1987b, *Re-constructing Archaeology: Theory and Practice* (Cambridge)

Shay, T. 1989, 'Israeli archaeology – ideology and practice', *Antiquity* 63, 768-72

Shennan, S.J. 1975, 'The social organisation at Branc', *Antiquity* 49, 279-88

Shennan, S. 1978, 'Archaeological cultures: an empirical investigation', in I. Hodder (ed.), *The Spatial Organisation of Culture* (London), 113-39

———— 1989, *Archaeological Approaches to Cultural Identity* (London)

———— 1991, 'Tradition, rationality and cultural transmission', in R.W. Preucel (ed.), *Processual and Post-processual Archaeologies* (Carbondale, Illinois), 107-208

———— 1993, 'After social evolution: a new archaeological agenda?', in N. Yoffee and A. Sherratt (eds), *Archaeological Theory: Who Sets the Agenda?* (Cambridge), 53-9

Shepherd, J. 1979, 'The social identity of the individual in isolated barrows and barrow cemeteries in Anglo-Saxon England', in B.C. Burnham and J. Kingsbury (eds), *Space, Hierarchy and Society* (Oxford), 47-80

Sheridan, A. and Bailey, G. (eds) 1981, *Economic Archaeology: Toward an Integration of Ecological and Social Approaches* (Oxford)

Sherratt, A.G. 1981, 'Plough and pastoralism: aspects of the secondary products revolution', in I. Hodder, G. Isaac and N. Hammond (eds), *Pattern of the Past: Studies in Honour of David Clarke* (Cambridge), 261-305

———— 1983, 'The secondary exploitation of animals in the Old World', *World Archaeology* 15, 90-104

Simek, J.F. 1987, 'Integrating pattern and context in spatial archaeology', *Journal of Archaeological Science* 11, 405-20

Sims-Williams, P. 1990, *Religion and Literature in Western England 600-800* (Cambridge)

Skeates, R. 1990, 'What can the Annaliste approach offer the archaeologist?', *Papers from the Institute of Archaeology* 1, 56-61

Small, D. 1987, 'Toward a competent structuralist archaeology', *Journal of Anthropological Archaeology* 6, 105-21

Sneath, P.H.A. and Sokal, R.R. (eds) 1973, *Numerical Taxonomy: The Principle and Practice of Numerical Classification* (San Francisco)

Sokal, R.R. and Sneath, P.H.A. 1963, *Principles of Numerical Taxonomy* (San Francisco)

Sommer, U. 1990, 'Dirt theory, or archaeological sites seen as rubbish heaps', *Journal of Theoretical Archaeology* 1, 47-60

Sorenson, M.L. 1988, 'Is there a feminist contribution to archaeology?', *Archaeological Review from Cambridge* 7, 9-20

South, S. 1977a, *Method and Theory in Historical Archaeology* (New York)

———— 1977b, *Research Strategies in Historical Archaeology* (London)

Spaulding, A.C. 1968, 'Explanation in archaeology', in S.R. Binford and L.R. Binford (eds), *New Perspectives in Archaeology* (Chicago), 33-9

Spencer, C.S. 1990, 'On the tempo and mode of state formation: Neoevolutionism reconsidered', *Journal of Anthropological Archaeology* 9, 1-30

Spencer-Wood, S.M. 1987, *Consumer Choice in Historical Archaeology* (New York)

Speth, J.D. and Spielmann, K.A. 1983, 'Energy source, protein metabolism, and hunter-gatherer subsistence strategies', *Journal of Anthropological Archaeology* 2, 1-31

Spratt, D.A. 1981, 'Prehistoric boundaries on the North Yorkshire Moors', in G. Barker (ed.), *Prehistoric Communities in Northern England*, 87-104

———— 1989, 'Innovation theory made plain', in S.E. Van der Leeuw and R. Torrence (eds), *What's New? The Process of Innovation* (London), 245-57

Spriggs, M. 1984, *Marxist Perspectives in Archaeology* (Cambridge)

Stapert, D. 1984, 'The ring and sector method. Intrasite spatial analysis of Stone Age sites, with special reference to Pincevent', *Palaeohistoria* 31, 1-57

———— 1990, 'Within the tent or outside? Spatial patterns in Later Palaeolithic sites', *Helinium* 19, 14-35

Staski, E. and Sutro, L.D. (eds) 1991, *The Ethnoarchaeology of Refuse Disposal* (Tempe)

Steiger, W.L. 1971, 'Analytical archaeology?', *Mankind* 8, 67-70

Steinsland, G. (ed.) 1986, *Words and Objects: Towards a Dialogue between Archaeology and the History of Religion* (Oslo)

Steward, J.H. 1937, 'Ecological aspects of southwestern society', *Anthropos* 32, 87-104

———— 1942, 'The direct historical approach to archaeology', *American Antiquity* 7, 337-43

———— 1955, *Theory of Culture Change* (Urbana)

Stewart, M. 1990, 'Burnt stone at West Heath, Hampstead', *Papers from the Institute of Archaeology* 1, 37-44

Stone, P. and MacKenzie R. (eds) 1989, *The Excluded Past* (London)

Stopford, J. 1994, 'Some approaches to the archaeology of Christian pilgrimage', *World Archaeology* 26.1, 57-72

Strong, W.D. 1936, 'Anthropological theory and archaeological fact', in R.H. Lowie (ed.), *Essays in Anthropology* (Berkeley), 359-68

Struever, S. (ed.) 1971, *Approaches to the Social Dimensions of Mortuary Practices* (= *American Antiquity* 36, 3)

Swain, P.H. and Fu, K.S. 1972, 'Stochastic programmed grammars for syntactic pattern recognition', *Pattern Recognition* 4, 83-100

Taçon, P.S.C. 1991, 'The power of stone: symbolic aspects of stone use and tool development in Western Arnhem, Australia', *Antiquity* 65, 192-207

Tainter, J.A. 1980, 'Behavior and status in a Middle Woodland mortuary population from the Illinois valley', *American Antiquity* 45, 308-13

———— 1988, *The Collapse of Complex Societies* (Cambridge)

Tarlow, S. forthcoming, 'Scraping the bottom of the barrow: an agricultural metaphor in Neolithic/Bronze Age European burial practice', *Journal of Theoretical Archaeology* 3-4

Taylor, C., Everson, P. and Wilson-North, R. 1990, 'Bodiam Castle, Sussex', *Medieval Archaeology* 34, 155-7

Taylor, P. 1989, *Political Geography* (London)

Taylor, W.W. 1948, *A Study of Archaeology* (Manasha)

———— 1969, 'Review of *New Perspectives in Archaeology*', *Science* 165, 382-4

Thom, A. 1967, *Megalithic Sites in Britain* (Oxford)

Thomas, C. 1981, *Christianity in Roman Britain to AD 500* (London)

———— 1986, 'Recognising Christian origins: an archaeological and historical dilemma', in L.A.S. Butler and R.H. Morris (eds), *The Anglo-Saxon Church* (London), 121-5

Thomas, D.H. 1971, 'On the use of cumulative curves and numerical taxonomy', *American Antiquity* 36, 206-9

———— 1972, 'The use and abuse of numerical taxonomy in archaeology', *Archaeological and Physical Anthropology in Oceana* 7, 31-49

———— 1974, 'An archaeological perspective on Shoshonean Bands', *American*

Anthropologist 76, 11-23

———— 1978, 'The awful truth about statistics in archaeology', *American Antiquity* 43, 231-44

Thomas, J. 1987, 'Relations of production and social change in the Neolithic of north-west Europe', *Man* 22, 405-30

———— 1988b, 'Neolithic explanations revisited: the Mesolithic-Neolithic transition in Britain and south Scandinavia', *Proceedings of the Prehistoric Society* 54, 59-66

———— 1991a, *Rethinking the Neolithic* (Cambridge)

———— 1991b, 'The Hollow Men? A reply to Steve Mithen', *Proceedings of the Prehistoric Society* 57-2, 15-20

Thompson, M. 1979, *Rubbish Theory: The Creation and Destruction of Value* (Oxford)

Thomson, D. 1939, 'The seasonal factor in human culture', *Proceedings of the Prehistoric Society* 30, 400-22

Thorpe, I. 1984, 'Ritual, power and ideology: a reconstruction of earlier Neolithic rituals in Wessex', in R. Bradley and J. Gardiner (eds), *Neolithic Studies* (Oxford), 41-60

———— and Richards, C.C. 1984, 'The decline of ritual authority and the introduction of Beakers into Britain', in R. Bradley and J. Gardiner (eds), *Neolithic Studies* (Oxford), 67-86

Tilley, C. 1984, 'Ideology and the legitimation of power in the Middle Neolithic of southern Sweden', in D. Miller and C. Tilley (eds), *Ideology, Power and Prehistory* (Cambridge), 111-46

———— 1989a, 'Discourse and power: the genre of the Cambridge Inaugural Lecture', in D. Miller, M. Rowlands and C. Tilley (eds), *Domination and Resistance* (London), 41-62

———— 1989b, 'Excavation as theatre', *Antiquity* 63, 275-80

———— 1989c, *Reading Material Culture* (Oxford)

———— 1991, *Material Culture and Text* (London)

———— (ed.) 1993, *Interpretative Archaeology* (Oxford)

Tolstoy, P. 1966, 'Method in long range comparison', *Congreso Internacional de Americanistas* 36, 68-89

Tooker, E. (ed.) 1982, *Ethnography by Archaeologists* (Washington)

Trigger, B.G. 1978, *Time and Tradition* (Edinburgh)

———— 1980a, 'Archaeology and the image of the American Indian', *American Antiquity* 45, 662-76

———— 1980b, *Gordon Childe* (London)

———— 1981, 'Anglo-American archaeology', *World Archaeology* 13, 138-55

———— 1982, 'Archaeological analysis and concepts of causality', *Culture* 2 (2), 31-42

———— 1984a, 'Marxism and archaeology', in J. Maquet and N. Daniels (eds), *On Marxian Perspectives in Anthropology* (Malibu)

———— 1984b, 'Alternative archaeologies: Nationalist, Colonialist, Imperialist', *Man* 19, 355-70

———— 1985a, *Archaeology as Historical Science*, Banaras Hindu University, Department of Ancient Indian History, Culture and Archaeology Monograph 14

———— 1985b, 'The past as power: anthropology and the North American Indian', in I. McBryde (ed.), *Who Owns the Past?* (Melbourne), 11-40

———— 1985c, 'Marxism in archaeology: real or spurious?', *Reviews in*

Anthropology 12, 114-23

———— 1989, *A History of Archaeological Thought* (Cambridge)

Turner, V. and Turner, E. (eds) 1978, *Image and Pilgrimage in Christian Culture. Anthropological Perspectives* (Oxford)

Tyldesley, J.A., Johnson, J.S. and Snape, S.R. 1985, ' "Shape" in archaeological artifacts: two case studies using a new analytical method', *Oxford Journal of Archaeology* 4, 19-30

Tylecote, R.F. and Gilmour, B.J.J. 1986, *The Metallography of Early Ferrous Edge Tools and Edged Weapons* (Oxford)

Ucko, P.J. 1969, 'Ethnography and the archeological interpretation of funerary remains', *World Archaeology* 1, 262-80

————, Tringham, R. and Dimbleby, G.W. (eds) 1972, *Man, Settlement and Urbanism* (London)

Uhr, L. 1973, *Pattern Recognition, Learning, and Thought: Computer-Programmed Models of Higher Mental Processes* (Englewood Cliffs)

Upham, S. (ed.) 1990, *The Evolution of Political Systems* (Cambridge)

Ussher, S. 1969, *The Historians of Greece and Rome* (London)

Van der Leeuw, S.E. 1977, 'Towards a study of the economics of pottery making', in B.L. van Beek, R.W. Brandt and W. Greunman-van Waateringe (eds), *Ex Horreo, Cyngyla IV* (Amsterdam), 68-76

———— 1981a, 'Information flows, flow structures and the explanation of change in human institutions', in S.E. Van der Leeuw (ed.), *Archaeological Approaches to the Study of Complexity* (Amsterdam), 230-312

———— 1982, 'How objective can we become? Some reflections on the nature of the relationship between the archaeologist, his data, and his interpretation', in C. Renfrew, M. Rowland and B. Segraves (eds), *Theory and Explanation in Archaeology* (New York), 431-57

———— 1983, 'Acculturation as information processing', in R. Brandt and J. Slofstra (eds), *Roman and Native in the Low Countries. Spheres of Interaction* (Oxford), 11-41

———— 1987, 'Revolutions revisited', in C. Manzanilla (ed.), *Studies in the Neolithic and Urban Revolutions* (Oxford), 215-41

———— (ed.) 1981b, *Archaeological Approaches to the Study of Complexity* (Amsterdam)

———— and Pritchard, A. (eds) 1984, *The Many Dimensions of Pottery* (Amsterdam)

———— and Torrence, R. (eds) 1989, *What's New?* (London)

van Dommelen, P. 1992, 'Blurred genes: archaeology as anthropology or ...', *Helinium* 32, 215-26

van Velzen, D.T. 1992, 'A game of tombs: the use of funerary practices in the conflict between Etruscans and Romans in the second and first centuries B.C. in Chiusi, Tuscany', *Archaeological Review from Cambridge* 11, 65-76

Venc, S. 1984, 'War and warfare in archaeology', *Journal of Anthropological Archaeology* 3, 116-32

Vickers, M. 1990, 'The impoverishment of the past: the case of Classical Greece', *Antiquity* 64, 455-63

Vierck, H. 1978, 'Die Anglische Frauentracht', in C. Ahrens (ed.), *Sachsen un Angelsachsen* (Hamburg), 245-53

Vincent, J. 1982, 'Las tendencias metodoligicas en prehistoria', *Trabajos de Prehistoria* 39, 9-54

Vita-Finzi, C. 1978, *Archaeological Sites in their Setting* (London)

———— and Higgs, E.S. 1970, 'Prehistoric economy in the Mount Carmel area of Palestine: site catchment analysis', *Proceedings of the Prehistoric Society* 36, 1-37

Wacher, J. 1974, *The Towns of Roman Britain* (London)

Wagstaff, J.M. (ed.) 1987, *Landscape and Culture* (Oxford)

Wahle, E. 1964, *Tradition und Auftrag prähistorischer Forschung: Ausgewählte Abhandlungen* (Berlin)

Walde, D. and Willows, N. (eds) 1991, *The Archaeology of Gender* (Calgary)

Walker, M.J. 1988, 'Like what? A practical question of analogical inference and archaeological meaningfulness', *Journal of Anthropological Archaeology* 7, 248-87

Wallerstein, I. 1974, *The Modern World-System: Capitalist Agriculture and the Origins of the European World-Economy in the Sixteenth Century* (New York)

Walters, H.B. 1934, *The English Antiquaries of the Sixteenth, Seventeenth and Eighteenth Centuries* (London)

Washburn, D.K. (ed.) 1983, *Structure and Cognition in Art* (Cambridge)

Watson, P.J. 1984, *Archaeological Explanation: The Scientific Method in Archaeology* (New York)

————, Le Blanc, S.A. and Redman, C.L. 1971, *Archaeological Explanation: The Scientific Method in Archaeology* (New York)

Watts, D.J. 1989, 'Infant burials and Romano-British Christianity', *Archaeological Journal* 146, 372-83

———— 1991, *Christians and Pagans in Roman Britain* (London)

Wedel, W.R. 1938, *The Direct-Historical Approach in Pawnee Archaeology* (Washington D.C.)

Weide, M. 1969, 'Seasonality of Pisamo Clam collection at O'a-82. Los Angeles', *University of California Archaeological Survey Annual Report 1968-9* 11, 127-41

Welinder, S. 1975, *Prehistoric Agriculture in Eastern Middle Sweden* (Lund)

———— 1977, *Ekonomiska processar i förhistorisk expansion* (Acta Archaeologica Lundensia 7)

———— 1979, *Prehistoric Demography* (Acta Archaeologica Lundensia 8)

———— 1983, *The Ecology of Long-term Change* (Acta Archaeologica Lundensia 9)

Wells, C. 1964, *Bones, Bodies and Disease* (London)

Wells, P.S. 1980, *Culture Contact and Culture Change: Early Iron Age Central Europe and the Mediterranean World* (Cambridge)

Wenham, S.J. 1989, 'Anatomical interpretations of Anglo-Saxon weapon injuries', in S.C. Hawkes (ed.), *Weapons and Warfare in Anglo-Saxon England* (Oxford), 123-39

Wenke, R.J. 1985, *Patterns in Prehistory*, 2nd ed. (Oxford)

West, A. 1991, 'Knowing the past, telling the past: putting emotion into archaeology', *Archaeological Review from Cambridge* 10, 94-101

Whallon, R. and Brown, J.A. (eds) 1982, *Essays on Archaeological Typology* (Evanston)

Wheeler, R.E.M. 1954, *Archaeology from the Earth* (Harmondsworth)

White, J.P. and Thomas, D.H. 1972, 'Ethno-taxonomic models and archaeological interpretations in the New Guinea Highlands: what mean these stones?', in D.L. Clarke (ed.), *Models in Archaeology* (London), 275-308

White, L.A. 1949, *The Science of Culture: A Study of Man and Civilization* (New York)

———— 1959, *The Evolution of Culture* (New York)

Whitelaw, T.M. 1983, 'People and space in hunter gatherer camps: a generalising approach in ethnoarchaeology', *Archaeological Review from Cambridge* 2 (2), 48-66

Wiessner, P. 1983, 'Style and social information in Kalahari San projectile points', *American Antiquity* 48, 253-76

Williams, E. 1988, *Complex Hunter-Gatherers* (Oxford)

Wilson, D.M. 1976, *The Archaeology of Anglo-Saxon England* (London)

Wiseman, J. 1980, 'Archaeology as archaeology', *Journal of Field Archaeology* 7, 149-51

Wittfogel, K.A. 1957, *Oriental Despotism* (New Haven)

Wobst, M. 1977, 'Stylistic behaviour and information exchange', in C.E. Cleland (ed.), *For the Director: Research Essays in Honor of James B. Griffin* (Michigan), 317-42

———— 1978, 'The archaeo-ethnology of hunter-gatherers or the tyranny of the ethnographic record in archaeology', *American Antiquity* 43, 303-9

Woolf, G. 1990, 'World-systems analysis and the Roman Empire', *Journal of Roman Archaeology* 3, 44-58

Wylie, A. 1982, 'Epistemological issues raised by a structuralist archaeology', in I. Hodder (ed.), *Symbolic and Structural Archaeology* (Cambridge), 39-46

———— 1985, 'The reaction against analogy', in M. Schiffer (ed.), *Advances in Archaeological Method and Theory* (New York), 63-111

———— 1988, ' "Simple" analogy and the role of relevance assumptions: implications of archaeological practice', *International Studies in the Philosophy of Science* 2, 134-50

———— 1990, 'Feminist theories of social power: some implications for a processual archaeology', *Norwegian Archaeological Review* 23, 51-68

———— 1992, 'The interplay of evidential constraints and political interests: recent archaeological research on gender', *American Antiquity* 57, 15-35

Yellen, J.E. 1977, *Archaeological Approaches to the Present* (New York)

Yengoyan, A.A. 1985, 'Digging for symbols: the archaeology of everday material culture', *Proceedings of the Prehistoric Society* 51, 329-34

Yentsch, A.E. forthcoming, *A Chesapeake Family and their Slaves* (Cambridge)

Yoffee, N. 1993, 'Too many chiefs? (Or, safe texts for the '90s)', in N. Yoffee and A. Sherratt (eds), *Archaeological Theory: Who Sets the Agenda?* (Cambridge), 60-78

———— and Cowgill, G.L. (eds) 1988, *The Collapse of Ancient States and Civilizations* (Tucson)

———— and Sherratt, A. (eds) 1993, *Archaeological Theory: Who Sets the Agenda?* (Cambridge)

Zeeman, E.C. 1982, 'Decision making and evolution', in C. Renfrew, M.J. Rowlands and B.A. Segraves (eds), *Theory and Explanation in Archaeology* (New York), 315-46

Zubrow, E.B.W. 1975, *Prehistoric Carrying Capacity: A Model* (Menlo Park)

———— 1978, 'Simulation as a heuristic device in archaeology', in J. Sabloff (ed.), *Simulations in Archaeology* (Albuquerque), 143-88

Zvelebil, M. 1986, *Hunters in Transition* (Cambridge)

———— and Rowley-Conwy, P. 1984, 'Transition to farming in Northern Europe: a hunter-gatherer perspective', *Norwegian Archaeological Review* 17, 104-27

Index

Numbers in **bold** type indicate that there is a relevant illustration on that page.